E. H.
GOMBRICH

A LITTLE
HISTORY of
THE WORLD

TRANSLATED BY CAROLINE MUSTILL

YALE UNIVERSITY PRESS
NEW HAVEN AND LONDON

Published in German as *Eine kurze Weltgeschichte für junge Leser* by
Ernst H. Gombrich
Originally published under the title *Weltgeschichte von der Urzeit bis zur
Gegenwart* by Steyrermühl-Verlag, Vienna in 1936

For information about this and other Yale University Press publications,
please contact:
U.S. Office: sales.press@yale.edu   www.yalebooks.com
Europe Office: sales @yaleup.co.uk   www.yaleup.co.uk

Set in Minion by Northern Phototypesetting Co. Ltd, Bolton
Printed in the United States of America

Library of Congress Cataloging-in-Publication Data

Gombrich, E. H. (Ernst Hans), 1909–
  [Kurze Weltgeschichte für Junge Leser. English]
  A little history of the world/Ernst Gombrich.
    p. cm.
  ISBN 0–300–10883–4 (cl.: alk. paper)
  1. World history—Juvenile literature. I. Title.
  D23.G64 2005
  909—dc22

                                                    2005011802

A catalogue record for this book is available from the British Library.

10 9 8 7 6 5 4

The publishers would like to thank the Estate of E. H. Gombrich for
permission to reproduce photographs from the family albums, taken by Ilse
Gombrich.

Für Ilse

Wie Du stets Dir's angehört
Also stets Dir's angehört

CONTENTS

Preface

c. 1935.

My grandfather, Ernst Gombrich, is best known as an art historian. Besides many important academic publications, his popular introduction to art history, *The Story of Art*, has made him known to millions of readers around the world. But had it not been for *A Little History of the World*, *The Story of Art* would never have been written.

To understand how it happened – and why this, his very first book, has never appeared in English until now despite being available in eighteen other languages – we need to start in Vienna in 1935, when my grandfather was still a young man.

After Ernst Gombrich had finished his studies at the University of Vienna, he was unemployed and, in those difficult times, without prospect of a job. A young publisher with whom he was acquainted asked him to take a look at a particular English history book for children, with a view to translating it into German. It was intended for a new series called *Wissenschaft für Kinder* ('Knowledge for Children') and had been sent by a mutual friend who was studying medicine in London.

My grandfather was not impressed by what he read: so little so that he told the publisher – Walter Neurath who later founded the publishing house Thames & Hudson in England – that it was probably not worth translating. 'I think I could write a better one myself,' he said. To which Neurath responded that he was welcome to submit a chapter.

It so happened that, in the final stages of writing his doctoral thesis, my grandfather had been corresponding with a little girl who was the daughter of some friends. She wanted to know what was keeping him so busy, and he enjoyed trying to explain his subject to her in ways she would understand. He was also, he said later, feeling a little impatient with academic writing, having waded through so much of it in the course of his studies, and was convinced that it should be perfectly possible to explain most things to an intelligent child without jargon or pompous language. So he wrote a lively chapter on the age of chivalry and submitted it to Neurath – who was more than happy with it. 'But,' he said, 'in order to meet the schedule that was intended for the translation, I will need a finished manuscript in six weeks' time.'

My grandfather wasn't sure that it could be done, but he liked the challenge and agreed to try. He plotted out the book at speed, selecting episodes for inclusion by asking himself simply which events of the past had touched most lives and were best remembered. He then set out to write a chapter a day. In the morning, he would read up on the day's topic from what books were available in his parents' house – including a big encyclopaedia. In the afternoon, he would go to the library to seek out, wherever possible, some texts belonging to the periods he was writing about, to give authenticity to his account. Evenings were for writing. The only exceptions were Sundays – but to explain about these, I must first introduce my grandmother.

Ilse Heller, as my grandmother was then called, had come to Vienna from Bohemia about five years earlier to pursue her piano studies. She was soon taken on as a pupil by Leonie Gombrich, after whom I am named. Leonie introduced Ilse to Ernst, and encouraged my grandfather to show her pupil some of the galleries and architectural splendours of Vienna. By 1935 their weekend outings together were well established – and in fact, they married the following year. And one Sunday, as my grandmother remembers it, they were walking in the Wienerwald and had stopped for a break – 'Perhaps in a sunny clearing,' she says, 'sitting on the grass or on a fallen tree . . .' – when my grandfather pulled a sheaf of papers from inside his jacket and said, 'Do you mind if I read you something?'

'Well, it was better that he read it,' says my grandmother now. 'Even then, you know, Ernst's handwriting was very difficult.'

That something, of course, was the *Little History*. Evidently she liked it, and the readings continued for the next six weeks until the book was done – for he delivered it to Neurath on time. If you read it aloud, you will find how beautifully those readings shaped the telling of it; the dedication gives an idea of how he appreciated them. The original illustrations were produced by a former riding instructor, and my grandfather liked to point out that the numerous horses he included in his pictures were more skilfully drawn than the people.

When the book came out in 1936, titled *Eine kurze Weltgeschichte für junge Leser*, it was very well received, reviewers assuming that my grandfather must be an experienced teacher. Within quite a short time, it had been translated into five other languages – but by then, my grandparents were already in England, where they were to remain. In the end, the Nazis stopped publication, not for racial reasons but because they considered the outlook 'too pacifist'.

However, the seed had been planted and, despite his other concerns, my grandfather eventually responded to requests for a sequel, this time focusing on art history. This became *The Story of Art* – not for children because, my grandfather said, 'The history of art is not a topic for children', but for slightly older readers. It has remained in print since 1950 and continues to make new friends in more than thirty nations.

But the first edition of the *Little History*, which preceded its better-known cousin, lay in a drawer in North London. Some time after the war had ended, my grandfather managed to reclaim his copyright, but by then the world in which he had written the book seemed very far away. So nothing happened until, more than thirty years later, he received an enquiry from a German publisher who, on reading the book, was captivated by its energy and vivid language. A second German edition was published with a new final chapter – and once again, my grandfather was surprised and delighted by the book's success and the many translations that have followed. He took a cheerful interest in tailoring editions for audiences of different nationalities, and was always ready to listen to the suggestions of the various translators. There was one caveat, though. Apart from the *Little History*, my grandfather wrote all his books in English: if there was ever to be an English edition, he was going to translate it himself.

Then, for ten years, and despite repeated approaches, he refused to do so. It wasn't just that he was busy, although that was also true. English history, he said, was all about English kings and queens – would a European perspective mean anything to English-speaking children? It took the events of the 1990s, and Britain's increasing involvement in the European Union – as well as my grandmother's tactful encouragement – to convince him that they might.

And so, at the very end of his long and distinguished life, he embarked on producing a new, English version of the book with which he had started. 'I've been looking at my *Little History*,' he told me with modest surprise, shortly after he began, 'and there's actually a lot in it. You know, I really think it's good!'

Of course, he made corrections. He added new information about prehistoric man. He asked his son – my father – who is an expert on Early Buddhism, to advise on changes to Chapter 10, while his assistant, Caroline Mustill, helped with the sections on Chinese history. It is our great good fortune that Caroline worked with him so closely, for he was still engaged in the task of translating and updating when he died, at the age of ninety-two. With his blessing, she has completed this difficult task meticulously and beautifully. Clifford Harper produced new illustrations, which I know my grandfather would have loved to see. But some changes, of course, could not be made without him: we know that he intended to add chapters about Shakespeare and about the Bill of Rights, and no doubt he would have expanded on, for example, his very brief treatment of the English Civil War and the birth of parliamentary democracy, which carried less weight for the Viennese graduate who wrote the book than for the British citizen he became. But how he would have explained these things we could not guess, and so the areas he did not revise himself have been left as his thousands of readers in other countries already appreciate them.

Revisions, in any case, are perhaps beside the point. What matters is his obvious sense that the pursuit of history – indeed, all learning – is an enquiry to be enjoyed.

'I want to stress,' he wrote, in his preface to the Turkish edition a few years ago, 'that this book is not, and never was, intended to replace any textbooks of history that may serve a very different purpose at school. I would like my readers to relax, and to follow the story without having to take notes or to memorise names and dates. In fact, I promise that I shall not examine them on what they have read.'

Leonie Gombrich
April 2005

With Carl and Leonie, 1972.

*The Estate of E. H. Gombrich would like to thank, for information and advice:
Patrick Boyde, Henry French, Rhodri Hayward, the Oxford University Museum
of Natural History, J. B. Trapp and, in particular, Adrian Lyttelton.*

1

❖

ONCE UPON A TIME

All stories begin with 'Once upon a time'. And that's just what this story is all about: what happened, once upon a time. Once you were so small that, even standing on tiptoes, you could barely reach your mother's hand. Do you remember? Your own history might begin like this: 'Once upon a time there was a small boy' – or a small girl – 'and that small boy was me.' But before that you were a baby in a cradle. You won't remember that, but you know it's true. Your father and mother were also small once, and so was your grandfather, and your grandmother, a much longer time ago, but you know that too. After all, we say: 'They are old.' But they too had grandfathers and grandmothers, and they, too, could say: 'Once upon a time'. And so it goes on, further and further back. Behind every 'Once upon a time' there is always another. Have you ever tried standing between two mirrors? You should. You will see a great long line of shiny mirrors, each one smaller than the one before, stretching away into the distance, getting fainter and fainter, so that you never see the last. But even when you can't see them any more, the mirrors still go on. They are there, and you know it.

And that's how it is with 'Once upon a time'. We can't see where it ends. Grandfather's grandfather's grandfather's grandfather ... it makes your head spin. But say it again, slowly, and in the end you'll be able to imagine it. Then add one more. That gets us quickly back into the past, and from there into the distant past. But you will never reach the beginning, because behind every beginning there's always another 'Once upon a time'.

It's like a bottomless well. Does all this looking down make you dizzy? It does me. So let's light a scrap of paper, and drop it down into that well. It will fall slowly, deeper and deeper. And as it burns it will light up the sides of the well. Can you see it? It's going down and down. Now it's so far down it's like a tiny star in the dark depths. It's getting smaller and smaller ... and now it's gone.

Our memory is like that burning scrap of paper. We use it to light up the past. First of all our own, and then we ask old people to tell us what they remember. After that we look for letters written by people who are already dead. And in this way we light our way back. There are buildings that are just for storing old scraps of paper that people once wrote on – they are called archives. In them you can find letters written hundreds of years ago. In an archive, I once found a letter which just said: 'Dear Mummy, Yesterday we ate some lovely truffles, love from William.' William was a little Italian prince who lived four hundred years ago. Truffles are a special sort of mushroom.

But we only catch glimpses, because our light is now falling faster and faster: a thousand years ... five thousand years ... ten thousand years. Even in those days there were children who liked good things to eat. But they couldn't yet write letters. Twenty thousand ... fifty thousand ... and even then people said, as we do, 'Once upon a time'. Now our memory-light is getting very small ... and now it's gone. And yet we know that it goes on much further, to a time long, long ago, before there were any people and when our mountains didn't look as they do today. Some of them were bigger, but as the rain poured down it slowly turned them into hills. Others weren't there at all. They grew up gradually, out of the sea, over millions and millions of years.

But even before the mountains there were animals, quite different from those of today. They were huge and looked rather like dragons. And how do we know that? We sometimes find their bones, deep in the ground. When I was a schoolboy in Vienna I used to visit the Natural History Museum, where I loved to gaze at the great skeleton of a creature called a Diplodocus. An odd name, Diplodocus. But an even odder creature. It wouldn't fit into a room at home – or even two, for that matter. It was as tall as a very tall tree, and its tail was half as long as a football pitch. What a tremendous noise it must have made, as it munched its way through the primeval forest!

But we still haven't reached the beginning. It all goes back much further – thousands of millions of years. That's easy enough to say, but stop and think for a moment. Do you know how long one second is? It's as long as counting: one, two, three. And how about a thousand million seconds? That's thirty-two years! Now, try to imagine a thousand million years! At that time there were no large animals, just creatures like snails and worms. And before then there weren't even any plants. The whole earth was a 'formless void'. There was nothing. Not a tree, not a bush, not a blade of grass, not a flower, nothing green. Just barren desert rocks and the sea. An empty sea: no fish, no seashells, not even any seaweed. But if you listen to the waves, what do they say? 'Once upon a time . . .' Once the earth was perhaps no more than a swirling cloud of gas and dust, like those other, far bigger ones we can see today through our telescopes. For billions and trillions of years, without rocks, without water and without life, that swirling cloud of gas and dust made rings around the sun. And before that? Before that, not even the sun, our good old sun, was there. Only weird and amazing giant stars and smaller heavenly bodies, whirling among the gas clouds in an infinite, infinite universe.

'Once upon a time' – but now all this peering down into the past is making me feel dizzy again. Quick! Let's get back to the sun, to earth, to the beautiful sea, to plants and snails and dinosaurs, to our mountains, and, last of all, to human beings. It's a bit like coming home, isn't it? And just so that 'Once upon a time' doesn't keep dragging us back down into that bottomless well, from now on we'll always shout: 'Stop! *When* did that happen?'

And if we also ask, 'And *how* exactly did that happen?' we will be asking about history. Not just *a* story, but *our* story, the story that we call the history of the world. Shall we begin?

2

❖

THE GREATEST INVENTORS
OF ALL TIME

Near Heidelberg, in Germany, somebody was once digging a pit when they came across a bone, deep down under the ground. It was a human bone. A lower jaw. But no human beings today have jaws like this one. It was so massive and strong, and had such powerful teeth! Whoever owned it must have been able to bite really hard. And must have lived a long time ago for the bone to be buried so deep.

On another occasion, but still in Germany – in the Neander valley – a human skull was found. And this was also immensely interesting because nobody alive today has a skull like this one either. Instead of a forehead like ours it just had two thick ridges above the eyebrows. Now, if all our thinking goes on behind our foreheads and these people didn't have any foreheads, then perhaps they didn't think as much as we do. Or at any rate, thinking may have been harder for them. So the people who examined the skull concluded that once upon a time there were people who weren't very good at thinking, but who were better at biting than we are today.

But now you're going to say: 'Stop! That's not what we agreed. *When* did these people live, *what* were they like, and *how* did they live?'

Your questions make me blush, as I have to admit that we don't know, precisely. But we will find out one day, and maybe you will want to help. We don't know because these people didn't yet know how to write things down, and memory only takes us a little way back. But we are making new discoveries all the time. Scientists have found that certain materials, such as wood and plants and volcanic rocks, change slowly but regularly over a very long period of time. This means that we can work out when they grew or were formed. And since the discoveries in Germany, people have carried on searching and digging, and have made some startling finds. In Asia and Africa, in particular, more bones have been found, some at least as old as the Heidelberg jaw. These were our ancestors who may have already been using stones as tools more than a hundred and fifty thousand years ago. They were different from the Neanderthal people who appeared about seventy thousand years earlier and inhabited the earth for about two hundred thousand years. And I owe the Neanderthal people an apology, for despite their low foreheads, their brains were no smaller than those of most people today.

'But all these "about"s, with no names and no dates . . . this isn't history!' you say, and you are right. It comes before history. That is why we call it 'prehistory', because we only have a rough idea of when it all happened. But we still know something about the people whom we call prehistoric. At the time when real history begins – and we will come to that in the next chapter – people already had all the things we have today: clothes, houses and tools, ploughs to plough with, grains to make bread with, cows for milking, sheep for shearing, dogs for hunting and for company, bows and arrows for shooting and helmets and shields for protection. Yet with all of these things there must have been a first time. Someone must have made the discovery. Isn't it an amazing thought that, one day, a prehistoric man – or a woman – must have realised that meat from wild animals was easier to chew if it was first held over a fire and roasted? And that one day someone discovered how to make fire? Do you realise what that actually means? Can you do it? Not with matches, because they didn't exist. But by rubbing two sticks together until they become so hot that in the end they catch fire. Have a go and then you'll see how hard it is!

Tools must have been invented by someone too. The earliest ones were probably just sticks and stones. But soon stones were being shaped and sharpened. We have found lots of these shaped stones in the ground. And because of these stone tools we call this time the Stone Age. But people didn't yet know how to build houses. Not a pleasant thought, since at that time it was often intensely cold – at certain periods far colder than today. Winters were longer and summers shorter. Snow lay deep throughout the year, not only on mountain tops, but down in the valleys as well, and glaciers, which were immense in those days, spread far out into the plains. This is why we say that the Stone Age began before the last Ice Age had ended. Prehistoric people must have suffered dreadfully from the cold, and if they came across a cave where they could shelter from the freezing winds, how happy they must have been! For this reason they are also known as 'cavemen', although they may not have actually lived in caves.

Do you know what else these cavemen invented? Can't you guess? They invented *talking*. I mean having real conversations with each other, using words. Of course animals also make noises – they can cry out when they feel pain and make warning calls when danger threatens, but they don't have names for things as human beings do. And prehistoric people were the first creatures to do so.

They invented something else that was wonderful too: pictures. Many of these can still be seen today, scratched and painted on the walls of caves. No painter alive now could do better. The animals they depict don't exist any more, they were painted so long ago. Elephants with long, thick coats of hair and great, curving tusks – woolly mammoths – and other Ice Age animals. Why do you think these prehistoric people painted animals on the walls of caves? Just for decoration? That doesn't seem likely, because the caves were so dark. Of course we can't be sure, but we think they may have been trying to make magic, that they believed that painting pictures of animals on the walls would make those animals appear. Rather like when we say 'Talk of the devil!' when someone we've been talking about turns up unexpectedly. After all, these animals were their prey, and without them they would starve. So they may have been trying to invent a magic spell. It would be nice to think that such things worked. But they never have yet.

The Ice Age lasted for an unimaginably long time. Many tens of thousands of years, which was just as well, for otherwise these people would not have had time to invent all these things. But gradually the earth grew warmer and the ice retreated to the high mountains, and people – who by now were much like us – learnt, with the warmth, to plant grasses and then grind the seeds to make a paste which they could bake in the fire, and this was bread.

In the course of time they learnt to build tents and tame animals which until then had roamed freely around. And they followed their herds, as people in Lapland still do. Because forests were dangerous places in those days, home to large numbers of wild animals such as wolves and bears, people in several places (and this is often the case with inventors) had the same excellent idea: they built 'pile dwellings' in the middle of lakes, huts on stilts rammed deep in the mud. By this time they were masters at shaping and polishing their tools and used a different, harder stone to bore holes in their axe-heads for handles. That must have been hard work! Work which could take the whole of the winter. Imagine how often the axe-head must have broken at the last minute, so that they had to start all over again.

The next thing these people discovered was how to make pots out of clay, which they soon learnt to decorate with patterns and fire in ovens, although by this time, in the late Stone Age, they had stopped painting pictures of animals. In the end, perhaps six thousand years ago (that is, 4000 BC), they found a new and more convenient way of making tools: they discovered metals. Not all of them at once, of course. It began with some green stones which turn into copper when melted in a fire. Copper has a nice shine, and you can use it to make arrowheads and axes, but it is soft and gets blunt more quickly than stone.

But once again, people found an answer. They discovered that if you add just a little of another, very rare, metal, it makes the copper stronger. That metal is tin, and a mixture of tin and copper is called bronze. The age in which people made themselves helmets and swords, axes and cauldrons, and bracelets and necklaces out of bronze is, naturally, known as the Bronze Age.

Now let's take a last look at these people dressed in skins, as they paddle their boats made of hollowed-out tree trunks towards their villages of huts on stilts, bringing grain, or perhaps salt from mines in the mountains. They drink from splendid pottery vessels, and their wives and daughters wear jewellery made of coloured stones, and even gold. Do you think much has changed since then? They were people just like us. Often unkind to one another. Often cruel and deceitful. Sadly, so are we. But even then a mother might sacrifice her life for her child and friends might die for each other. No more but also no less often than people do today. And how could it be otherwise? After all, we're only talking about things that happened between three and ten thousand years ago. There hasn't been enough time for us to change!

So, just once in a while, when we are talking, or eating some bread, using tools or warming ourselves by the fire, we should remember those early people with gratitude, for they were the greatest inventors of all time.

3

❖

THE LAND BY THE NILE

Here – as I promised – History begins. With a *when* and a *where*. It is 3100 BC (that is, 5,100 years ago), when, as we believe, a king named Menes was ruling over Egypt. If you want to know exactly where Egypt is, I suggest you ask a swallow. Every autumn, when it gets cold, swallows fly south. Over the mountains to Italy, and on across a little stretch of sea, and then they're in Africa, in the part that lies nearest to Europe. Egypt is close by.

In Africa it is hot, and for months on end it doesn't rain. In many regions very little grows. These are deserts, as are the lands on either side of Egypt. Egypt also gets very little rain. But here they don't need it, because the Nile flows right through the middle of the country, from one end to the other. Twice a year, when heavy rain filled its sources, the river would swell and burst its banks, flooding the whole land. Then people were forced to take to boats to move among the houses and the palm trees. And when the waters withdrew, the earth was wonderfully drenched and rich with oozing mud. There, under the hot sun, the grain grew as it did nowhere else. Which is why, from earliest times, the Egyptians worshipped the Nile as if it were God himself. Would you like to hear a hymn they sang to their river, four thousand years ago?

> Glory be to thee, Oh Nile! You rise out of the earth and come to nourish Egypt! You water the plains and have the power to feed all cattle. You quench the thirsty desert, far from any water. You bring forth the barley, You create the wheat. You fill the granaries and storehouses, not forgetting the poor. For You we pluck our harps, for You we sing.

So sang the ancient Egyptians. And they were right. For, thanks to the Nile, their land grew rich and powerful. Mightiest of all was their king. One king ruled over all the Egyptians, and the first to do so was King Menes. Do you remember when that was? It was in 3100 BC. And can you also remember – perhaps from Bible stories – what those kings of Egypt were called? They were called pharaohs. A pharaoh was immensely powerful. He lived in a great stone palace with massive pillars and many courtyards, and his word was law. All the people of Egypt had to toil for him if he so decreed. And sometimes he did.

One such pharaoh was King Cheops, who lived in about 2500 BC. He summoned all his subjects to help construct his tomb. He wanted a building like a mountain, and he got it. You can still see it today. It's the Great Pyramid of Cheops. You may have seen pictures of it, but you still won't be able to imagine how big it is. A cathedral would fit comfortably inside. Clambering up its huge stone blocks is like scaling a mountain peak. And yet it was human beings who piled those gigantic stones on top of each other. They had no machines in those days – rollers and pulleys at most. They had to pull and shove every single block by hand. Just think of it, in the heat of Africa! In this way, it seems, for thirty years, some hundred thousand people toiled for the pharaoh, whenever they weren't working in the fields. And when they grew tired, the king's overseer was sure to drive them on with his hippopotamus-skin whip, as they dragged and heaved those immense loads, all for their king's tomb.

Perhaps you're wondering why the pharaoh should want to build such a gigantic tomb? It was all part of his religion. The Egyptians believed in many gods. Some had ruled over them as kings long ago – or at least, that's what they thought – and among these were Osiris and his consort, Isis. The sun god, Amon, was a special god. The Kingdom of the Dead had its own god, Anubis, and he had a jackal's head. Each pharaoh, they believed, was a son of the sun god, which explains why they feared him so much and obeyed all his commands. In honour of their gods they chiselled majestic stone statues, as tall as a five-storey house, and built temples as big as towns. In front of the temples they set tall pointed stones, cut from a single block of granite. These are called 'obelisks' (a Greek word meaning something like 'little spear'). In some of our own cities you can still see obelisks that people brought back from Egypt. There's one in London by the Thames.

In the Egyptian religion, certain animals were sacred: cats, for example. Other gods were represented in animal form. The creature we know as the Sphinx, which has a human head on a lion's body, was a very powerful god. Its statue near the pyramids is so vast that a whole temple would fit inside. Buried from time to time by the desert sands, the Sphinx has now been guarding the tombs of the pharaohs for more than five thousand years. Who can say how long it will continue to keep watch?

And yet the most important part of the Egyptians' strange religion was their belief that, although a man's soul left his body when he died, for some reason the soul went on needing that body, and would suffer if it crumbled into dust.

So they invented a very ingenious way of preserving the bodies of the dead. They rubbed them with ointments and the juices of certain plants, and bandaged them with long strips of cloth, so that they wouldn't decay. A body preserved in this manner is called a mummy. And today, after thousands of years, these mummies are still intact. A mummy was placed in a coffin made of wood, the wooden coffin in one of stone, and the stone one buried, not in the earth, but in a tomb that was chiselled out of the rock. If you were rich and powerful like King Cheops, 'Son of the Sun', a whole stone mountain would be made for your tomb. Deep inside, the mummy would be safe – or so they thought! But the mighty king's efforts were in vain: his pyramid is empty.

But the mummies of other kings and those of many ancient Egyptians have been found undisturbed in their tombs. A tomb was intended to be a dwelling for the soul when it returned to visit its body. For this reason they put in food and furniture and clothes, and there are lots of paintings on the walls showing scenes from the life of the departed. His portrait was there too, to make sure that when his soul came on a visit it wouldn't go to the wrong tomb.

Thanks to the great stone statues, and the wonderfully bright and vivid wall paintings, we have a very good idea of what life in ancient Egypt was like. True, these paintings do not show things as we see them. An object or a person that is behind another is generally shown on top, and the figures often look stiff. Bodies are shown from the front and hands and feet from the side, so they look as if they have been ironed flat. But the Egyptians knew what they were doing. Every detail is clear: how they used great nets to catch ducks on the Nile, how they paddled their boats and fished with long spears, how they pumped water into ditches to irrigate the fields, how they drove their cows and goats to pasture, how they threshed grain, made shoes and clothes, blew glass – for they could already do that! – and how they shaped bricks and built houses. And we can also see girls playing catch, or playing music on flutes, and soldiers going off to war, or returning with loot and foreign captives, such as black Africans.

In noblemen's tombs we can see embassies arriving from abroad, laden with tribute, and the king rewarding faithful ministers with decorations. Some pictures show the long-dead noblemen at prayer, their arms raised before the statues of their gods, or holding banquets in their houses, with singers plucking harps, and clowns performing somersaults.

Next to these brightly coloured paintings you often see lots of tiny pictures of all sorts of things, such as owls and little people, flags, flowers, tents, beetles and vases, together with zigzag lines and spirals, all jumbled up together. Whatever can they be? They aren't pictures, they are hieroglyphs – or 'sacred signs' – the Egyptian form of writing. The Egyptians were immensely proud of their writing – indeed, they were almost in awe of it. And of all professions, that of scribe was the most highly esteemed.

Would you like to know how to write using hieroglyphs? In fact, learning this sort of writing must have been incredibly hard, as it's more like constructing a picture puzzle. If they wanted to write the name of their god, Osiris, they would draw a throne (ḥ), which was pronounced 'Oos', and an eye (👄), which was pronounced 'iri', so that the two together made 'Os-iri'. And to make sure that no one thought they meant 'Throne-eye', they often drew a little flag like this beside it (P). Which meant that person was a god. In the same way that Christians used to draw a cross after a name, if they wanted to show that that person was dead.

So now you can write 'Osiris' in hieroglyphs! But think what a job it must have been to decipher all that Egyptian writing when people became interested in hieroglyphs again, two hundred years ago. In fact, they were only able to decipher them because a stone had been found on which the same words were written in three scripts: ancient Greek, hieroglyphs and another Egyptian script. It was still a tremendous puzzle, and great scholars devoted their lives to it. You can see that stone – it's called the Rosetta Stone – in the British Museum in London.

We are now able to read almost everything the Egyptians wrote. Not just on the walls of palaces and temples, but also in books, though the books are no longer very legible. For the ancient Egyptians *did* have books, even that long ago. Of course they weren't made of paper like ours, but from a certain type of reed that grows on the banks of the Nile. The Greek name for these reeds is papyrus, from which our name for paper comes.

They wrote on long strips of this papyrus, which were then rolled up into scrolls. A whole heap of these scrolls has survived. And when we read them we discover just how wise and clever those ancient Egyptians really were. Would you like to hear a saying written more than five thousand years ago? But you must listen and think about it carefully: 'Wise words are rarer than emeralds, yet they come from the mouths of poor slave girls who turn the millstones.'

Because the Egyptians were so wise and so powerful their empire lasted for a very long time. Longer than any empire the world has ever known: nearly three thousand years. And they took just as much care as they did with their corpses, when they preserved them from rotting away, in preserving all their ancient traditions over the centuries. Their priests made quite sure that no son did anything his father had not done before him. To them, everything old was sacred.

Only rarely in the course of all that time did people turn against this strict conformity. Once was shortly after the reign of King Cheops, about 2100 BC, when the people tried to change everything. They rose up in rebellion against the pharaoh, killed his ministers, and dragged the mummies from their tombs: 'Those who formerly didn't even own sandals now hold treasures, and those who once wore precious robes go about in rags,' the ancient papyrus tells us. 'The land is turning like a potter's wheel.' But it did not last long, and soon everything was as strict as before. If not more so.

On another occasion it was the pharaoh himself who tried to change everything. Akhenaton was a remarkable man who lived around 1370 BC. He had no time for the Egyptian religion, with its many gods and its mysterious rituals. 'There is only one God,' he taught his people, 'and that is the Sun, through whose rays all is created and all sustained. To Him alone you must pray.'

The ancient temples were shut down, and King Akhenaton and his wife moved into a new palace. Since he was utterly opposed to tradition, and in favour of fine new ideas, he also had the walls of his palace painted in an entirely new style. One that was no longer severe, rigid and solemn, but freer and more natural. However, this didn't please the people at all. They wanted everything to look as it had always done for thousands of years. As soon as Akhenaton was dead, they brought back all the old customs and the old style of art. So everything stayed as it had been, for as long as the Egyptian empire endured. Just as in the days of King Menes, and for nearly three and a half more centuries, people continued to put mummies into tombs, write in hieroglyphs, and pray to the same gods. They even went on worshipping cats as sacred animals. And if you ask me, I think that in this, at least, the ancient Egyptians were right.

4

❖

SUNDAY, MONDAY ...

There are seven days in a week. I don't need to tell you their names because you know them already. But have you any idea where and when it was that the days were each given a name? Or who first had the idea of arranging them into weeks, so that they no longer flew past, nameless and in no order, as they did for people in prehistoric times? It wasn't in Egypt, but in another country which was no less hot, but where, instead of just one river, there were two: the Tigris and the Euphrates. And because the important part of that country lay between two rivers, it was called Mesopotamia, which is Greek for the land 'between the rivers'. Mesopotamia is not in Africa, but in Asia, though still not so very far from our part of the world, in a region called the Middle East, in the country we know as Iraq. The Tigris and the Euphrates join together and then flow out into the Persian Gulf.

Picture a vast plain, crossed by these two rivers. A land of heat and swamp and sudden floods. Here and there tall hills rise out of the plain. But if you dig into them you find that they aren't hills at all. First you come across a lot of bricks and rubble, and when you dig deeper you meet stout, high walls. For these hills are really ruined towns and great cities laid out with long, straight streets, tall houses, palaces and temples. But unlike Egypt's stone temples and pyramids, they were built with sun-baked bricks which cracked and crumbled over time, and eventually collapsed into great mounds of rubble.

One such mound, standing in the desert, is all that remains of Babylon, once the greatest city on earth, a city swarming with people who came there from every part of the world to trade their wares. Upstream, at the foot of the mountains, sits another. This was Nineveh, the second greatest city in the land. Babylon was the capital of the Babylonians – that's easy enough to remember – Nineveh was that of the Assyrians.

Unlike Egypt, Mesopotamia was rarely ruled by just one king. Nor did any single empire survive long within firm frontiers. Many tribes and many kings held power at different times. The most important of these were the Sumerians, the Babylonians and the Assyrians. For a long time it was thought that the Egyptians were the first people to have everything that goes to make up what we call a culture: towns and tradesmen, noblemen and kings, temples and priests, administrators and artists, writing and technical skills.

Yet we now know that, in some respects, the Sumerians were ahead of the Egyptians. Excavations of rubble mounds on plains near the Persian Gulf have revealed that the people living there had already learnt how to shape bricks from clay and build houses and temples by 3100 BC. Deep inside one of the largest of these mounds were found the ruins of the city of Ur where, so the Bible tells us, Abraham was born. A great number of tombs were also found that appeared to date from the same time as Cheops's Great Pyramid in Egypt. But while the pyramid was empty, these tombs were packed with the most astonishing treasures. Dazzling golden headdresses and gold vessels for sacrifices, gold helmets and gold daggers set with semi-precious stones. Magnificent harps decorated with bulls' heads, and – would you believe it – a gameboard, beautifully crafted and patterned like a chessboard. The explorer who found these treasures took many of them to

England, where you can see them in the British Museum. Others are in the University of Pennsylvania and the Museum of Baghdad in Iraq.

They also found round seals and inscribed clay tablets in those tombs. However, the inscriptions were not in hieroglyphs, but in a totally different script that was, if anything, even harder to decipher. This was because pictures had been replaced by neatly incised single strokes ending in a small triangle, or wedge. The script is called *cuneiform*, meaning wedge-shaped. Books made of papyrus were unknown to the Mesopotamians. They inscribed these signs into tablets of soft clay, which they then baked hard in ovens. Huge numbers of these ancient tablets have been found, some recounting long and wonderful stories, such as that of the hero Gilgamesh and his battles with monsters and dragons. On other tablets kings boast of their deeds: the temples they have built for all eternity, and all the nations they have conquered.

There are also tablets on which merchants recorded their business dealings – contracts, receipts and inventories of goods – and thanks to these we know that, even before the Babylonians and Assyrians, the ancient Sumerians were already great traders. Their merchants could calculate with ease, and plainly knew the difference between what was lawful and what was not.

One of the first Babylonian kings to rule over the whole region left a long and important inscription, engraved in stone. It is the oldest law-book in the world, and is known as the Code of Hammurabi. His name may sound as if it comes out of a storybook, but there is nothing fanciful about his laws – they are strict and just. So it is worth remembering when King Hammurabi lived: around 1700 BC, that is some 3,700 years ago.

The Babylonians, and the Assyrians after them, were disciplined and hardworking, but they didn't paint cheerful pictures like the Egyptians. Most of their statues and reliefs show kings out hunting, or inspecting kneeling captives bound in chains, or foreign tribes-people fleeing before the wheels of their chariots, and warriors attacking fortresses. The kings look forbidding, and have long black ringlets and rippling beards. They are also sometimes shown making sacrifices to Baal, the sun god, or to the moon goddess Ishtar or Astarte.

For both the Babylonians and the Assyrians worshipped the sun and the moon, and also the stars. On clear, warm nights, throughout the year and over centuries, they observed and recorded everything they saw in the skies. And because they were intelligent, they noticed that the stars revolved in a regular way. They soon learnt to recognise those that seemed fixed to the vault of heaven, reappearing each night in the same place. And they saw shapes in the constellations and gave them names, just as we do when we speak of the Great Bear. But the stars which seemed to move over the vault of heaven, now, say, towards the Great Bear, and now towards the Scales, were the ones that interested them most. In those days people thought that the earth was a flat disk, and that the sky was a sort of hollow sphere cupped over the earth, that turned over it once each day. So it must have seemed miraculous to them that, although most of the stars stayed fixed to the heavens, some seemed, as it were, only loosely fastened, and able to move about.

Today we know that these are the stars that are close to us, and that they turn with the earth around the sun. They are called planets. But the ancient Babylonians and Assyrians couldn't know that, and so they thought some strange magic must lie behind it. They gave a name to each wandering star and observed them constantly, convinced that they were powerful beings whose positions influenced the destinies of men, and that by studying them they would be able to predict the future. This belief in the stars has a Greek name: astrology.

Some planets were believed to bring good luck, others misfortune: Mars meant war and Venus, love. To each of the five planets known to them they dedicated a day, and with the sun and the moon, that made seven. This was the origin of our seven-day week. In English we still say Satur (Saturn)-day, Sun-day and Mon (moon)-day, but the other days are named after different gods. In other languages – such as French or Italian – most of the days of the week still belong to the planets that the Babylonians first named. Would you ever have guessed that our weekdays had such

a strange and venerable history, reaching back all those thousands
of years?

To be nearer to their stars, and also to see them better in a misty
land, the Babylonians, and the Sumerians before them, erected
strange buildings with a wonderful name: ziggurats. These are tall,
broad towers made up of terraces piled one on top of another, with
formidable ramps and steep, narrow staircases. Right at the very
top was a temple dedicated to the moon, or one of the other planets. People came from far and wide to ask the priests to read their
fortunes in the stars, and brought offerings of great value. These
half-ruined ziggurats can still be seen today, poking out of the
rubble mounds, with inscriptions telling how this or that king built
or restored them. The earliest kings in this region lived as long ago
as 3000 BC, and the last around 550 BC.

The last great Babylonian king was Nebuchadnezzar. He lived
around 600 BC and is remembered for his feats of war. He fought
against Egypt and brought a vast number of foreign captives home
to Babylon as slaves. And yet his truly greatest deeds were not his
wars: he had huge canals and water cisterns dug in order to retain
the water and irrigate the land, so that it became rich and fertile.
Only when those canals became blocked with silt and the cisterns
filled with mud did the land become what it is today: a desert
wasteland and marshy plain with, here and there, one of those hills
I mentioned.

So, whenever we are glad that the week is nearly over, and Sun-
day is coming round again, we must spare a thought for those hills
of rubble in that hot and marshy plain, and for those fierce kings
with their long, black beards. For now we know how it all fits
together.

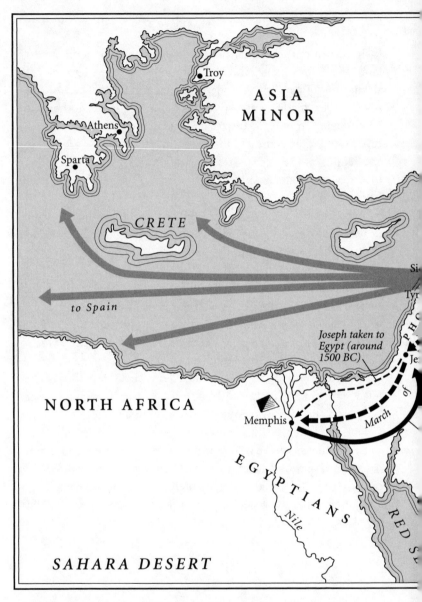

It was in this part of the world, between Mesopotamia and Egypt, that
the history of mankind began, with bloody battles and daring voyages by
Phoenician trading ships. You can look at this map again as you read the
next chapters.

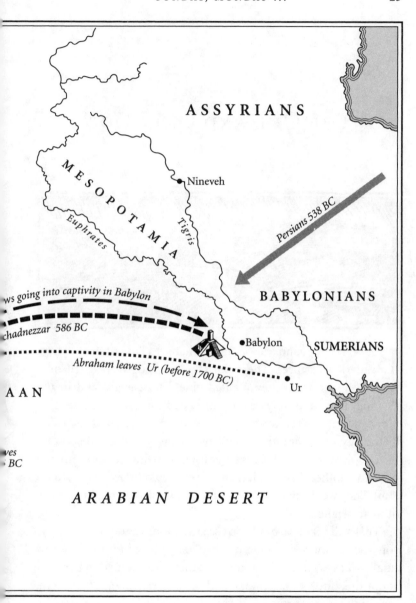

5

❖

The One and Only God

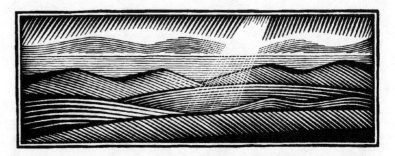

Between Egypt and Mesopotamia there is a land of deep valleys and rich pastures. There, for thousands of years, herdsmen tended their flocks. They planted vines and cereals, and in the evenings they sang songs, as country people do. But because it lay between those two countries, first it would be conquered and ruled by the Egyptians, and then the Babylonians would invade, so that the people who lived there were constantly being driven from one place to another. They built themselves towns and fortresses, to no avail. They were still not strong enough to resist the mighty armies of their neighbours.

'That's all very sad, but I can't see what it has to do with history,' you say, 'for the same thing must have happened to thousands of small tribes.' And you're right. But there was something special about this one, because, small and defenceless though they were, they didn't just become *part* of history, they *made* history – and by that I mean they shaped the course of all history to come. And this special something was their religion.

All other peoples prayed to many gods – you remember Isis and Osiris, Baal and Astarte. But these herdsmen only prayed to one god, their own special protector and leader. And when they sat beside their camp fires in the evening, and sang songs about their deeds and their battles, they sang of *his* deeds and *his* battles. *Their* god, they sang, was better and stronger and more exalted than all the gods of the heathen put together. Indeed, they insisted as the years went by, he was the only god there was. The One and Only God, Creator of heaven and earth, sun and moon, land and river, plant and beast, and of all mankind as well. It was he who raged furiously against them in the storm, but he never abandoned his people. Not when they were persecuted by the Egyptians, nor when they were carried off by the Babylonians. For that was their faith and their pride: they were *his* people, and he was *their* God.

You may have already guessed who these strange and powerless herdsmen were. They were the Jews. And the songs of their deeds, which were the deeds of their god, are the Old Testament of the Bible.

One day – but there's no hurry – you may come to read the Bible. Nowhere else will you find so many stories about ancient times so vividly told. And if you read them carefully, you may find that you now understand many of them better. There's the story of Abraham, for example. Do you remember where he came from? The answer is in the Book of Genesis, in chapter 11. He came from Ur in the Chaldees. Ur – that mound of rubble near the Persian Gulf, where they dug up all those ancient things like harps and game-boards and weapons and jewellery. But Abraham didn't live there in the earliest times. He was probably alive at the time of Hammurabi, the great lawgiver, which was – as you remember! – around 1700 BC. And many of Hammurabi's strict and just laws turn up again in the Bible.

But that isn't all the Bible has to say about ancient Babylon. Do you know the story of the Tower of Babel, when the people of a great city tried to build a tower that would reach up to heaven, and God was angry at their pride and stopped them building any higher by making them all speak different languages so that they could no longer understand one another? Well, Babel is Babylon. So now you will be able to understand the story better. For, as you know, the Babylonians really did build gigantic towers 'the top of which reached even to the heavens', and they built them so as to be nearer to the sun, the moon and the stars.

The story of Noah and the Flood is also set in Mesopotamia. A number of clay tablets have been dug up, inscribed with cuneiform script telling a story very similar to the one in the Bible.

One of Abraham of Ur's descendants (the Bible tells us) was Joseph, son of Jacob, whose brothers took him to Egypt and sold him, despite which he became a counsellor and minister to the pharaoh. You may know how the story goes on: how there was a famine throughout the land, and how Joseph's brothers travelled to Egypt to buy corn. At that time, the pyramids were already over a thousand years old, and Joseph and his brothers must have marvelled at them, just as we do today.

Rather than return to their own country, Joseph's brothers and their children settled in Egypt, and before long had to toil for the pharaoh as the Egyptians did at the time of the pyramids. In the first chapter of Exodus we read: 'And the Egyptians made the children of Israel to serve with rigour: and they made their lives bitter with hard bondage, in mortar and in brick . . .' In the end, Moses led them out of Egypt into the desert – probably in around 1250 BC. From there they tried to win back the promised land – that is, the land in which their ancestors had lived since the time of Abraham. And finally, after long, cruel and bloody battles, they succeeded. So now they had their own small kingdom, with its capital: Jerusalem. Their first king was Saul, who fought against a neighbouring tribe, the Philistines, and died on the battlefield.

The Bible has lots of good stories about the next kings, King David and King Solomon. Solomon was a wise and just king who ruled soon after 1000 BC, which was about seven hundred years after King Hammurabi and 2,100 years after King Menes. He built the first Temple of Jerusalem, although his architects weren't Jews, but foreign artisans from neighbouring lands. It was as large and as splendid as any built by the Egyptians or the Babylonians. But in one respect it was different: deep inside the heathen temples there were images of Anubis with his jackal's head, or of Baal, to whom even human sacrifices were made. Whereas in the innermost part of the Jewish temple – the Holy of Holies – there was no image at all. For of the God, whose first appearance in the history of the world was to the people of the Jews – God, the Almighty, the One and Only God – no image could or might be made. All that was there were the tablets of the Laws with their Ten Commandments. In these God had represented himself.

After Solomon's reign things went less well for the Jews. Their kingdom split in two: the kingdom of Israel and the kingdom of Judah. Many battles followed, at the end of which one half, the kingdom of Israel, was invaded by the Assyrians in 722 BC, and was conquered and destroyed.

Yet what is so remarkable is that the effect of so many disasters on the few Jews who survived them was to make them even more devout. Men arose among them – not priests, but simple people – who felt compelled to speak to their people, because God spoke through them. Their sermon was always the same: 'You yourselves are the cause of your misfortunes. God is punishing you for your sins.' Through the words of these prophets the Jewish people heard again and again that suffering was God's way of punishing them and testing their faith, and that one day salvation would come in the form of the Messiah, their Saviour, who would restore their people to its former glory and bring unending joy.

But their suffering was still far from over. You will remember the mighty Babylonian warrior and ruler, King Nebuchadnezzar. On his way to war with the Egyptians he marched through the Promised Land, where he destroyed the city of Jerusalem in 586 BC, put out the eyes of King Zedekiah and led the Jews in captivity to Babylon.

There they remained for nearly fifty years, until, in its turn, the Babylonian empire was destroyed by its Persian neighbour in 538 BC. When the Jews returned to their homeland they had changed. They were different from the surrounding tribes and saw them all as idol worshippers, who had failed to recognise the one true God. So they kept themselves apart and had nothing to do with their neighbours. It was at this time that the Old Testament was first written down as we know it today, 2,500 years later. To those around them, however, it was the Jews who seemed odd, if not ridiculous, with their ceaseless talk of a unique and invisible god, and their strict observance of the most tiresome and inflexible rules and practices ordained by a god whom no one could see. And if the Jews had been the first to distance themselves from other tribes, it was not long before those others were taking even greater care to avoid the Jews, that tiny remnant of a people that called itself 'chosen', who pored night and day over their sacred songs and scriptures as they tried to understand why the one and only God allowed his people to suffer so.

6

❖

I C-A-N R-E-A-D

How do you do it? Why, every schoolchild knows the answer: 'You spell out the words.' Yes, all right, but what *exactly* do you mean? 'Well, there's an I, which makes "I", and then a "C" and an "A" and an "N", which spells "can" – and so on, and with twenty-six letters you can write anything down.' Anything? Yes, anything. In any language? Just about.

Isn't that amazing? With twenty-six simple signs, each no more than a couple of squiggles, you can write down anything you like, be it wise or silly, angelic or wicked. It wasn't anything like as easy for the ancient Egyptians with their hieroglyphs. Nor was it for the people who used the cuneiform script, for they kept on inventing new signs that didn't stand just for single letter sounds, but for whole syllables or more. The idea that each sign might represent one sound, and that just twenty-six of those signs were all you needed to write every conceivable word, was a wholly new invention, one that can only have been made by people who did a lot of writing. Not just sacred texts and songs, but all sorts of letters, contracts and receipts.

These inventors were merchants. Men who travelled far and wide across the seas, bartering and trading in every land. They lived quite near the Jews, in the ports of Tyre and Sidon, cities much larger and more powerful than Jerusalem, and quite as noisy and bustling as Babylon. And in fact, their language and their religion were not unlike those of the peoples of Mesopotamia, though they didn't share their love of war. The Phoenicians (for this was the name of the people of Tyre and Sidon) made their conquests by other means. They sailed across the seas to unknown shores, where they landed and set up trading posts. The wild tribes living there brought them furs and precious stones in exchange for tools, cooking pots and coloured cloth. For Phoenician craftsmanship was known throughout the world – indeed, their artisans had even helped in the construction of Solomon's Temple in Jerusalem. Most popular of all their goods was their dyed cloth, especially the purple, which they sold throughout the world. Many Phoenicians stayed in their trading posts on foreign shores and built towns. Everywhere they went they were welcomed, in Africa, Spain and in southern Italy, on account of the beautiful things they brought.

Nor did they ever feel cut off from home, because they could write letters to their friends in Tyre and Sidon, using the wonderfully simple script they had invented, which we still use today. It's true! Take this 'B', for example: it is almost identical to the one used by the ancient Phoenicians, three thousand years ago, when they wrote home from distant shores, sending news to their families in those noisy, bustling harbour towns. Now you know this, you'll be sure not to forget the Phoenicians.

7

❖

HEROES AND THEIR WEAPONS

Here are some lines to be chanted aloud while tapping their
  rhythm,
Lines that were used by the poets of Greece in their stories
  of warfare,
Telling the contests of gods and of heroes in earlier ages.

(Verses like this, with six beats to each line, were called 'hexam-
eters' by the Greeks. The rhythm suits the Greek language, but it
sounds a little unnatural in English.)

You will have heard of the war that arose when Paris, the
  Trojan,
Sided with Venus and gave her the apple of gold in the
  contest,
How, as reward, she helped him to seize the beautiful Helen,
Wife of the King of the Greeks, Menelaus the Caller in
  Battle,
How an army of Greeks laid siege to the city of Troy to
  regain her,

With Agamemnon and Nestor the sage, Achilles and Ajax,
And countless heroes who fought in that war with the sons
    of King Priam,
Paris and Hector, for ten long summers and winters before
    the
City at last was conquered and razed to the ground by the
    victors.
Do you also remember the tale of the wily Odysseus?
How, returning from Troy, he experienced the strangest
    adventures,
Till, at last, on miraculous ships, he returned to his
    homeland,
To the wife who awaited her lord all the years of his absence.

Verses like these were chanted at feasts by Greek minstrels as they played their lyres. Later, they were written down and people came to believe that one poet, called Homer, had composed them all. They are read to this day and you, too, can enjoy them, for they are as fresh and vivid as ever – full of beauty and wisdom.

'Now wait a minute,' you're going to say. 'These are stories, not history. What I want to know is, *when* and *how* did these events take place?' A German businessman called Schliemann asked himself that same question, more than a hundred years ago. He read Homer over and over again, and longed to see all the beautiful places described by the poet. If only he could hold in his hands, just once, the wonderful weapons with which these heroes fought. And one day he did. For it turned out that all of it was true. Not in every detail, of course: the heroes named in the songs were no more real than the giants and witches in fairy tales. But the world that Homer describes – the drinking cups, the weapons, the buildings and the ships, the princes who were at the same time shepherds, and the heroes who were also sea raiders – were not inventions. When Schliemann told people this they laughed at him. But he didn't give up. He just kept putting money aside, so that one day he could go to Greece and see for himself. And when he had finally raised enough money, he hired labourers and set about digging in search of all the cities mentioned in Homer. At Mycenae he discovered palaces and the tombs of kings, armour and shields, just as the Homeric songs had described them. And he found Troy, too, and dug there. And it turned out that it really *had* been destroyed by fire. But in all those tombs and palaces there wasn't one inscription, so that for a long time no one could put a date to them until, one day, quite by chance, a ring was found in Mycenae that didn't come from there. On it, in hieroglyphs, was the name of an Egyptian king who had lived around 1400 BC, and had been the predecessor of Akhenaton, the great reformer.

Now at that time there was living in Greece, and on the many neighbouring islands and shores, a warlike people who had amassed great treasures. Greece was not so much a kingdom as a collection of small fortified cities, each with its own palace and king. The people were mostly seafarers, like the Phoenicians, only they traded less and fought more. They were often at war with one another, but on occasion would gang together to plunder other shores. And as their fortunes grew bigger, they grew bolder – and not just bolder, but braver, because to be a sea raider takes courage as well as cunning. So sea raiding was a task which fell to the nobility. The rest of the population were simple peasants and shepherds.

Now, unlike the Egyptians, the Babylonians and the Assyrians, these noblemen weren't interested in preserving the ways of their ancestors. Their many raids and battles with foreign peoples had opened their eyes to new ideas and taught them to relish variety and change. And it was at this point, and in this part of the world, that history began to progress at a much greater speed, because people no longer believed that the old ways were best. From now on, things were constantly changing. And this is why, nowadays, when we find even a fragment of pottery – in Greece, or anywhere else in Europe – we can say: 'this dates from roughly this or that period.' Because a hundred years later a pot like that would have gone out of fashion, and nobody would have wanted it.

It is now thought that all the beautiful things that Schliemann found in his excavations of Greek cities – the fine vessels and daggers decorated with hunting scenes, the golden shields and helmets, the jewellery and even the colourful paintings on the walls of the halls – were not invented there. They were first made not in Greece or in Troy, but on an island nearby. This island is called Crete. There, at the time of King Hammurabi – do you remember when that was? – the Cretans had already built splendid royal palaces, with innumerable rooms, staircases running up and down in all directions, great pillars, courtyards, corridors and cellars – a veritable labyrinth!

Speaking of labyrinths, have you ever heard the story of the evil Minotaur, half man, half bull, who lived in a labyrinth and made the Greeks send him seven youths and seven maidens each year as human sacrifices? Do you know where that was? It was in Crete, so there may be some truth in the story. Cretan kings may once have ruled over Greek cities, and those Greeks may have had to send them tribute. In any event, these Cretans were clearly a remarkable people, even if we still don't know much about them. You only have to look at the paintings on the walls of their palaces to see that they are unlike any made at the same time in Egypt or in Babylon. If you remember, the Egyptian pictures were very beautiful, but rather severe and stiff, a bit like their priests. This was not the case in Crete. What mattered most to them was to catch animals or people in rapid motion: hounds chasing wild boar, and people leaping over bulls – nothing was too hard for them to paint. The kings of the Greek cities clearly learnt a great deal from them.

But by 1200 BC this time of splendour was over. For it was at around that time (some two hundred years before the reign of

King Solomon) that new tribes came down from the north. Whether they were related to the former builders of Mycenae nobody knows for sure, but it is likely. In any event, they drove out the kings and installed themselves in their place. Meanwhile, Crete had been destroyed. But the memory of its magnificence lived on in the minds of the invaders, even when they founded new cities and built their own shrines. And as the centuries went by, the tales of the kings of ancient Mycenae became confused with those of their own battles and conquests, until they became part of their own history.

These newcomers were the Greeks, and the myths and songs sung in the courts of their nobles were the very same Homeric poems with which this chapter began. It is worth remembering that they were composed shortly before 800 BC.

When the Greeks came to Greece, they were not yet Greeks. Does that sound strange? Yet it is true. For the fact is that when the tribes from the north first invaded the lands they were to occupy, they weren't yet a unified people. They spoke different dialects and were obedient to different chieftains. They were tribes rather like the Sioux or the Mohicans you read about in stories of the Wild West, and had names such as the Dorians, Ionians and Aeolians. Like the American Indians they were warlike and brave, but in other ways they were quite different. The native Americans were familiar with iron, while the people of Mycenae and Crete – just as the songs of Homer tell us – had weapons made of bronze. And so these tribes arrived, with their wives and their children. The Dorians pushed furthest, right down into the southernmost tip of Greece which looks like a maple leaf and is called the Peloponnese. There they subdued the inhabitants, and set them to work in the fields. They themselves founded a city where they lived, and called it Sparta.

The Ionians who arrived after the Dorians found there was not enough room for them all in Greece. Many of them settled above the maple leaf, to the north of its stalk, on a peninsula called Attica. They made their homes by the sea and planted vines, cereals and olive trees. And they, too, founded a city, which they dedicated to the goddess Athena – she who, in the Homeric songs, so often came to the rescue of Ulysses the sailor. That city is Athens.

Like all the members of the Ionian tribe, the Athenians were great seafarers, and in due course they took possession of a number of small islands, known since that time as the Ionian Islands. Later, they went even further, and founded cities far across the sea away from Greece, along the fertile coast of Asia Minor, with its many sheltering bays. No sooner did the Phoenicians hear of these cities than they sailed there to trade. And the Greeks will have sold them olive oil and cereals, as well as silver and other metals found in those regions. But they soon learnt so much from the Phoenicians that they, too, sailed onwards, to distant shores, where they founded their own outposts, or colonies as we call them. And the Phoenicians passed on to them their wonderful way of writing using letters. You shall see what use they made of it.

8

❖

AN UNEQUAL STRUGGLE

Something very strange happened between 550 and 500 BC. I don't really understand it myself, but perhaps that's what makes it so interesting. In the high mountain chain that runs north of Mesopotamia a wild mountain tribe had long been living. They had a beautiful religion: they worshipped light and the sun and believed it to be in a state of constant warfare with the dark – that is, with the dark powers of evil.

These mountain people were the Persians. For hundreds of years they had been dominated, first by the Assyrians, and then by the Babylonians. One day they had had enough. Their ruler was a man of exceptional courage and intelligence called Cyrus, who was no longer prepared to put up with the oppression of his people. He led his band of horsemen down onto the plain of Babylon. The Babylonians looked down from their mighty ramparts and laughed at the little band of warriors that dared attack their city. Yet, under Cyrus's leadership, they succeeded, through courage and guile. And so Cyrus became lord of that great realm. His first act was to free all the peoples held in captivity by the Babylonians.

Among them were the Jews, who went home to Jerusalem (that was, as you remember, in 538 BC). Not content with his great kingdom, however, Cyrus marched on to conquer Egypt, only to die on the way. But his son, Cambyses, succeeded. Egypt fell and the pharaoh was deposed. That was the end of the Egyptian empire, which had lasted almost three thousand years! And with its end, this little Persian tribe became master of nearly all the known world. But only nearly: they hadn't yet swallowed up Greece. That was still to come.

It came after the death of Cambyses, during the reign of a great king named Darius. He governed the vast Persian empire – which now stretched from Egypt to the frontiers of India – in such a way that nothing happened anywhere that he himself had not decreed. He built roads so that his orders might be carried without delay to the furthest parts of his kingdom. And even his highest officials, the satraps, were spied on by informers known as 'the king's eyes and ears'. Darius now began to extend his empire out into Asia Minor, along whose coasts lay the cities of the Ionian Greeks.

Now the Greeks were not used to being part of a great empire, with a ruler who sent orders from God knows where in the heart of Asia, expecting instant obedience. Many of the people who lived in the Greek colonies were rich merchants, used to running their own affairs and making their own decisions about the administration of their cities, jointly and independently. They had no wish to be ruled by a Persian king, nor would they pay him tribute. So they rebelled, and threw out the Persian governors.

In this they were supported by the Greeks in the motherland, the original founders of the colonies, and in particular by the Athenians, who sent them ships. Never before had the king of Persia, the King of Kings – for that was his title – been so insulted. That this insignificant tribe, these nobodies, should dare to challenge *him*, the ruler of the world! He dealt with the Ionian cities in Asia Minor in less than no time. But he wasn't finished yet. He was furious with the Athenians for meddling in his affairs. With the aim of destroying Athens and conquering Greece, he equipped a large fleet. But his ships were caught in a violent storm, dashed against the cliffs and sunk. At this his anger knew no bounds. The story goes that he appointed a slave to call out three times at every meal: 'Sire, remember the Athenians!' So great was his fury.

He then sent his son-in-law, with a new and mighty fleet, to sail against Athens. They conquered many islands on their way and destroyed a lot of cities. They finally dropped anchor not far from Athens, at a place called Marathon. There, the whole great Persian army disembarked, ready to march on Athens. It is said that they numbered seventy thousand men, as many as the entire population of Athens. With roughly ten thousand soldiers the Athenian army was outnumbered seven to one. Their fate was surely sealed.

But not quite. For the Athenians had a general named Miltiades, a brave and able man, who had lived for many years among the Persians, and knew their fighting tactics. Added to which, the Athenians all knew what was at stake: their freedom and their lives, and those of their wives and children. So there at Marathon they formed ranks, and fell upon the startled Persians. And they were victorious. The Persians suffered heavy losses. Those remaining took to their ships and fled.

Such a victory! And against such odds! Others in his place might have thought of nothing but celebration. But Miltiades was shrewd as well as brave. He had noted that instead of sailing back the way they had come, the Persian ships had turned towards Athens, which lay undefended and open to attack. But as luck would have it, the distance from Marathon to Athens was greater by sea than by land. For ships had to negotiate a long spit of land easily crossed on foot. This Miltiades did. He sent a messenger ahead, who was to run as fast as he could, to warn the Athenians. This was the famous Marathon Run after which we call our race. Famous, because the messenger ran so far and so fast that all he could do was deliver his message before he fell down dead.

Meanwhile Miltiades and his army had taken the same route, marching in tremendous haste. This was just as well, for no sooner had they reached the harbour at Athens than the Persian fleet appeared over the horizon. But there was no more fighting: at the sight of their heroic enemy, the disheartened Persians turned tail

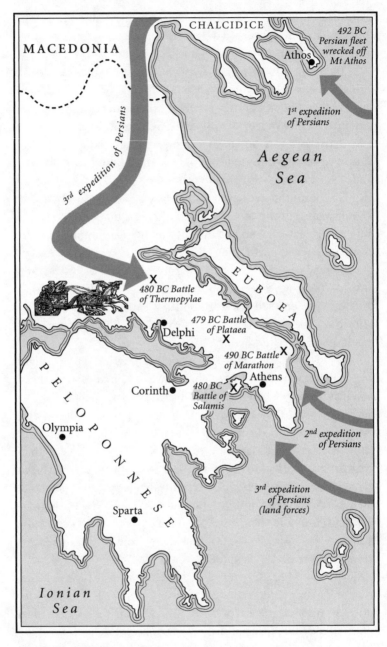

The battles of the Persians in Greece.

and sailed for home. And not just Athens, but the whole of Greece was saved. This was 490 BC.

How the great Darius, King of Kings, must have cursed when he learnt of the defeat at Marathon! But at the time there was little he could do about Greece, for a revolt had broken out in Egypt which had to be suppressed. He died soon after, leaving his son and successor, Xerxes, to take revenge on Greece once and for all.

Xerxes, a hard, ambitious man, needed no urging. He assembled an army from among all the subject peoples of his empire. Dressed in their traditional costumes, with their weapons, their bows and arrows, shields and swords, lances, war-chariots and slings, they were a vast, swirling multitude, said by some to number more than a million men. What hope had the Greeks in the face of such a host? This time Xerxes himself took command. But when the Persians tried to cross the narrow neck of sea which separates Asia Minor from today's Istanbul, on a bridge made of boats, rough waves tore the bridge apart. In his fury Xerxes had the waves lashed with chains. But I doubt if the sea took any notice.

One part of this gigantic army attacked Greece by sea, while another part marched overland. In northern Greece, a small army of Spartans, who had made an alliance with the Athenians, tried to block the Persian advance in a narrow pass called Thermopylae. The Persians called on the Spartans to throw down their weapons. 'Come and get them yourselves!' was the reply. 'We've enough arrows here to blot out the sun!' threatened the Persians. 'So much the better', cried the Spartans, 'then we'll fight in the shade!' But a treacherous Greek showed the Persians a way over the mountains and the Spartan army was surrounded and trapped. All three hundred Spartans and seven hundred of their allies were killed in the battle, but not one of them tried to run away, for that was their law. Later, a Greek poet wrote these words in their memory:

Go tell the Spartans, thou who passest by,
That here obedient to their laws we lie.

Now the Athenians had not been idle since their great victory at Marathon. And they had a new leader called Themistocles, an astute and far-sighted man, who repeatedly warned his fellow citizens that a miracle like Marathon could only happen once, and that if Athens were to continue to hold out against the Persians, it must have a fleet. So a fleet was built.

Themistocles had the whole of Athens evacuated – not that the population can have been very large in those days – and sent to the little island of Salamis nearby. The Athenian fleet then positioned itself by this island. When the Persian land army arrived and found Athens abandoned, they set fire to the city and razed it to the ground, while the Athenians on their island remained unharmed as they watched their burning city from afar. But now the Persian fleet appeared, and threatened to surround Salamis.

The allies panicked, and were all for taking to their ships and leaving the Athenians to their fate. At this moment Themistocles demonstrated his extraordinary ingenuity and daring. Having finally succeeded in persuading the allies not to leave, he secretly sent a messenger to Xerxes saying: 'Make haste and attack, or the Athenians' allies will escape you!' Xerxes, who must have heard from his spies that the allies were set on leaving, fell for it. The next morning he attacked with his many small and nimble warships. And he lost. The Greek ships were larger and less easy to manoeuvre, but once again they were fighting desperately for their freedom. Not only that, but their victory ten years earlier at Marathon had inspired them with confidence. From a vantage point Xerxes was forced to look on while his smaller, lighter galleys were rammed and sunk by the Greeks' heavy ships. Aghast, he ordered the retreat. And so for the second time the Athenians were victorious, and against an even greater army than before. This was in 480 BC.

Shortly afterwards, in 479 BC, the Persian land army was also defeated by the combined forces of the Greeks and their allies, near Plataea. After this the Persians never again dared attack the Greeks. And this is very interesting, because it wasn't as if the Persians were weaker or more stupid than the Greeks – far from it. But, as I said before, the Greeks were different. For, whereas the great empires of the East bound themselves so tightly to the traditions and teachings of their ancestors that they could scarcely move, the Greeks – and the Athenians in particular – did the opposite. Almost every year they came up with something new. Everything was always changing. The same went for their leaders. Miltiades and Themistocles, the great heroes of the Persian wars, learnt this to their cost: one moment it was high praise, honours and monuments to their achievements, the next it was accusations, slander and exile. This was not the best feature of the Athenians, yet it was part of their nature. Always trying out new ideas, never satisfied, never at rest. Which explains why, during the hundred years that followed the Persian wars, more went on in the minds of the people of the little city of Athens than in a thousand years in all the great empires of the East. The ideas, the painting, sculpture and architecture, the plays and poetry, the inventions and experiments, the discussions and arguments which the young brought to the marketplaces and the old to their council chambers still continue to concern us today. It is strange that it should be so, and yet it's true. And what would it have been like if the Persians had won at Marathon? Or at Salamis, ten years later? That I cannot say.

9

❖

TWO SMALL CITIES
IN ONE SMALL LAND

I said earlier that Greece, when set against the Persian empire, was no more than a small peninsula, dotted here and there with little cities of busy merchants, a country of barren mountain ranges and stony fields, able to sustain only a handful of people. And also, as you may remember, that the Greeks belonged to a number of tribes, the most important of them being the Dorians in the south and the Ionians and the Aeolians in the north. These tribes differed little from one another, either in appearance or in language. They spoke different dialects, which they could all understand if they chose. But they very rarely did. For, as is often the case, these close-related, neighbouring tribes were unable to get on with one another. They spent all their time exchanging insults and ridicule, when actually they were jealous of each other. For Greece had no one king or administration in common. Instead, each city was a kingdom in itself.

But one thing united the Greeks: their religion and their sport. And I say 'one thing' because, strangely enough, sport and religion weren't two separate things – they were closely connected. For instance, in honour of Zeus, the Father of the Gods, great sporting contests were held every four years in his sanctuary at Olympia. As well as large temples there was a stadium at Olympia, and all the Greeks – the Dorians, Ionians, Spartans and Athenians – came there to show how well they could run, throw the discus and the javelin, fight hand to hand and race chariots. To be victorious at Olympia was the greatest honour in a man's life. The prize was no more than a simple garland made from sprigs of wild olive, but what fame for the winners: the greatest poets sang their praises, the greatest sculptors carved their statues to stand for ever in Olympia. They were shown in their chariots, throwing the discus, or rubbing oil into their bodies before the fight. Victory statues like these can still be seen today – there may even be one in your local museum.

Since the Olympic Games took place once every four years, and were attended by all the Greeks, they provided everyone with a convenient way to measure time. This was gradually adopted throughout Greece. Just as we say BC meaning 'Before the birth of Christ' or AD for after the birth of Christ (*Anno Domini* which means the year of our Lord in Latin), the Greeks would say: 'At the time of this or that Olympiad'. The first Olympiad was in 776 BC. Can you work out when the tenth would have been? But don't forget! They only happened every four years.

But it wasn't only the Olympic Games that brought all the Greeks together. There was another sanctuary which they all held sacred. This one was at Delphi, and belonged to the sun god Apollo, and there was something most peculiar about it. As sometimes happens in volcanic regions, there was a fissure in the ground from which vapour issued. If anyone inhaled it, it literally clouded their mind. It was as if they were drunk or delirious, and nothing they said made any sense.

The very meaninglessness of these utterances seemed deeply mysterious to the Greeks, who said that 'the god himself speaks through a mortal mouth'. So they had a priestess – whom they called Pythia – sit over the fissure on a three-legged stool, while other priests interpreted her babble as predictions of the future.

The shrine was known as the Delphic Oracle, and at difficult moments of their lives Greeks from everywhere made pilgrimages to Delphi, to consult the god Apollo. The answer they received was often far from clear, and could be understood in a variety of ways. And in fact we still say that a vague or enigmatic answer is 'oracular'.

Let us now take a closer look at two of Greece's most important cities: Sparta and Athens. We already know something about the Spartans: they were Dorians, who, when they arrived in Greece, in around 1100 BC, enslaved the former inhabitants and put them to work on the land. But the slaves outnumbered their masters, and the danger of rebellion meant that the Spartans had to be constantly on the alert lest they find themselves homeless again. They only had one aim in life: to be fighting fit, ready to crush any uprising by their slaves, and to protect themselves from the surrounding peoples still at liberty.

And they really did think of nothing else. Their lawgiver, Lycurgus, had already seen to that. A Spartan baby that appeared weak, and unlikely to grow up to be a warrior, was killed at birth. A strong infant had to be made stronger. From a very young age he must train from dawn till dusk, learn to endure pain, hunger and cold, must eat poorly and be denied all pleasure. Boys were beaten just to harden them to pain. A harsh upbringing is still called 'spartan' today, and as you know, it worked: at Thermopylae, in 480 BC, in obedience to their law, the Spartans allowed themselves to be massacred by the Persians. Knowing how to die like that isn't easy. But knowing how to live is, perhaps, even harder. And this is what the Athenians aimed to do. They weren't looking for an easy, comfortable life, but one which had meaning. A life of which something remained after one's death. Something of benefit to those who came after. You shall see how they succeeded.

Had they not lived in fear – fear of their own slaves – the Spartans might never have become so warlike and brave. Athenians had fewer reasons to be afraid and they didn't live under the same pressures. Things were different for them even though, as in Sparta, the nobles who once ruled Athens imposed harsh laws drawn up by an Athenian named Draco. (These laws were so strict that people still speak of 'Draconian' severity.) But the people of Athens, who had roamed the seas in their ships, and had heard and seen so many different things, did not consent to this for long.

It was, in fact, a nobleman who had the wisdom to try to give the little state a new system of government. His name was Solon, and the laws he introduced in 594 BC – at the time of Nebuchadnezzar – were named after him. They stated that the people, that is, the city's inhabitants, should decide the city's affairs themselves. They should assemble in the marketplace of Athens and vote. The majority should decide and should elect a council of experts to put those decisions into effect. This sort of government is called democracy, or 'the rule of the people', in Greek. This didn't mean that everyone who lived in Athens was entitled to vote in the Assembly. Citizenship depended on wealth and influence, and many people, including women and slaves, played no part in government. But many Athenians could at least have their say, and so they took an interest in how their city was run. 'Polis' is Greek for city, 'politics', the affairs of a city.

For a while individual noblemen curried favour with the people to win their votes, and then seized power. Rulers like these were called tyrants. But the people soon expelled them and took better care next time to ensure that it was they themselves who really governed. I have already told you about the wayward nature of the Athenians. And it was this, together with a real fear of losing their freedom once again, which led them to banish any politician who showed signs of becoming too popular, lest he seize power for himself and rule as a tyrant. The same free people of Athens who defeated the Persians later treated Miltiades and Themistocles with just such ingratitude.

But there was one politician who avoided this fate. His name was Pericles. When he spoke in the Assembly, the Athenians always believed that it was they who had made the decisions, whereas in fact it was Pericles, who had made up his mind long before. This wasn't because he held any special office or had any particular power – he was simply the wisest and the most intelligent. And so he gradually worked his way up until, by 444 BC – a number as beautiful as the time it represents – he was, in effect, the city's sole ruler. His chief concern was that Athens should maintain its power at sea, and this he achieved through alliances with other Ionian cities who paid Athens for its protection. In this way the Athenians grew rich and could at last afford to make use of their great gifts.

And now I can hear you asking: 'But what exactly *did* they do that was so great?' And I can only say 'everything'. But two things interested them most and these were truth and beauty.

Their assemblies had taught the Athenians how to discuss all matters openly, with arguments for and against. This was good training in learning how to think. Soon they were using arguments and counter-arguments, not just when they were debating every-day matters like whether or not to increase taxation, but in discussions about the whole of nature. The Ionians in the colonial outposts may have been ahead of them here, for they had already reflected on what the world was actually made of, and what might be the cause of all events and experiences.

This sort of reflection is what we call philosophy. In Athens, however, their reflecting – or philosophising – went much further. They also wanted to know how people should act, what was good and what was evil, and what was just and what was unjust. They wanted to find an explanation for human existence and discover the essence of all things. Of course, not everyone agreed on matters as complex as these – there were various theories and opinions that were argued back and forth, just as in the people's Assembly. And since that time, the sort of reflection and reasoned argument we call philosophy has never stopped.

But the Athenians didn't only pace up and down their porticos and sports fields talking about things like the essence of life and how to recognise it, and where it came from. They didn't just picture the world in a new way in their minds, they saw it with new eyes. When you look at the works of Greek artists, and see how fresh and simple and beautiful they are, it is as if their creators were seeing the world for the first time. We spoke of the statues of Olympic champions earlier. They show fine human beings, not posed, but looking as if the position they are shown in is the most natural one in the world. And it is *because* they seem so natural that they are so beautiful.

The Greeks portrayed their gods with the same beauty and humanity. The most famous sculptor of such statues was Phidias. He did not create mysterious and supernatural images, like the colossal statues in Egyptian temples. Although some of his temple statues were large and splendid and made of precious materials like ivory and gold, their beauty was never insipid, and they had a noble and natural grace which must have inspired confidence in the gods they represented, and the same can be said for Athenian paintings and buildings. But nothing remains of the pictures they painted on the walls of their halls and assembly rooms. All we have are little paintings on pottery – on vases and urns. Their loveliness tells us what we have lost.

However, the temples are still standing. Even in Athens. And best of all, the citadel of Athens is still there – the Acropolis – where new sanctuaries made of marble were erected in the time of Pericles, because the old ones had been burnt and destroyed by the Persians while the Athenians watched from the island of Salamis. The Acropolis still contains the most beautiful buildings we know. Not the grandest, or the most splendid. Simply the most beautiful. Every detail is so clear and so simple that one cannot imagine it otherwise. All the forms which the Greeks employed in these buildings were to be used again and again in architecture. You will find Greek columns – of which there are several kinds – in almost every city of the world, once you have learnt to recognise them. But none of them is as beautiful as those on the Acropolis where they are used not for show and decoration but for the purpose for which they were invented: as elegant supports for the roof.

Both wisdom of thought and beauty of form were to be united by the Athenians in a third art: the art of poetry. And here, too, they invented something new: the theatre. Their theatre, like their sport, was also once bound up with their religion, with festivals held in honour of their god Dionysus (also known as Bacchus). On his feast-day a performance was held which could last all day. It took place in the open air, and the actors wore huge masks and high heels, so that they could be easily seen from a distance. We still have plays which they performed. Some are serious, grand and solemn. They are called tragedies. But there were other ones that were very sharp, witty and lively, which made fun of certain Athenian citizens. These are called comedies. I could tell you lots more about the Athenians – about their historians and their doctors, their singers, their thinkers and their artists, but I think it would be better for you to find out about them yourself, one day. Then you'll see that I haven't exaggerated.

10

❖

THE ENLIGHTENED ONE
AND HIS LAND

A nd now let us go to the opposite end of the world. To India and then to China, so that we can find out what was going on in these vast lands at the time of the Persian wars. Like Mesopotamia, India also had a very ancient civilisation, and at about the same time as the Sumerians were holding sway at Ur – that is, around 2500 BC – there was a mighty city in the valley of the Indus. (The Indus is a great river which flows through what is Pakistan today.) It had well-drained streets, canals, granaries and workshops, and was called Mohenjo Daro, and until its discovery in the 1920s nobody had even dreamt of its existence. When it was excavated, things came to light that were as remarkable as any found in the rubble mounds at Ur. Although we know almost nothing about the people who built Mohenjo Daro, we do know that different people arrived much later, and that they are ancestors of the people who inhabit northern India and Pakistan today. These people spoke a language similar not only to those spoken by the Persians and Greeks, but also to those of the Romans and the Teutons. An example of this is the word for 'father': in ancient Indian it was *pitar*, the Greek is *patèr*, the Latin, *páter*.

Since both Indians and Europeans speak these languages, they are known as the Indo-European family of languages. Whether the fact that the languages are similar means that the people who speak them are actually distant relatives we don't yet know for sure. But in any event, the people who spoke an Indo-European language invaded India much as the Dorians invaded Greece, and may have enslaved the native population just as they did.

In time, most of the continent was subdued by the descendants of these invaders, who, like the Spartans, maintained a distance between themselves and the peoples they had conquered. Traces of this division persist today in what is known as the 'caste system'. In it, professions or occupations are strictly separated from each other. Men who were warriors had to remain warriors, and their sons had to be warriors too, because they belonged to the warrior caste. Other castes were similarly closed, like those of farmers and craftsmen. A farmer could never become a craftsman, or a crafts-man a farmer – nor could their sons. Someone who was a member of one caste couldn't marry a girl from another – or even share a meal with a member of another caste.

At the top were the priests, or Brahmins – even higher than the warriors. Their task was to perform sacrifices to the gods and look after the temples, and, as in Egypt, they were in charge of sacred knowledge. They had to learn all the chants and prayers off by heart so that they were preserved and handed down, unchanged. They did this for more than a thousand years until the texts were finally written down.

A tiny part of the population was excluded from any caste. They were pariahs – people who were given the dirtiest and most unpleas-ant tasks. Not even members of the lowest castes could associate with them – their very touch was thought to be defiling. So they became known as the 'untouchables'. They weren't allowed to fetch water from the streams that other Indians used, and had to make sure that their shadow never touched another person, because even that was thought to be defiling. People can be very cruel.

But it would be wrong to say that the Indians were a cruel people. On the contrary, their priests were serious and profound thinkers, who often withdrew into the forest to meditate, alone and undisturbed, on the most difficult questions. They meditated on their many fierce gods, and on Brahma, the Sublime, the highest divinity of all. They seemed to sense the breath of this one Supreme Being throughout the natural world – in gods as well as men, and in every animal and plant. They felt him active in all things: in the shining of the sun and in the sprouting of crops, in growing and in dying. He was everywhere, just as a little salt dropped in water makes all the water salty, down to the last drop. In all the variety of nature, in all her cycles and transformations, we only see the surface. A soul may inhabit the body of a man, and after his death, that of a tiger, or a cobra, or any other living creature – the cycle will only end when that soul has become so pure that it can at last become one with the Supreme Being. For the divine breath of Brahma is the essence of all things. To help their pupils understand this, Indian priests had a lovely formula which you may turn over in your mind. All they said was 'This is you', by which they meant that everything around you – all the animals and plants and your fellow human beings – are, with you yourself, part of the breath of God.

The priests had invented an extraordinary way of actually *feeling* this all-embracing unity. They would sit down somewhere in the depths of the ancient Indian forest and think about it, and nothing else, for hours, days, weeks, months, years. They sat on the ground, upright and still, their legs crossed and their eyes lowered. They breathed as little as possible and they ate as little as possible – indeed, some of them even tormented themselves in special ways to purify themselves and help them sense the divine breath within them.

Holy men like these penitents and hermits, were common in India three thousand years ago, and there are still many there today. But one of them was different from all the others. He was a nobleman called Gautama, and he lived about five hundred years before Christ.

The story goes that Gautama, whom they were later to call the 'Enlightened One', the 'Buddha', grew up in Eastern luxury and

splendour. It is said that he had three palaces which he never left –
one for summer, one for winter, and one for the rainy season – and
that they were always filled with the most beautiful music. His
father wouldn't allow him to leave their lofty terraces because he
wanted to keep him far away from all the sorrows of the world. And
no one who was sick or unhappy was ever allowed near him. However, one day Gautama summoned his carriage and went out. On
the way he caught sight of a man, bent with age, and he asked his
driver what it was. The driver was forced to explain that this was an
old man. Deep in thought, Gautama returned to his palace. On
another occasion he saw someone who was sick. No one had ever
told him about illness. Pondering even more deeply, he went home
to his wife and his small son. The third time he went out he saw a
dead man. This time he didn't go home to his palace. Coming
across a hermit in the road, he decided that he, too, would go into
the wilderness, where he would meditate on the sufferings of this
world which had been revealed to him in the forms of old age, sickness and death.

Later in his life Gautama told the story of his decision in a
sermon: 'And so it came about that, in the full freshness and enjoyment of my youth, in glowing health, my hair still black, and
against the wishes of my weeping and imploring elders, I shaved
my head and beard, dressed in coarse robes, and forsook the shelter of my home.'

For six years he led the life of a hermit and penitent. But his
meditations were deeper and his sufferings greater than those of
any other hermit. As he sat, he almost stopped breathing altogether, and endured the most terrible pains. He ate so little that he
would often faint with weakness. And yet, in all those years, he
found no inner peace. For he didn't only reflect on the nature of
the world, and whether all things were really one. He thought
about its sadness, of all the pain and suffering of mankind – of old
age, sickness and death. And no amount of penitence could help
him there.

And so, gradually, he began to eat again. His strength returned, and he breathed like other people. Other hermits who had

formerly admired him now despised him, but he took no notice of them. Then, one night, as he sat beneath a fig tree in a beautiful clearing in a wood, understanding came. Suddenly he realised what he had been seeking all those years. It was as if an inner light had made everything clear. Now, as the 'Enlightened One', the Buddha, he went out to proclaim his discovery to all men.

It wasn't long before he found like-minded people who were soon convinced that he had found a way out of human suffering. And because these followers admired the Buddha, they formed what we would call an 'order' of monks and nuns. This order lived on after his death, and still exists today in many Eastern countries. You can recognise its members by their yellow robes and their austere way of life.

I imagine that you'd like to know exactly what happened to Gautama, as he sat under that fig tree – the Tree of Enlightenment, as it became known – that took away his doubts and brought him inner peace. But if you want me to try and explain it, you will have to do some hard thinking too. After all, Gautama spent six whole years thinking about this and nothing else. The idea that came to him, his great Enlightenment, the solution to human suffering, was this: if we want to avoid suffering, we must start with ourselves, because all suffering comes from our own desires. Think of it like this. If you are sad because you can't have something you want – maybe a book or a toy – you can do one of two things: you can do your best to get it, or you can stop wanting it. Either way, if you succeed, you won't be sad any more. This is what the Buddha taught. If we can stop ourselves wanting all the beautiful and pleasant things in life, and can learn to control our greed for happiness, comfort, recognition and affection, we shan't feel sad any more when, as so often happens, we fail to get what we want. He who ceases to wish for anything ceases to feel sad. If the appetite goes, the pain goes with it.

I can already hear you saying: 'That's all very well, but people can't help wanting things!' The Buddha thought otherwise. He said that it is possible to control our desires, but to do so we need to work on ourselves, perhaps even for years, so that in the end we only have the desires we want to have. In other words, we can become masters of ourselves, in the same way that an elephant driver learns to control his elephant. A person's highest achievement on earth is to reach the point at which he or she no longer has any desires. This is the Buddha's 'inner calm', the blissful peace of someone who no longer has any wishes, someone who is kind to everyone and demands nothing. The Buddha also taught that a person who is master of all his wishes will no longer be reborn after his death. Only souls which cling to life are reborn – or so the Buddha's followers believe. He who no longer clings to life is released from the unending cycle of birth and death, and is at last freed from all suffering. Buddhists call this state 'Nirvana'.

So this was the Enlightenment that the Buddha experienced under the fig tree: the realisation that, instead of giving in to our wishes, we can break free from them – rather like when we are feeling thirsty and take no notice, and the feeling goes away. You can see that the way to do this is far from easy. The Buddha called it the 'middle way', because it lay between useless self-torment and thoughtless pleasure-seeking. The important thing is to find the right balance: in what we believe, in the decisions we make, in what we say and what we do, in the way we live, in our ambitions, in our conscience and our innermost thoughts.

That was the essential message of the Buddha's sermons, and these sermons made such a deep impression on people that many followed him and worshipped him as a god. Today there are almost as many Buddhists in the world as there are Christians, especially in South East Asia, in Sri Lanka, Tibet, China and Japan. But not many of them are able to live their lives in accordance with the Buddha's teachings, and so achieve that inner calm.

11

❖

THE GREAT TEACHER
OF A GREAT PEOPLE

When I was a schoolboy, China was to us, as it were, 'at the other end of the world'. At most we had seen the odd picture on a teacup or a vase, so that we imagined a country of stiff little men with long plaits down their backs, and artful gardens full of hump-backed bridges and little turrets hung with tinkling bells.

Of course there never was such a fairyland, although it is true that for more than two hundred years, until 1912, Chinese men were made to wear their hair plaited in a pigtail, and that we first learnt about them through delicate objects of porcelain and ivory made by skilled craftsmen. From their palace in the capital emperors had ruled over China for more than a thousand years. The fabled emperors of China who called themselves the 'Son of Heaven', just as the Egyptian pharaoh called himself 'Son of the Sun'. But at the time I am going to talk about, around 2,500 years ago, all this was yet to come, though China was already a vast and ancient kingdom. In its fields many millions of hard-working peasants grew rice and other crops, while in the towns people strolled through the streets in sumptuous, silken gowns.

Over all these people a king ruled, and beneath him many princes who governed the many provinces of this immense country which was larger than Egypt, and larger than Assyria and Babylonia put together. But soon these princes had become so mighty that the king could no longer command their obedience. They were constantly at war with each other, the big provinces gobbling up the smaller ones. And because the empire was so vast that in all its corners the Chinese spoke quite different languages, it would probably have fallen apart altogether had they not had one thing in common. This was their script.

'But wait a minute!' you say. 'If they all spoke different languages, how could using the same script make any difference?' Well, Chinese writing is special. You can read and understand it even if you don't know a single word of the spoken language. That must be magic! No, absolutely not, it is really quite simple. Instead of writing words you write things. If you want to write 'sun', you make a picture like this: ⊟. Then you can read it in any language: sun in English, *soleil* in French or *jih* in Mandarin Chinese. Everyone who knows the sign will know what it means. Now I'll show you how to make the sign for 'tree'. Again it is quite easy, just a couple of strokes like this: 木. In Mandarin it is pronounced 'mu', but you hardly need know the sign to guess it is a tree.

'All right,' you say, 'I can see that works quite well for things you can draw, but what if you want to write "white"? Do you just paint a blob of white paint? And what if you want to write "East"? You can hardly draw a picture of "East"!' On the contrary, you'll see that it's all quite straightforward. We can write 'white' by drawing something that is white – in this case, a sunbeam. A stroke coming out of a sun 白 stands for 'white' – *blanc* – *pai*, and so on. 'And "East"?' East is where the sun rises, behind the trees. So I draw a picture of a sun behind a tree: 東!

That is clever, isn't it? Well, it is and it isn't. There are two sides to everything! For when you think how many words and things there are in the world, in Chinese each one has its own sign which must be learnt. There are already more than forty thousand of them, and some are really complicated and hard to learn. So I think we should congratulate our Phoenicians on their twenty-six letters, don't you? However, the Chinese have been writing like this for many thousands of years, and their signs are read in many parts of Asia, even where no Chinese is spoken. And this meant that the thoughts and principles of the great men of China were able to spread quickly and influence many people.

Now at the same time as the Buddha was seeking to relieve man's suffering in India (as you remember, that was around 500 BC), there was in China another great man who was also trying to make people happy through his teachings. And yet he was as different from the Buddha as he could possibly be. He wasn't a wealthy nobleman's son but came from a family that had fallen on hard times. He didn't become a hermit, but an adviser and teacher. Rather than helping individuals not to want things, and therefore not to suffer, what mattered most to Confucius was that everybody should live peacefully together – parents with their children and rulers with their subjects. That was his goal: to teach the right way of living together. And he succeeded. Thanks to his teachings all the peoples of China lived together for thousands of years, more contentedly and more peacefully than many other peoples of the world. So I am sure you will be interested in the teachings of Confucius – or K'ung Fu-tzu, as he was called in Chinese. They aren't hard to understand. Nor to remember. Perhaps that's why he was so successful.

What Confucius proposed is quite simple. You may not like it, but there is more wisdom in it than first meets the eye. What he taught was this: outward appearances are more important than we think – bowing to our elders, letting others go through a door first, standing up to speak to a superior, and many other similar things for which they had more rules in China than we have. All such practices, so he believed, were not just a matter of chance. They meant something, or had done once. Usually something beautiful. Which is why Confucius said: 'I believe in Antiquity, and I love it.' By this he meant that he believed in the sound good sense of all the many-thousand-year-old customs and habits, and he repeatedly urged his fellow countrymen to observe them. He thought that everything in life ran more smoothly if people did. Almost by itself, as it were, without the need to think too hard about it. Of course such behaviour does not *make* people good, but it helps them *stay* good.

For Confucius had a very good opinion of humanity. He said that all people were born honest and good, and that, deep down, they remained so. Anyone seeing a small child playing near the water's edge will worry lest it fall in, he said. Concern for our fellow human beings and sympathy for the misfortunes of others are inborn sentiments. All we need do is to make sure we do not lose them. And that, said Confucius, is why we have families. Someone who is always good to his parents, who obeys them and cares for them – and this comes naturally to us – will treat others in the same way, and will obey the laws of the state in the same way that he obeys his father. Thus, for Confucius, the family, with its brotherly and sisterly love and respect for parents, was the most important thing of all. He called it 'the root of humanity'.

However, he didn't mean that respect and obedience should be shown only by a subject to his ruler, and not the other way round as well. On the contrary, Confucius and his disciples often came up against obstinate princes, and would usually tell them exactly what they thought of them. For a prince must take the lead in observing the forms. He must demonstrate a father's love in providing for his people and deal with them justly. If he neglects to do so, and brings suffering on his subjects, then it serves him right if they rise up and overthrow him. So taught Confucius and his followers. For a prince's first duty was to be an example to all who lived in his kingdom.

It may seem to you that what Confucius taught was obvious. But that was exactly his intention. He wanted to teach something that everyone would find easy to grasp, because it was so just and fair. Then living together would become much easier. I have already told you that he succeeded. And, thanks to his teaching, that enormous empire, with all its provinces, was saved from falling apart.

But you mustn't think that in China there weren't other people more like the Buddha, for whom what mattered was not living together and bowing to one another, but the great mysteries of the world. A wise man of this sort lived in China at about the same time as Confucius. His name was Lao-tzu. He is said to have been an official who became tired of the way people lived at court. So he gave up his job and wandered off into the lonely mountains at the frontier of China to be a hermit.

A simple border guard at a frontier pass asked him to set down his thoughts in writing, before leaving the world of men. And this Lao-tzu did. But whether the border guard could make head or tail of them I do not know, for they are very mysterious and hard to grasp. Their meaning is roughly this: in all the world – in wind and rain, in plants and animals, in the passage from day to night, in the movements of the stars – everything acts in accordance with one great law. This he calls the 'Tao', which means the Way, or the Path. Only man in his restless striving, in his many plans and projects, even in his prayers and sacrifices, resists, as it were, this law, obstructs its path and prevents its fulfilment.

Therefore the one thing we must do, said Lao-tzu, is: do nothing. Be still within ourselves. Neither look nor listen to anything around us, have no wishes or opinions. Only when a person has become like a tree or a flower, empty of all will or purpose, will he begin to feel the Tao – that great universal law which makes the heavens turn and brings the spring – begin to work within him. This teaching, as you see, is hard to grasp and harder still to follow. Perhaps, in the solitude of the distant mountains, Lao-tzu was able to take 'doing nothing' so far that the law began to work within him in the way he described. But maybe it is just as well that it was Confucius, and not Lao-tzu, who became the great teacher of his people. What do you think?

12

❖

The Greatest Adventure
of All

Greece's age of splendour was short-lived. The Greeks could do everything but live in peace with one another. Above all, it was Athens and Sparta who could not put up with one another for long. By 430 BC the two states were locked in a long and bitter conflict. This was the Peloponnesian War. The Spartans marched on Athens, savagely laying waste to the countryside all around. They uprooted all the olive trees and this was a terrible misfortune because it takes years for a newly planted olive tree to bear fruit. The Athenians hit back, attacking the Spartan colonies to the south of Italy, at Syracuse in Sicily. There was a great deal of fighting and retaliation, a terrible plague in Athens in which Pericles died and, in the end, Athens lost the war and the city walls were torn down. As is usually the case with wars, not only Athens but the whole country was exhausted by the conflict, and the victors were no exception. To add to it all, a small tribe near Delphi, provoked by the priests of the Oracle, invaded and plundered the sanctuary of Apollo. Utter confusion followed.

A foreign tribe – though not so very foreign – took advantage of this confusion to interfere. These were the Macedonians, a people who lived in the mountains to the north of Greece. The Macedonians were related to the Greeks, but they were barbarous and warlike. Their king, Philip, was a man of great cunning. He spoke excellent Greek and was familiar with Greek customs and culture, and his aim was to be king of all Greece. Since the invasion of the sanctuary at Delphi concerned all tribes loyal to the Greek religion, he had a good excuse to intervene. There was a politician in Athens, however, who was suspicious of Philip of Macedon. This was the famous orator Demosthenes, whose fulminating speeches at the Assembly, in which he repeatedly warned people against King Philip's schemes, are known as 'Philippics'. But Greece was too divided to put up any real defence.

At Chaeronea, in 338 BC, the Greeks, who hardly a hundred years before had held their own against the gigantic Persian host, were defeated by King Philip and tiny Macedonia. So ended the freedom of the Greeks – not that it could be said that they had made good use of it lately. But it wasn't Philip's intention to enslave or plunder Greece. He had other ideas: he planned to create a great army made up of Greeks and Macedonians with which to invade and conquer Persia.

At the time of the Persian wars such a task would have proved impossible, but things had changed. The great kings of Persia were no longer able and ambitious like Darius or mighty like Xerxes. They had long given up ruling the country themselves and contented themselves with the money their satraps sent back from the provinces. They used it to build themselves magnificent palaces and held court in great style. They ate off golden dishes and even their slaves – both male and female – were dressed in splendid robes. They loved good food, and good wines even more. So did their satraps. A kingdom like this, thought King Philip, should be easy to conquer. But before he had even completed the preparations for his campaign he was assassinated.

His son, who now inherited the whole of Greece, along with his native Macedonia, was barely twenty years old at the time. His name was Alexander. The Greeks were convinced that freedom was in their grasp – he was only a boy and they'd make short work of him. But Alexander was no ordinary boy. From his youth he had been impatient to be king. When he was little, he was said to cry whenever his father, King Philip, conquered another Greek city, saying: 'Father won't leave anything for me to conquer when I'm king!' Now his father had left him everything. A Greek city that tried to free itself was razed, and its inhabitants sold into slavery as a warning to all. Then Alexander summoned all the Greek leaders to a meeting in the town of Corinth, to discuss the Persian campaign.

Now Alexander wasn't just a brave and ambitious warrior – there was much more to him than that. He was exceptionally handsome, with long curly hair, and he knew just about everything there was to know at the time. His tutor was the most famous teacher living: the Greek philosopher Aristotle. And if I tell you that Aristotle wasn't just Alexander's tutor but – in a manner of speaking – the teacher of mankind for 2,000 years, you'll have an idea of what I mean. In the 2,000 years that followed, whenever people failed to agree on one thing or another, they turned to his writings. He was their referee. What Aristotle said must be right. For what he had done was to gather together all the knowledge of his time. He wrote about the natural sciences – the stars, animals and plants; about history and people living together in a state – what we call politics; about the right way to reason – logic; and the right way to behave – ethics. He wrote about poetry and its beauty. And last of all he wrote down his own thoughts on a god who hovered impassive and unseen above the vault of heaven.

All this Alexander studied too, and no doubt he was a good student. Best of all he loved the stories about heroes in Homer's great lyric poems – they say he kept them under his pillow at night. But Alexander didn't spend all his time with his nose in a book. He loved sport, and riding more than anything. No one rode better than he. His father once bought a beautiful stallion that no one could tame. His name was Bucephalus. Whenever anyone tried to mount him they were thrown off. But Alexander worked out why he did it: the horse was afraid of his own shadow. So Alexander turned the horse's head towards the sun so that he couldn't see his shadow on the ground. Stroking him gently, he swung himself onto his back and rode round to the applause of the whole court. From that time on, Bucephalus would always be his favourite horse.

Now when Alexander appeared before the Greek leaders in Corinth they greeted him warmly and paid him lavish compliments – all of them, that is, but one. A funny fellow, a philosopher named Diogenes. He had views not unlike those of the Buddha. According to him, possessions and all the things we think we need only serve to distract us and get in the way of our simple enjoyment of life. So he had given away everything he owned and now sat, almost naked, in a barrel in the market square in Corinth where he lived, as free and independent as a stray dog. Curious to meet this strange fellow, Alexander went to call on him. Dressed in shining armour, the plume on his helmet waving in the breeze, he walked up to the barrel and said to Diogenes: 'I like you. Let me know your wish and I shall grant it.' Diogenes, who had until then been comfortably sunning himself, replied: 'Indeed, Sire, I have a wish.' 'Well, what is it?' 'Your shadow has fallen over me: stand a little less between me and the sun.' Alexander is said to have been so struck by this that he said: 'If I weren't Alexander I should like to be Diogenes.'

A king like this was soon as popular with the Greek soldiers as he was with the Macedonians. They were more than willing to fight for him. So, with increasing confidence, Alexander marched on Persia. He gave everything he owned to his friends. They were horrified and said: 'But what are you leaving for yourself?' 'Hope', he is said to have replied. And that hope didn't deceive him. His army reached Asia Minor first. There he came up against the first Persian army. Although larger than his own, it turned out to be no more than a milling host of soldiers with no effective leader. The Persians were quickly put to flight, for Alexander's army fought bravely, and Alexander most bravely of all in the heat of the fray.

It so happens that vanquished Asia Minor is the scene of the famous story of the Gordian Knot. It went like this. In the city of Gordium there was a temple, and in it an old chariot whose shaft was held fast by a strap that was tightly and intricately knotted. Now it had been foretold that he who could untie the enchanted knot would become master of the world. Alexander wasted little time fiddling with a knot that was clearly far worse than the sort you get in your shoelace when you are in a hurry. He did something my mother never let me do: he took his sword and simply chopped it through. The story's meaning is twofold: Alexander would conquer the world in fulfilment of the ancient prophecy, and he would do it with the sword. As indeed he did.

You will find it easier to follow the rest of this story of conquest if you take a look at the map (on pages 70 and 71). Alexander could have gone on to attack Persia directly, but rather than risk an attack from the rear by the Persian provinces of Phoenicia and Egypt, he chose to subdue them first. The Persians tried to block his way near a town called Issus, but Alexander crushed them. He plundered the magnificent royal tents and made off with the king's treasure. He captured the king's wife and sisters, too, and treated them with the utmost respect and courtesy. That was in 333 BC, an easy date to remember.

Phoenicia was less easy to conquer. For seven long months Alexander laid siege to the city of Tyre. Its destruction, when it came, was all the more brutal. Egypt was easier. Glad to be rid of the Persians, the Egyptians soon surrendered to Persia's foe. But Alexander was determined to be a true ruler of Egypt, the sort they were used to. He marched across the desert to a temple of the sun god and had the priests proclaim him Son of the Sun, and therefore righteous Pharaoh. Before he left Egypt to continue his campaign, he founded a new city by the sea and named it after himself: Alexandria. It is still there today, and was for a long time one of the richest and most powerful cities in the world.

Only now did he march on Persia. In the meantime the Persian king had assembled a huge army and was waiting for Alexander near ancient Nineveh at a place called Gaugamela. He sent messengers ahead to meet Alexander and offered him half his kingdom and his daughter in marriage, if only he would agree not to fight. 'If I were Alexander, I'd take it,' said Alexander's friend, Parmenios.

'And so would I, if I were Parmenios,' was Alexander's reply. Half the world wasn't enough for Alexander. With that, he defeated the last and greatest Persian army. The king of Persia fled into the mountains, where he was assassinated.

Alexander punished the assassins. Now he was king of the whole of Persia. Greece, Egypt, Phoenicia, Palestine, Babylonia, Assyria, Asia Minor and Persia – all these were now part of his empire. He set about putting it in order. His commands could now be said to reach all the way from the Nile to Samarkand.

This would probably have been enough for you or me, but Alexander was far from satisfied. He wanted to rule over new, undiscovered lands. He longed to see the mysterious, far-off peoples merchants talked about when they came to Persia with rare goods from the East. Like Dionysus in the Greek legend, he wanted to ride in triumph to the sun-burnished Indians of the East, and there receive their tribute. So he spent little time in the Persian capital, and in 327 BC led his army on the most perilous adventures over unknown and unexplored mountain passes and down along the valley of the Indus into India. But the Indians did not submit to him willingly. The hermits and penitents in the forests denounced the conquerors from the distant West in their sermons. And the soldiers of the warrior caste fought valiantly, so that every city had to be besieged and conquered in its turn.

Alexander himself was no less valiant, as is shown by his encounter with an Indian king. King Porus had lain in wait for him on a branch of the Indus River, with a mighty army of war elephants and foot soldiers. When Alexander reached the river the king's army was positioned on the far bank, and Alexander and his soldiers had no choice but to cross the river in the face of the enemy host. His success was one of his greatest feats. Yet even more remarkable was his victory over that army, in the stifling heat of India. Porus was brought before him in chains. 'What do you want of me?' asked Alexander. 'Only that you treat me as befits a king.' 'And that is all?' 'That is all,' came the reply, 'there is no more to be said.' Alexander was so impressed that he gave Porus back his kingdom.

He himself wished to march on even further towards the east, to the even more mysterious and unknown peoples who lived in the valley of the River Ganges. But his soldiers had had enough. They didn't want to march on to the end of the world. They wanted to go home. Alexander begged and pleaded and threatened to go on alone. He shut himself up in his tent and refused to come out for three whole days. But in the end the soldiers had their way, and he was forced to turn back.

But they did agree to one thing: they wouldn't go home by the same route. Of course it would have been far the simplest thing to do, since those regions had already been conquered. But Alexander wanted new sights and new conquests. So they followed the Indus down as far as the sea. There he put part of his army onto ships and sent them home that way. He himself chose to endure new and terrible hardships as he marched with the rest of the army over pitiless desert wastes. Alexander bore all the privations his army endured and took no more water and slept no more than the next man. He fought in the foremost ranks.

On one occasion, he only escaped death by a miracle. That day they were besieging a fortress. Ladders had been set in place to scale the walls. Alexander was first up. He had reached the top when the ladder snapped under the weight of the soldiers behind, leaving him alone on top of the wall. His men shouted to him to jump back down. Instead he leapt straight into the city and, with his back to the ramparts, defended himself with his shield against overwhelming odds. By the time the others were able to scale the wall to rescue him, he had already been hit by an arrow. It must have been thrilling!

In the end they returned to the Persian capital. But since Alexander had burnt it down when he conquered it, he chose to set up his court in Babylon. This was no idle choice: Son of the Sun to the Egyptians, King of Kings to the Persians, with troops in India and in Athens, he was determined to show the world that he was its rightful ruler.

It may not have been pride that prompted him to do so. As a pupil of Aristotle he understood human nature and knew that power needs pomp and dignity if it wants to make the right impression. So he introduced all the age-old ceremonies of the Babylonian and Persian courts. Anyone who came into his presence had to fall on their knees before him and speak to him as if he were a god. And in the manner of Oriental kings he had several wives, among them the daughter of the Persian king, Darius, which made him that king's rightful successor. For Alexander didn't wish to be seen as a foreign conqueror. His aim was to combine the wisdom and splendour of the East with the clear thinking and vitality of the Greeks, and so create something entirely new and wonderful.

But this idea didn't please the Greeks and Macedonians at all. They were the conquerors, so they should be the masters. What was more, they were free men, and used to their freedom. They weren't going to bow down to any man on earth – or, as they put it, lick any man's boots. His Greek friends and the soldiers became increasingly rebellious, and he was forced to send them home. Alexander never realised his great ambition of mingling the two peoples, even though he handed out rich dowries to ten thousand Macedonian and Greek soldiers so that they could marry Persian women, and laid on a great wedding feast for all.

He had great plans. He wanted to found many more cities like Alexandria. He wanted to build roads, and change the face of the world with his military campaigns, whether the Greeks liked it or not. Just imagine, in those days, to have a regular postal service running from India to Athens! But in the midst of all his plans he died, in Nebuchadnezzar's summer palace, in 323 BC. He was thirty-two years old – an age when most people's lives have barely begun.

To the question of who should succeed him, he answered, in his fever: 'He who is most worthy.' But there was no one. The generals and princes in his entourage were greedy, dissolute and dishonest. They fought over the empire until it fell apart. Egypt was then governed by a family of generals – the Ptolemies. The Seleucids ruled Mesopotamia, and the Attalids Asia Minor. India was simply abandoned.

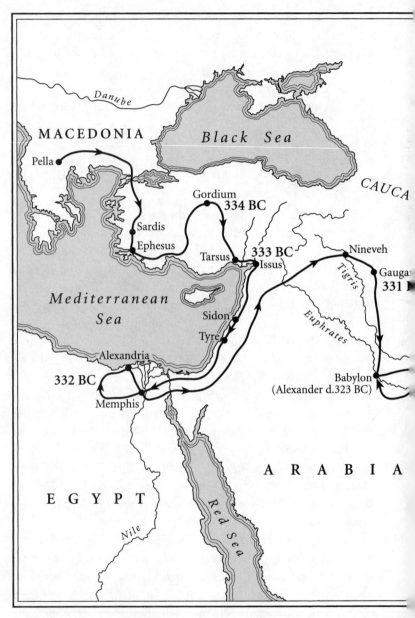

Follow the arrows! They will take you in Alexander's footsteps as he conquers half the world.

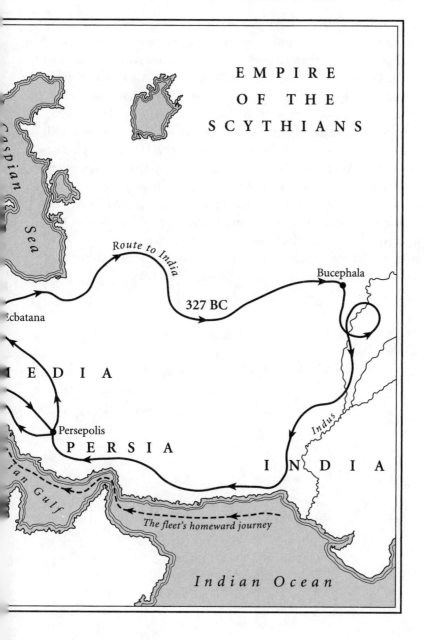

But although the empire was in pieces, Alexander's grand project slowly went on taking shape. Greek art and the spirit of Greece had penetrated Persia and passed on through India to China. Meanwhile the Greeks themselves had learnt that there was more to the world than Athens and Sparta, and more to do than waste their lives in endless squabbling between Dorians and Ionians. And, having lost the little political power they once had, the Greeks went on to be the bearers of the greatest intellectual force there has ever been, the force we know as Greek culture. This force was protected and preserved in some very special fortresses. Can you guess what those fortresses were? They were libraries. Alexandria, for instance, had a Greek library that held around seven hundred thousand scrolls. Those seven hundred thousand scrolls were the Greek soldiers who set off to conquer the world. And that empire is still standing today.

13

❖

New Wars and New Warriors

Alexander only went east. Although 'only' may not be quite the right word! But the lands that lay to the west of Greece did not tempt him – just a couple of Phoenician and Greek colonies and a handful of densely wooded peninsulas inhabited by tribes of stubborn and unruly peasants. One of these peninsulas was Italy, and one of the peasant tribes, the Romans. At the time of Alexander the Great, the Roman empire was no more than a little patch of land in the heart of Italy, and Rome a tiny city of twisting streets within strong walls. But Rome's inhabitants were a proud people. They loved recounting stories of the greatness of their past and were convinced of a great future. Their history, as they told it, went back to ancient Troy. A Trojan named Aeneas fled to Italy. His descendants were the twin brothers Romulus and Remus, sons of Mars, the god of war, who were suckled and raised in the forest by a wild she-wolf. Romulus, so the myth goes, founded Rome. They even had a date for it, 753 BC, and would later count the years from that date as the Greeks did from the Olympiads. They would say: in such-and-such a year after the city's founding. So, for example, the

Roman year 100 is what we would call the 653rd year before the birth of Christ – or 653 BC.

The Romans had lots of other stories about the glorious past of their little city. Tales of kings, both good and bad, and their wars with neighbouring cities – I almost said with neighbouring villages. The seventh and last king was called Tarquin the Proud, and he was said to have been assassinated by a nobleman named Brutus. From that time onwards, power was in the hands of the nobility. These were the patricians – the word means something like 'city fathers' – although in those days they weren't citizens as we know them, but old landowning families with vast estates of fields and meadows. And they alone had the right to choose officials to govern the city, once there were no more kings.

In Rome the highest officials were the consuls. There were always two of them ruling jointly, and they held office for just one year. Then they had to stand down. Of course, the patricians weren't the only people who lived in the city, but if you didn't have illustrious ancestors or great estates you weren't noble. The others were the plebeians, and they were almost a caste of their own as in India. A plebeian couldn't marry a patrician. Still less could he become a consul. He wasn't even allowed to voice his opinion at the People's Assembly on the Field of Mars outside the city gates. But the plebeians were many and every inch as strong-willed and stubborn as the patricians. Unlike the gentle Indians they didn't willingly submit. On more than one occasion they threatened to leave the city unless they were treated better and given a share of the fields and pastures which the patricians liked to keep for themselves. After a relentless struggle which went on for more than a hundred years, the plebeians of Rome finally succeeded in obtaining the same rights as the patricians. Of the two consuls, one would be a patrician, the other a plebeian. So justice was done. The end of this long and complicated struggle coincided with the time of Alexander the Great.

From this struggle you will have gained some idea of what the Romans were like. They were not as quick-thinking or as inventive as the Athenians. Nor did they take such delight in beautiful things, in buildings, statues and poetry. Nor was reflecting on the world and on life so vital to them. But when they set out to do something, they did it, even if it took two hundred years, for they were peasants through and through, not restless seafarers like the Athenians. Their homes, their livestock and their land – these were what mattered. They cared little for travel, they founded no colonies. They loved their native city and its soil and would do anything and everything to increase its prosperity and power. They would fight for it and they would die for it. Beside their native soil there was one other thing that was important to them: their law. Not the law that is just and fair and before which all men are equal, but the law which is law. The law that is laid down. Their laws were inscribed on twelve bronze tablets set out in the marketplace. And those few, stern words meant precisely what they said. No exceptions, no compassion, no mercy. For these were the laws of their ancestors and they must be right.

There are many old and wonderful stories telling of the love Romans had for their native land and of their faithfulness to its laws. Stories of fathers who sentenced their own sons to death without turning a hair, because the law so demanded, and of heroes who didn't hesitate to give their lives for their fellow countrymen on the battlefield or in captivity. While we don't have to believe every word of them, such stories give us an idea of what was expected of a Roman: the harshness and discipline that it was his duty to show towards himself and to others whenever his native land or the law were involved. Nothing could shake these Romans. They never gave up. Not even when their city was captured and burnt to the ground by tribesmen from the north called Gauls, in 390 BC. They just rebuilt it, fortified it, and gradually brought the small surrounding towns back under their control.

After the time of Alexander the Great, however, small wars against small towns ceased to satisfy them and they set about conquering the entire peninsula. Not, as Alexander had done, in one single great campaign, but in easy stages – town by town, region by region, and with all their characteristic single-mindedness and determination. It usually went like this. Because Rome was a powerful city, other Italian cities wanted to be its allies. This suited the

Romans very well, and all would go smoothly as long as the allies behaved themselves. But if a disagreement arose that led to an ally's refusing to follow Rome's instructions, it would mean war – a war which Rome's regiments or legions usually won. Now it so happened that one day a city in the south of Italy asked a Greek prince and commander called Pyrrhus to come to its aid against Rome. He arrived with war elephants – whose use the Greeks had learnt from the Indians – and succeeded in defeating the Roman legions. But at a cost: he lost so many of his men that he is said to have cried out, 'One more such victory and we are lost!' Which is why people still speak of a 'Pyrrhic victory' if it has been won at too great a cost.

Pyrrhus soon withdrew his forces, leaving the Romans to become lords of the whole of southern Italy. But even that was not enough for them. They aimed to conquer Sicily as well, drawn by the island's fertile soil which produced such good crops, and by its wealthy Greek colonies. But Sicily didn't belong to the Greeks any more: it was under the control of the Phoenicians.

Now as you remember, even before the Greeks, the Phoenicians had set up trading posts and founded cities everywhere they went. These were mainly in southern Spain and along the coasts of North Africa. One of the African cities was Carthage, and it lay immediately opposite Sicily. Carthage was the richest and mightiest city for miles around and the Romans referred to its Phoenician inhabitants as 'Punics'. Its ships went far across the seas, taking goods from one country to another and, since they were so near Sicily, they fetched grain from there.

Because of this the Carthaginians had become Rome's first real opponents – and very dangerous ones too. Unlike the Romans they didn't usually fight themselves, but could afford to pay foreign mercenaries to fight on their behalf. In the war which now broke out in Sicily they won the early battles – not least because the Romans didn't have many ships, weren't used to sea voyages and sea warfare, and knew next to nothing about shipbuilding. But one day a Carthaginian ship ran aground off Italy. Using it as a model, and working in furious haste, the Romans managed to build a whole fleet of identical ships within two months. It took all the

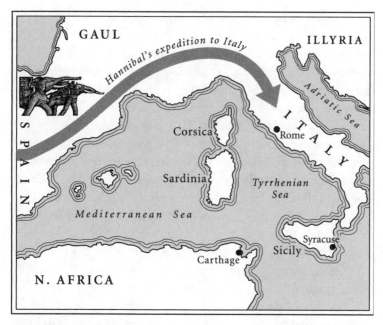

Carthage and Rome, fighting for the possession of Sicily, drove Hannibal to bring his army over the Alps.

money they had, but with their brand new fleet they defeated the Carthaginians, who were soon forced to cede Sicily to the Romans. This happened in 241 BC.

However, it was only the start of the war between the two cities. They've taken Sicily, the Carthaginians said to themselves, so we'll take Spain. Now at the time we're talking about there weren't any Romans in Spain, only wild tribes. Even so, the Romans would not allow it. It so happened that there was a Carthaginian commander in Spain whose son Hannibal was a truly extraordinary young man. Reared among soldiers, he knew everything there was to know about warfare. Hunger and cold, heat and thirst, forced marches night and day, he had seen them all. He was fearless, unbelievably tenacious and a born leader. He could outwit the enemy with his cunning and sum up a situation in an instant, and he had a cool head. He was that rare thing: a man who made war like a chess-player, carefully considering each move before he made it.

But above all he was a good Carthaginian. He already hated the Romans for trying to subdue his native city, and their meddling in Spain was the last straw. He left Spain immediately for Italy, equipped with war elephants and a large army – a truly formidable force. To reach Italy he had to take his army and all his elephants across the whole of southern France, across rivers and over mountains and right up over the Alps. He may have taken the pass that goes over the shoulder of Mount Cenis, as it is known today. I've been there myself, following a wide, winding road. But how they found their way over those wild mountains in those days, with no roads to follow, is impossible to imagine. Surrounded by deep ravines, sheer precipices and slippery grass ledges – I wouldn't want to be up there with one elephant, let alone forty, and by then it was already September and there was snow on the mountain tops. But Hannibal found a way through for his army and they finally reached Italy. There he was confronted by the Romans, but he defeated them in a bloody battle. Later a second Roman army surprised his camp under cover of darkness. But Hannibal, having been forewarned, saved himself with a cunning trick. He tied flaming torches to the horns of a herd of cattle and drove them down the mountainside where his camp was billeted. In the darkness the Roman soldiers mistook them for Hannibal's soldiers and rushed off in hot pursuit. How I would love to have seen their faces when they finally caught up with them and found they were cows!

The Romans had a very gifted general called Quintus Fabius Maximus, who wanted to avoid meeting Hannibal in battle. He believed that Hannibal would eventually become impatient and, being in a foreign country, was bound to make a blunder. But the Romans didn't like his waiting game and mocked Quintus Fabius Maximus, calling him 'Cunctator' – 'Hesitator'. Ignoring his advice, they attacked Hannibal at a place called Cannae. There they were decisively beaten: forty thousand dead on the Roman side. This battle, which took place in 217 BC, was their bloodiest defeat. Yet despite his victory Hannibal did not march on Rome. Favouring caution, he stayed put and waited for reinforcements from home. And this was his undoing. For Carthage sent no fresh troops and his men began to run wild, robbing and plundering the Italian cities. Though the Romans no longer dared attack him directly, they called up all their men to fight. Every one of them – even young boys and slaves. Every man in Italy became a soldier, and these weren't hired soldiers like Hannibal's. They were Romans, and you know what that means. They fought the Carthaginians both in Sicily and in Spain. And everywhere they fought, as long as it wasn't Hannibal they were fighting, they always won.

After fourteen years in Italy Hannibal finally returned to Africa, where his countrymen needed him. The Romans, led by Scipio their general, had reached the gates of Carthage. And there Hannibal met his defeat. In 202 BC the Romans conquered Carthage. The Carthaginians were made to burn their entire fleet and pay the Romans a huge sum of money. Hannibal fled, and later poisoned himself rather than fall into the hands of the Romans. Emboldened by its great victory, Rome now conquered Greece, still under Macedonian rule and as disunited and fragmented as ever. They brought home the most beautiful works of art from Corinth and reduced the city to ashes.

Rome also expanded northwards into the land of the Gauls who, two hundred years earlier, had sacked Rome. They conquered the region we know as northern Italy. Yet even this was not enough. Carthage was still standing, a fact which many Romans would not accept, in particular a patrician named Cato. Cato was a just and honourable man, but notoriously severe. Whenever the city council met at the Senate, no matter what was discussed, he is said to have ended every speech with the words: 'For the rest, I propose that Carthage be destroyed.' And in the end that is precisely what they did. The Romans invented a pretext to attack. The Carthaginians defended themselves desperately, and even after the city had fallen the Roman soldiers had to fight on, house by house, through the streets for six more days. When the city was finally conquered, every Carthaginian had either been killed or captured. The Romans razed all the houses and turned the land where Carthage had once stood into a plain. It was 146 BC. And that was the end of Hannibal's city. Now Rome was the mightiest city in the world.

14

❖

An Enemy of History

I f you have always found history boring, you are going to enjoy this chapter.

At about the same time as Hannibal was in Italy (that is, shortly after 220 BC), an emperor was ruling over China who hated history so much that, in 213 BC, he ordered all history books and all old reports and records to be burnt, along with all collections of songs and poems and the writings of Confucius and Lao-tzu – in fact everything he considered to be useless rubbish. The only books he permitted were ones on agriculture and other useful subjects. Anybody found in possession of any other sort of book was to be put to death.

This emperor was Shih Huang-ti, the first emperor of all China and one of the greatest warriors there has ever been. He was not born into an imperial family but was the son of one of the princes I told you about, who ruled the many Chinese provinces. His province was called Ch'in, from which his family took its name, and it is likely that the whole country now known as China was named after him.

There are certainly more than enough reasons for China to take its name from the Prince of Ch'in. Not only did he make himself the first emperor of all China, by conquering all the other provinces one by one, but he transformed the entire country. He threw out all the princes and totally reorganised his empire. And if you ask me why he hated history and destroyed all those books, it was because he wanted to wipe out every trace of how things had been done before, so he could build an entirely new China – *his* China – starting from scratch. He built roads everywhere and began work on an enormous project: the Great Wall of China. Today it is still a massive construction, a double wall made of stone with tall towers and castellations, winding its symmetrical way over plains, through deep ravines and up steep mountain slopes as it follows the line of the frontier for all of four thousand miles. Shih Huang-ti built it to protect China's many hardworking and peaceable peasants and townspeople from the wild tribes of the steppes, whose warlike horsemen roamed the vast plains of inner Asia. It had to be strong enough to resist their incessant raids, with all their looting and killing. And he succeeded. Of course, over the centuries the wall has often been rebuilt and strengthened, but it is still there today.

Shih Huang-ti didn't have a long reign. Soon a new family ascended the throne of the Son of Heaven. This was the Han family. They saw no need to undo all Shih Huang-ti's good works, and under their rule China remained strong and unified. But by now the Hans were no longer enemies of history. On the contrary, they remembered China's debt to the teachings of Confucius and set about searching high and low for all those ancient writings. It turned out that many people had had the courage not to burn them after all. Now they were carefully collected and valued twice as highly as before. And to become a government official, you had to know them all.

China is, in fact, the only country in the world to be ruled for hundreds of years, not by the nobility, nor by soldiers, nor even by the priesthood, but by scholars. No matter where you came from, or whether you were rich or poor, as long as you gained high marks in your exams you could become an official. The highest post went to the person with the highest marks. But the exams were far from easy. You had to be able to write thousands of characters, and you can imagine how hard that is. What is more, you had to know an enormous number of ancient books and all the rules and teachings of Confucius and the other ancient sages off by heart.

So Shih Huang-ti's burning of the books was all in vain, and if you thought he was right, you were mistaken. It's a bad idea to try to prevent people from knowing their own history. If you want to do anything new you must first make sure you know what people have tried before.

15

❖

RULERS OF THE WESTERN WORLD

It would never have occurred to the Romans to do what Alexander the Great had done. They had no wish to turn the lands they conquered into a single, vast empire in which everyone was treated equally. Certainly not. All the lands the Roman legions conquered – and their conquests came thick and fast – became Roman provinces, their towns occupied by Roman troops and Roman officials. These occupiers looked down on the native inhabitants, even when they were Phoenicians, Jews and Greeks – all peoples of very ancient culture. In the eyes of the Romans they were good for just one thing: paying up. They were subject to crushing taxes and had to keep sending grain to Rome – as much and as often as possible.

Provided they did so, they were left more or less in peace. They could practise their own religion and speak their own language, and in many ways they benefited from all the good things the Romans brought, such as roads. Many of these, splendidly paved, led out from Rome across the plains and over distant mountain passes to remote and inaccessible parts of the empire. It must be said that the Romans didn't build these roads out of consideration for the people living there. On the contrary, their aim was to send news and troops to all parts of the empire in the shortest possible time. The Romans were superb engineers.

Most impressive of all their works were their magnificent aqueducts. These brought water from distant mountains and carried it down through valleys and into the towns – clear, fresh water to fill innumerable fountains and bathhouses – so that Rome's provincial officials could enjoy all the comforts they were used to having at home.

A Roman citizen living abroad always retained his separate status, for he lived according to Roman law. Wherever he happened to be in that vast empire, he could turn to a Roman official and say: 'I am a citizen of Rome!' These words had the effect of a magic formula. If until then no one had paid him much attention, everyone would instantly become polite and obliging.

In those days, however, the true rulers of the world were the Roman soldiers. It was they who held the gigantic empire together, suppressing revolts where necessary and ferociously punishing all who dared oppose them. Courageous, experienced and ambitious, they conquered a new land – to the north, to the south or to the east – almost every decade.

People who saw the tight columns of well-drilled soldiers, marching slowly in their metal-plated tunics, with their shields and javelins, their slings and swords and their catapults for hurling rocks and arrows, knew that it was useless to resist. War was their favourite pastime. After each victory they returned in triumph to Rome, led by their generals, with all their captives and their loot. To the sound of trumpets they would march past the cheering crowds, through gates of honour and triumphal arches. Above their heads they held pictures and placards, like billboards to advertise their victories. The general would stand tall in his chariot, a crown of laurel on his head and wearing the sacred cape worn by the statue of Jupiter, God of Gods, in his temple. Like a second Jupiter, he would climb the steep path to the Capitol, the citadel of Rome. And there in the temple, high above the city, he would make his solemn sacrifice of thanksgiving to God, while below him the leaders of the vanquished were put to death.

A general who had many such victories, with plenty of booty for his troops and land for them to cultivate when they grew old and were retired from service, was loved by his men like a father. They would give their all for him. Not just on foreign soil but at home as well. For, in their eyes, a great hero of the battlefield was just what was needed to keep order at home, where there was often trouble brewing. For Rome had become a huge city with large numbers of destitute people who had no work and no money. If the provinces failed to send grain it meant famine in Rome.

Two brothers, living in about 130 BC (that is, sixteen years after the destruction of Carthage), thought up a plan to encourage this multitude of poor and starving people to move to Africa and settle there as farmers. These brothers were the Gracchi. But they were both killed in the course of political struggles.

The same blind devotion that the soldiers gave their general went to any man who gave grain to the multitudes and put on splendid festivals. For Romans loved festivals. But these were not at all like those of the Greeks, where leading citizens took part in sporting contests and sang hymns in honour of the Father of the Gods. These would have seemed ridiculous to any Roman. What serious, self-respecting man would sing in public, or take off his formal, many-pleated toga to throw javelins before an audience? Such things were best left to captives. It was they who had to wrestle and fight, confront wild beasts and stage whole battles in the arena under the eyes of thousands – sometimes tens of thousands – of spectators. It all got very serious and bloody, but that was just what made it so exciting for the Romans. Especially when, instead of trained professionals, men who had been condemned to death were thrown into the arena to grapple with lions, bears, tigers and even elephants.

Anyone who put on shows like these, with generous handouts of grain, was loved by the crowd and could do what he pleased. As you can imagine, many tried. If two rivals fought for power, one might have the army and the patricians on his side while the other had

Legionaries kept watch along all the frontiers of the vast Roman empire. They also built a palisade that stretched from the Rhine to the Danube.

the support of the plebeians and poor peasants. And in a long drawn-out struggle, now one and now the other would be uppermost. There were two such famous enemies called Marius and Sulla. Marius had been fighting in Africa and, several years later, took his army to rescue the Roman empire when it was in peril. In 113 BC, barbarians from the north had invaded Italy (as the Dorians had Greece or, seven hundred years later, the Gauls had Rome). These invaders were the Cimbri and the Teutones, ancestors of today's Germans. They had fought so bravely that they had actually succeeded in putting the Roman legions to flight. But Marius and his army had been able to halt and defeat them.

This made him the most celebrated man in Rome. But in the meantime, Sulla had fought on in Africa, and he too had returned triumphant. Both men got ready to fight it out. Marius had all Sulla's friends killed. Sulla in his turn made a long list of the Romans who supported Marius and had them murdered. He then generously presented all their property to the state. After which he and his soldiers ruled the Roman empire till 79 BC.

In the course of these turbulent times, Romans had changed a great deal. All the peasants had gone. A handful of rich people had bought up the smaller farms and brought in slaves to run their vast estates. Romans had, in fact, grown used to leaving everything to be managed by slaves. Not only those who worked in the mines and quarries, but even the tutors of patrician children were mostly slaves, prisoners of war or their descendants. They were treated as goods, bought and sold like cattle. Slave owners could do what they liked with their slaves – even kill them. Slaves had no rights at all. Some masters sold them to fight with wild beasts in the arena, where they were known as gladiators. On one occasion the gladiators rebelled against this treatment. They were urged on by a slave called Spartacus, and many slaves from the country estates rallied to him. They fought with a ferocity born of desperation and the Romans were hard put to suppress the revolt, for which the slaves paid a terrible price. That was in 71 BC.

By this time new generals had become the darlings of the Roman populace. The most popular of them all was Gaius Julius

Caesar. He too knew how to win the hearts of the masses, and had raised colossal sums of money for magnificent festivals and gifts of grain. But more than that, he was a truly great general, one of the greatest there has ever been. One day he went to war. A few days later, Rome received a letter from him with just these three Latin words: *veni, vidi, vici* – meaning 'I came, I saw, I conquered.' That is how fast he worked!

He conquered France – in those days known as Gaul – and made it a province of Rome. This was no small feat, for the peoples who lived there were exceptionally brave and warlike, and not easily intimidated. The conquest took seven years, from 58 to 51 BC. He fought against the Helvetii (who lived in what is now Switzerland), the Gauls and the Germans. Twice he crossed the Rhine into land that is now part of Germany and twice he crossed the sea to England, known to the Romans as Britannia. He did this to teach the neighbouring tribes a proper fear and respect for Rome. Although the Gauls continued to fight desperately, for years on end, he attacked them repeatedly, and everywhere he went he left troops in control behind him. Once Gaul had become a Roman province the inhabitants soon learnt to speak Latin, just as they had in Spain. And this is why French and Spanish, which come from the language of the Romans, are known as Romance languages.

After the conquest of Gaul, Caesar turned his army towards Italy. He was now the most powerful man in the world. Other generals who had previously been his allies he attacked and defeated. And after he had seduced Cleopatra, the beautiful queen of Egypt, he was able to add Egypt to the Roman empire. Then he set about putting it in order. For this he was ideally suited, for he had an exceptionally orderly mind. He was able to dictate two letters at the same time without getting his thoughts in a tangle. Imagine that!

He didn't just put the whole empire in order, he put time in order too. He put *time* in order? Whatever does that mean? He reformed the calendar, so that it ended up being more or less like ours, with twelve months and leap years. It is called after him, the Julian Calendar. And, because he was such a great man, one of the months is also named after him: the month of July. So July takes its name from a thin-faced bald-headed man, who liked to wear a laurel wreath made of gold on his head, a man whose weak and sickly body hid a shining intellect and a will of iron.

Since Caesar was now the mightiest man on earth, he could have become king of the Roman empire, and he might not have objected to that. But the Romans were jealous of him – even his best friend, Brutus – and they didn't want to be ruled by him. Fearing that Caesar would get the better of them, they decided to murder him. During a meeting in the Senate they surrounded him and raised their daggers to stab him. Caesar defended himself. But when, among his assailants, he caught sight of Brutus, he is reported to have said: 'You too, Brutus, my son?' and then let them strike him down, without making any further attempts to resist. This happened in 44 BC.

After July comes August. Caesar Octavianus Augustus was Caesar's adoptive son. Having fought for a long time against a number of generals on land and at sea, he finally succeeded in becoming the sole ruler of the empire in 31 BC, and so became the first to hold the title of Roman Emperor.

Since one month had been named after Julius Caesar, Augustus was given one too. He had certainly earned it. He may not have been extraordinary like Caesar, but he was a fair and prudent man who controlled himself at all times and so had earned the right to control others. It is said that he never gave an order or made a decision in anger. Whenever he felt his temper rising, he slowly recited the alphabet in his head, and by the time he had reached the end he had calmed down. This tells you what he was like: cool-headed, a man who ruled the empire fairly and wisely. He wasn't only a warrior and he didn't only enjoy going to gladiator fights. He lived simply and appreciated fine sculpture and fine poetry. And because the Romans were less gifted than the Greeks at such things, he had copies made of all the finest Greek statues and placed them in his palaces and gardens. The Roman poets of his time – and they are the most famous of all the Roman poets – also took the poems of the Greeks as their models. For even in those days people thought that all the most beautiful things came from

Greece. And for the same reason it was considered a sign of distinction for a Roman to speak Greek, to read the ancient Greek poets and to collect Greek works of art. This was lucky for us, for if they hadn't, we might never have heard about any of it.

16

❖

THE GOOD NEWS

Augustus ruled from 31 BC until AD 14, which tells you that Jesus Christ was born during his reign. He was born in Palestine, which was then a Roman province. You can read about the life and teachings of Jesus Christ in the Bible. You probably know the essentials of what he taught: that it doesn't matter if a person is rich or poor, of noble or of humble birth, a master or a slave, a great thinker or a child. That all men are God's children. And that the love of this father is infinite. That before him no man is without sin, but that God has pity on sinners. That what matters is not judgement but mercy.

You know what mercy is: the great giving and forgiving love of God. And that we should treat others as we hope God, our Father, will treat us. That is why Jesus said: 'Love your enemies, do good to those who hate you, bless those who curse you, pray for those who mistreat you. If someone strikes you on one cheek, turn to him the other also. If someone takes your cloak, do not stop him from taking your tunic. Give to everyone who asks you, and if anyone takes what belongs to you, do not demand it back.'

And you know that Jesus spent just a short time travelling all over the country, preaching and teaching, healing the sick and comforting the poor. That he was accused of wanting to be king of the Jews. And that, as a rebellious Jew, he was sentenced by a Roman official called Pontius Pilate to be nailed to a cross. This terrible punishment was only given to slaves, robbers and members of subject peoples, not to citizens of Rome. It was also seen as a dreadful humiliation. But Christ had taught that the world's worst sorrows had a meaning, that beggars, those in torment, the persecuted, the sick and the suffering were blessed in their misfortune. And so it was that the Son of God, martyred and in agony, became for the first Christians the very symbol of his teaching. Today we can hardly imagine what that meant. The cross was even worse than the gallows. And this cross of shame became the symbol of the new teaching. Just imagine what a Roman official or soldier, or a Roman teacher steeped in Greek culture, proud of his wisdom, his rhetoric and his knowledge of philosophy, would have thought when he heard Christ's teaching from one of the great preachers – perhaps the Apostle Paul in Athens or in Rome. We can read what he preached there today, in his First Letter to the Corinthians:

I will show you a more excellent way: If I speak with the tongues of men and of angels, but have not love, I am but a sounding gong or a tinkling cymbal. If I have the gift of prophecy and can see into all mysteries and have all knowledge and have all faith so that I can move mountains, but have not love, then I am nothing. If I give away everything that is mine, and offer up my body to be burnt, but have not love, I gain nothing. Love is long-suffering and kind, love does not envy, it does not boast, it is not proud, it does not behave improperly, it does not seek its own advantage, it is not easily provoked, it bears no grudge, delights not in evil but rejoices only in the truth. It shelters all, trusts all, always hopes, always endures. Love is everlasting.

When they heard Paul's sermons the Roman patricians must have shaken their heads in disapproval, for this was hardly the language of the law. But the poor and downtrodden heard in Paul's words something that was entirely new, something that had never been heard before: the extraordinary announcement of Divine Grace which was far greater than any law, and was called the Gospel, or the Good News. (Good news – or glad tidings – is a translation of the Greek *eu-angelion*, from which we get the word evangelical.) And this good and happy news of the mercy of God the Father – the unique and invisible God in whom the Jews had believed long before Christ had lived and preached among them – soon spread throughout the Roman empire.

Roman officials began to pay attention. As you know they hadn't previously involved themselves in matters of religion. But this was something new. The Christians, who believed in just one God, were refusing to scatter incense before images of the emperor, which had been the custom since Rome had had an emperor. Like the rulers of the Egyptians, the Chinese, the Babylonians and the Persians, Roman emperors allowed themselves to be worshipped as gods. Their statues were everywhere, and every good citizen was expected to place a few perfumed grains in front of these images as an offering. But the Christians were refusing to do so. And people wanted to make them.

Now about thirty years after Christ's death on the cross (that is, around sixty years after his birth – in AD 60), a cruel emperor was ruling over the Roman empire. He was called Nero. People still shudder when they hear the name of this monster. But what is truly repellent about him is that he didn't start out as a monster – ruthless and wicked through and through. He was simply weak, vain, suspicious and lazy. Nero fancied himself as a poet and composed songs which he performed himself. He ate – or, rather, gorged himself on – the rarest delicacies and was utterly devoid of decency or dignity. He was not unattractive, but there was something cruel and self-satisfied about his smile. He had his own mother murdered, and his wife and his tutor, along with a number of other relations and friends. He lived in constant fear of assassination, for he was a coward too.

One day a terrible fire broke out in Rome which, burning day and night, consumed house after house, district after district, and made hundreds of thousands of people homeless – for by then Rome was a huge city with more than a million inhabitants. And what do you think Nero did?

He stood on the balcony of his sumptuous palace with his lyre and sang a song he had composed about the burning of Troy. To him this seemed perfect for the occasion. The people, however, were enraged. Until then they had not hated him much because he had always given them splendid festivals and had only been cruel to close friends and acquaintances. Now the rumour spread that Nero himself had set Rome on fire. We do not know if it is true. But in any case Nero knew that people thought he was responsible. So he looked around for a scapegoat and found one in the Christians. The Christians had often said that this world must end so that a better, purer world might take its place. Of course, you and I know that they meant Heaven. But because people tend not to listen very carefully, soon they were saying: 'The Christians want the world to end because they hate mankind.' An extraordinary accusation, don't you think?

Nero had them arrested wherever he found them, and they were brutally put to death. Some were torn to pieces by wild beasts in the arena, while others were burnt alive as torches at a grand nocturnal banquet in his garden. But the Christians bore all these tortures and those of later persecutions with unbelievable courage. They were proud to testify to the power of their new faith. And these testifiers – or 'martyrs', to use the Greek word – later became the first saints. Christians used to pray at the tombs of their martyrs, whom they buried in a whole network of underground passages and burial chambers called catacombs, outside the city gates. The walls were painted with simple pictures inspired by Bible stories: pictures of Daniel in the Lion's Den, of Shadrach, Meshach and Abednego in the Burning Fiery Furnace, or Moses Striking Water from the Rock, which were there to remind Christians of the power of God and the Life Everlasting.

In these underground passages Christians gathered together at night to discuss Christ's teachings, to share the Lord's Supper and give each other encouragement when a new persecution threatened. And in the course of the next century, despite all the persecution, more and more men and women throughout the empire came to believe in the Good News and were ready to bear, for its sake, the suffering Christ had endured.

Christians were not the only ones to experience the severity of Roman rule for things were no better for the Jews. A few years after Nero's reign a revolt against the Romans broke out in Jerusalem. The Jews wanted their freedom. They fought with extraordinary determination and courage against the legions who were forced to lay siege to each Jewish town in turn to defeat them. Jerusalem itself was reduced to famine during two long years of siege by Titus, son of the ruling Roman emperor, Vespasian. Those who fled were caught and crucified by the Romans outside the city. When the Romans finally succeeded in forcing their way into the city in AD 70, Titus is said to have commanded that the sanctuary of the One God be spared, but the soldiers sacked and looted the temple all the same. The sacred vessels were carried home in triumph to Rome, as we can see today from the pictures carved on the arch which Titus erected in Rome to commemorate his triumph. Jerusalem was destroyed and the Jews scattered to the four winds. Long established as traders in many cities, the Jews had now lost their homeland. From now on they huddled together in their prayer schools, in cities like Alexandria and Rome and other foreign towns, scorned and derided by all because, even in the midst of heathens, they still clung to their ancient customs, reading the Bible and waiting for their Messiah who was to save them.

17

❖

LIFE IN THE EMPIRE
AND AT ITS FRONTIERS

If you weren't a Christian, a Jew or a close relative of the emperor, life in the Roman empire could be peaceful and pleasant. You could travel from Spain to the Euphrates, from the Danube to the Nile on wonderful Roman roads. The Roman postal service made regular visits to settlements at the empire's frontiers, carrying news back and forth. In all the great cities like Alexandria or Rome you could find everything you needed for a comfortable life. Of course, in Rome there were whole districts of barrack-like buildings, crudely built and many storeys high, where poor people lived. The private houses and villas of the well-to-do, in contrast, were luxuriously furnished with beautiful Greek works of art, and had delightful small gardens with cooling fountains. In winter months, rooms were warmed by a form of central heating in which hot air circulated through hollow bricks under the floor. Every rich Roman had several country houses, usually near the sea, with many slaves to run them, and fine libraries in which the works of all the best Greek and Latin poets were to be found. The villas of the rich even had their own sports grounds and cellars stocked with the best wines. If a Roman felt bored at home he would take himself to the marketplace, the law-courts or to the baths. The bath houses, or therms, were monumental buildings supplied by aqueducts with water from distant mountains. They were magnificently furnished and decorated and had halls for hot baths, cold baths and steam baths, and others for practising sports. Ruins of these colossal therms can still be seen. With their high vaulted ceilings, their brightly coloured marble pillars and their pools tiled with rare and precious stones, they look more like fairy-tale palaces.

Bigger still, and even more impressive were the theatres. The great amphitheatre in Rome known as the Colosseum held up to fifty thousand spectators – few of our modern stadiums hold more. They were mainly used for gladiatorial contests and animal-baiting, and, as you remember, many Christians died there. The tiers of seats for the spectators rose high above the arena, like a giant oval funnel. Imagine the noise fifty thousand people must have made when they were all in there together! The emperor sat below in the royal box beneath a magnificent awning to protect him from the sun. When he dropped his handkerchief into the arena, it was the signal for the games to begin. The gladiators would appear and, standing in front of the imperial box, cry: 'Hail Caesar! We who are about to die salute you!'

But you mustn't imagine that emperors did nothing but sit in amphitheatres, or that they were all layabouts and raving lunatics like Nero. On the contrary, they spent most of their time maintaining peace in the empire. Beyond the distant frontiers all around were fierce, barbarian tribes waiting to raid and pillage the rich provinces. The Germans, who lived in the north at the other side of the Danube and the Rhine, were especially troublesome – Caesar had already clashed with them during his conquest of Gaul. Tall and powerfully built, they towered over the Romans and frightened the life out of them. Not only that, but their country (now Germany) was in those days a land of swamps and dark forests in which Roman legions were forever losing their way. But, above all, the Germans simply weren't used to living in fine, centrally heated villas. They were peasants and herdsmen, as the Romans themselves had once been, and they preferred to live as they always had, in isolated wooden farmsteads.

Educated Romans from the cities liked to write about the great simplicity of the Germanic way of life, the plainness and austerity of their traditions, their love of warfare and their loyalty to their chieftains. By drawing attention to this seemingly simple, uncorrupted and natural way of life in the freedom of the forest, the authors of the accounts which have come down to us warned their fellow countrymen against what they saw as the Romans' own dangerously refined and self-indulgent way of life.

The German warriors really were dangerous enemies. The Romans had already learnt this to their cost during Augustus's rule. At that time the leader of a Germanic tribe called the Cherusci was a man called Arminius. Brought up in Rome, he knew all about Roman military tactics and, one day, when a Roman army was marching through Teutoburg Forest he ambushed it and annihilated it completely. After that, the Romans kept out of that region. But it was all the more vital for them to secure their frontiers against the Germans. Accordingly, during the first century AD, they did what the emperor Shih Huang-ti had done in China. They built a wall, known as the Limes, along the length of the frontier from the Rhine to the Danube. This wall, made of palisades with watchtowers and ditches, was intended to protect the empire from the nomadic Germanic tribes. For what worried the Romans most was that, instead of staying quietly on their farmsteads, cultivating the land, the tribes were always on the move looking for new hunting grounds or new pastures. They simply loaded their wives and children onto ox-carts and set off in search of somewhere else to live.

This meant that the Romans had to keep troops permanently stationed at the frontiers to defend the empire. Along the Rhine and the Danube there were soldiers from every country under the sun. Near Vienna there was an encampment of Egyptians, who even built themselves a temple beside the Danube which they dedicated to their goddess Isis. On that spot there is a town today called Ybbs, and Isis lives on in that name. Among the frontier guards any number of gods were worshipped – the Persian sun god Mithras, for example, and not long after, the unique and invisible god of the Christians. However, life in these outposts was not very different from life in Rome. Today we can still find Roman theatres and bath houses in Germany (in Cologne, Trier, Augsburg and Regensburg), in Austria (in Salzburg and Vienna), in France (in Arles and Nîmes), and in England (in Bath), together with villas for imperial officials and barracks for the soldiers. Older soldiers often bought themselves land in the district, married a local girl and settled near the camp. As a result, the populations within the provinces gradually became accustomed to the Roman presence, while those who lived beyond the Rhine and the Danube became increasingly restless as the years went by. It wasn't long before Roman emperors were spending more time in frontier towns than in their palaces in Rome. Among them were some remarkable men, one of whom was the Emperor Trajan. He lived about a hundred years after Christ and, long after his death, people were still talking about his justice and his gentleness.

Trajan's troops had crossed the Danube once again, into what is now Hungary and Romania. Making that land a Roman province would also make the empire safer. The country they conquered was known as Dacia. Once it had become Roman and its inhabitants began to speak Latin, Dacia became Romania. But Trajan didn't only lead military expeditions. He made Rome beautiful with glorious squares. Whole hills were levelled to make room for them. Then he commissioned a Greek architect to build temples and shops, law-courts, colonnades and monuments. You can still see their ruins in Rome today.

The emperors who followed Trajan also took good care of their empire and defended its frontiers, especially the Emperor Marcus Aurelius, who reigned between 161 and 180, and spent much of his time in garrisons on the Danube – at Carnuntum, and at Vindobona, which is what Vienna used to be called. And yet Marcus Aurelius hated war. He was a gentle, quiet man, a philosopher, who loved nothing better than reading or writing. We still have the diary he kept, much of which was written during his campaigns. Almost everything he wrote in it was about self-control and tolerance, about enduring pain and hardship, and about the silent heroism of the thinker. They are thoughts that would have pleased the Buddha.

But Marcus Aurelius couldn't retire into the forest to meditate. He had to wage war in the countryside near Vienna against the Germanic tribes, who were particularly restless at that time. The Romans are said to have taken lions with them to scare off the enemy from across the Danube. But since the Germans had never seen any lions before, they weren't frightened at all. They just killed what they thought were large dogs. While these battles were going on, Marcus Aurelius died suddenly at his headquarters in Vindobona, in AD 180.

The emperors who succeeded him spent even more time at the frontiers and even less in Rome. They were true soldiers, elected by their troops and often dismissed or even killed by them too. Many of these emperors weren't Romans, but foreigners, for by now the legions had only a very small number of Romans in them. The Italian peasants who, in earlier times, had gone out to conquer the world as soldiers, had virtually disappeared, while their farms had been absorbed into the huge estates owned by the rich and managed by foreign slaves, and the army was also made up of foreigners – you remember the Egyptians by the Danube. Most of these soldiers were Germans who, as you know, were excellent warriors. And it was these foreign troops, stationed at all four corners of the vast empire – at the frontiers of Germania and Persia and in Spain, Britain, North Africa, Egypt, Asia Minor and Romania – who now chose their favourite generals to be their emperors. Then they all fought for power and had each other murdered, just as at the time of Marius and Sulla.

Confusion and misery reigned in the years after AD 200. In the Roman empire there was almost no one to keep order but slaves or foreign troops who couldn't understand one another. The peasants in the provinces were unable to pay their taxes and rose up against their landowners. In those desperate times, when the land was in the grip of pestilence and lawlessness, many found consolation in the good news of the Gospel. More and more free men and slaves became Christians and refused to make sacrifices to the emperor.

At the height of the crisis a man from a poor family succeeded in wresting control of the empire. This was the Emperor Diocletian. He came to power in 284 and set about trying to rebuild the empire, which was by now in ruins. Famine was everywhere, so he fixed a limit on the price of all foods. Realising that the empire could no longer be governed from a single place, he chose four towns as his new imperial capitals and placed a deputy – or prefect – in each. To restore respect and dignity to the role of emperor, he introduced new rituals and court ceremony, and magnificent, richly embroidered robes for his courtiers and officials. He was particularly insistent that people should make sacrifices to the emperor, and so ruthlessly persecuted Christians throughout the empire. This was the last and most violent of all the persecutions. After a reign of more than twenty years, Diocletian renounced his imperial title and retired, a sick man, to his palace in Dalmatia. There he lived long enough to see the futility of his battle against Christianity.

It is said that his successor, the Emperor Constantine, abandoned this struggle on the eve of a battle against his rival, Maxentius. He had a dream in which he saw the Cross, and heard the words: 'Beneath this sign you will be victorious.' Victorious in that battle, he issued a decree in 313 that Christians should no longer be persecuted. He himself remained a pagan for a long time, and was only baptised on his death-bed. Constantine no longer ruled the empire from Rome. In those days the chief threat came from the east, the Persians having once again become powerful. So he chose as his seat the ancient Greek colony of Byzantium on the Black Sea, upon which it was renamed Constantine's City, or Constantinople. Today we know it as Istanbul.

By 395, the Roman empire didn't only have two capitals, it had two states: the Western Empire, consisting of Italy, Gaul, Britannia, Spain and North Africa, where people spoke Latin, and the Eastern Empire, consisting of Egypt, Palestine, Asia Minor, Greece and Macedonia, where they spoke Greek. In both states Christianity became the official religion from 380 onwards. This meant that bishops and archbishops became important dignitaries who wielded great influence in the affairs of state. Christians no longer met in underground passages, but in grand churches with fine pillars. And the Cross, symbol of the deliverance from suffering, now became the legions' battle emblem.

18

❖

THE STORM

Have you ever watched a storm approaching on a hot summer's day? It's especially spectacular in the mountains. At first there's nothing to see, but you feel a sort of weariness that tells you something is in the air. Then you hear thunder – just a rumble here and there – you can't quite tell where it is coming from. All of a sudden, the mountains seem strangely near. There isn't a breath of wind, yet dense clouds pile up in the sky. And now the mountains have almost vanished behind a wall of haze. Clouds rush in from all sides, but still there's no wind. There's more thunder now, and everything around looks eerie and menacing. You wait and wait. And then, suddenly, it erupts. At first it is almost a release. The storm descends into the valley. There's thunder and lightning everywhere. The rain clatters down in huge drops. The storm is trapped in the narrow cleft of the valley and thunderclaps echo and reverberate off the steep mountain sides. The wind buffets you from every angle. And when the storm finally moves away, leaving in its place a clear, still, starlit night, you can hardly remember where those thunderclouds were, let alone which thunderclap belonged to which flash of lightning.

The time I am now going to tell you about was like that. It was then that a storm broke that swept away the whole, vast Roman empire. We have already heard its rumblings: they were the movements of the Germanic tribes at the frontiers, the incursions of the Cimbri and the Teutones, and the campaigns led by Caesar, Augustus, Trajan, Marcus Aurelius and many others in their efforts to keep those tribes out of the empire.

But now the storm had come. It had started at the other end of the world – almost as far away as the wall built by the Chinese emperor Shih Huang-ti, the enemy of history. No longer able to mount their raids on China, Asiatic hordes from the steppes had turned westwards in search of new lands to plunder. This time it was the Huns. People like these had never been seen before in the West: small, yellow men with narrow, slit eyes and terrifying scars on their faces. Half man, half horse they seemed, for they rarely dismounted from their small, fast ponies. They slept on horseback, held meetings on horseback and ate, on horseback, the raw meat they had first made tender under their saddles. With fearful howls and a noise like thunder they charged down on their foes, showering them with arrows, before whirling round and rushing away, as if in headlong retreat. Then, if they were followed, they would twist in their saddles and shoot backwards at their pursuers. They were nimbler, more cunning and more bloodthirsty than any of the other tribes. Even the brave Germans fled before them.

One of these Germanic tribes, the Visigoths, or West Goths, sought refuge in the Roman empire, which agreed to accept them. However, it wasn't long before they were at war with their hosts. They marched as far as Athens, which they sacked. They also marched on Constantinople. Finally, under the leadership of their king, Alaric, they turned towards Italy where they besieged and sacked Rome in 410. When Alaric died they went north, this time to Gaul, and eventually to Spain, where they settled. In order to defend themselves against these armies the Romans were forced to recall large numbers of their troops from frontier garrisons in Gaul and Britannia, and from the Rhine and the Danube. Seizing their chance, other Germanic tribes now burst through into the empire in many places. It was the moment they had been waiting for, all those hundreds of years.

Some had names you can still see reflected on a map of Germany today: Swabians, Franks and Alemanni. Across the Rhine they came, their creaking ox-carts piled high with wives and children and all their goods and chattels. They fought, and they conquered. For when they fell there were always more behind to take their place. Thousands were slain, but tens of thousands followed. This period is known as the time of the Migrations. It was the storm that swept up the Roman empire and whirled it to extinction. For the Germanic tribes didn't stop when they reached Gaul and Spain. The Vandals, for instance, captured Carthage in 439 and used it as a base from which they launched their pirate ships to loot and burn the coastal towns. They ravaged Sicily and crossed into Italy. Today we still talk of 'vandalism', even though the Vandals were really no worse than many others.

As for the Huns, they *were* worse. They now had a new king: Attila. In 444 he was at the height of his power. Can you remember who was in power 444 years *before* Christ's birth? Pericles, in Athens. Those were the best of times. But Attila was in every way his opposite. People said that wherever he trod, the grass ceased to grow. His hordes burnt and destroyed everything in their path. And yet in spite of all the gold and silver and treasures the Huns looted, and in spite of all the magnificent finery worn by their leaders, Attila himself remained a plain man. He ate off wooden plates and he lived in a simple tent. Gold and silver meant nothing to him. Power was what mattered. It is said that he never laughed. He was a fearsome sovereign who had conquered half the world, and those he didn't kill had to fight for him. His army was immense. Many of his soldiers were Germans – largely East Goths, or Ostrogoths (for by this time the Visigoths had settled in Spain). From his camp in Hungary he sent an envoy to the emperor of the Roman Empire of the West with the following message: 'My Lord, and your Lord, Attila, bids me tell you that you will give him half of your empire and your daughter to be his wife.' When the emperor refused, Attila set out to punish him with his mighty army, and take by force what had been denied him. The two sides met in a tremendous battle on the Catalaunian plains in Gaul, in 451. All the armies of the Roman empire, assisted by Germanic troops, joined forces to repel the barbarian horde. The outcome being undecided, Attila turned towards Rome. Appalled and panic-stricken, the Romans could only look on as the Huns approached. Nearer and nearer they came, and no army there to save them.

It was at this point that one man dared defy Attila and his host: this was Pope Leo, known as Leo the Great. With priests and holy banners he went out to meet him. Everybody waited for the Huns to strike them down. But Attila was persuaded to turn back. He left Italy, and this time Rome was saved. Only two years later, in 453, Attila married a German princess and died on the same night.

Had the Pope not saved the Roman Empire of the West on that occasion it would have ceased to exist. For by this time the emperors had lost all authority, and such power as remained was in the hands of the soldiers, most of whom were Germans. The day came when the soldiers found that they could do without an emperor, so they decided to depose him. The last Roman emperor had a rather remarkable name: Romulus Augustulus. It is a curious coincidence that Rome's founder and first king was called Romulus and the first Roman emperor was the Emperor Augustus. Romulus Augustulus, the last one, was deposed in 476.

In his place, a German general called Odoacer proclaimed himself king of the Germans in Italy. This marked the end of the Roman Empire of the West and its Latin culture, together with the long period that goes all the way back to prehistoric times, which we call 'antiquity'.

So the date 476 marks the birth of a new era, the Middle Ages, given its name for no other reason than that it falls between antiquity and modern times. But at the time no one noticed that a new era had begun. Everything was just as confusing as before. The Ostrogoths, who had previously fought alongside the army of the Huns, had settled in the Roman Empire of the East. The Roman Emperor of the East, wishing to be rid of them, suggested that they might do better if they went to the Empire of the West and conquered Italy. So in 493, led by their great king, Theodoric, the Ostrogoths went to Italy. There, the battle-hardened soldiers made short work of a wretched, war-torn land. Theodoric captured Odoacer, but he promised to spare his life. Instead, he invited him to a banquet and stabbed him to death.

It has always puzzled me that Theodoric could have done something so monstrous, because in other ways he was a truly great ruler, a man of real merit and distinction. He made sure that the Goths lived in peace with the Italians and gave his warriors no more than one piece of land each to farm. He chose Ravenna, a harbour town in northern Italy, to be his capital and built beautiful churches decorated with wonderful brightly coloured mosaics.

This was all quite unexpected. That the Ostrogoths might succeed in building themselves a mighty and prosperous kingdom in Italy, one that would one day pose a threat to the imperial rule in Constantinople, is something that would never have occurred to the Emperor of the East, who must have regretted his advice.

From 527 onwards Constantinople was ruled by a mighty, luxury-loving and ambitious sovereign, whose name was Justinian. The emperor Justinian was possessed of one great ambition. This was to recover the whole of the old Roman empire and unite it under his rule. His court had all the splendour of the East. His wife, Theodora, was a former circus dancer and they both wore heavy robes of jewel-encrusted silk and great ropes of gold and pearls round their necks, which must have made a tremendous swishing and jangling when they moved.

In Constantinople Justinian built a gigantic church with a huge dome on top called the Hagia Sophia, and did his utmost to revive the lost grandeur of ancient Rome. He began by making a collection of all the laws of ancient Rome, together with the many commentaries made on them by great scholars and legislators. This great book of Roman law is known as the Pandects of Justinian. Even today, anyone who plans to become a lawyer or a judge should read it, as it forms the basis of many of our laws.

After Theodoric's death, Justinian tried to drive the Goths out of Italy and conquer the country, but the Goths put up a heroic defence and held out for decades. Given that they were in a foreign land whose inhabitants were also hostile to them, this was no easy task. Moreover, although they were also Christians, their beliefs were unlike those of either of their opponents – for instance, they did not believe in the Trinity (the existence of one God in three persons: the Father, Son and Holy Spirit). So they were attacked and persecuted as unbelievers as well. In the end most of the Goths were killed in these battles. After the last battle, those who were left – an army of less than a thousand men – were allowed to disband without reprisals, and vanished away towards the north. It was the end of that great tribe, the Ostrogoths. Now Justinian ruled over Ravenna as well. He built wonderful churches there which he had decorated with splendid portraits of his wife and himself.

But the rulers of the Empire of the East didn't stay long in Italy. In 586, new Germanic peoples called the Lombards came down from the north. The land was conquered yet again and today part of Italy is still called Lombardy after them. That was the last rumble of the storm. Then, slowly the clouds parted to reveal the starry night of the Middle Ages.

19

THE STARRY NIGHT BEGINS

You will probably agree that the peoples' migrations were a sort of thunderstorm. But you may be surprised to hear that the Middle Ages were like a starry night. Let me explain. Have you ever heard people talking about the Dark Ages? This is the name given to the period which followed the collapse of the Roman empire when very few people could read or write and hardly anyone knew what was going on in the world. And because of this, they loved telling each other all sorts of weird and wonderful tales and were generally very superstitious. 'Dark', too, because houses in those days were small and dark, and because the streets and highways that the Romans had built had all fallen into decay and were over-grown and their camps and cities had become grass-covered ruins. The good Roman laws were forgotten and the beautiful Greek statues had been smashed to pieces. All this is true. And it isn't really surprising, given all the dreadful upheavals and war-torn years of the Migrations.

But there was more to it than that. It wasn't all dark. It was more like a starry night. For above all the dread and uncertainty in which ignorant people lived like children in the dark – frightened of witches and wizards, of the Devil and evil spirits – above it all was the bright starlit sky of the new faith, showing them the way. And just as you don't get lost so easily in the woods if you can see stars like the Great Bear or the Pole Star, people no longer lost their way completely, no matter how much they stumbled in the dark. For they were sure of one thing: God had given souls to all men, and they were all equal in his eyes, beggars and kings alike. This meant there must be no more slaves – that human beings must no longer be treated as if they were things. That the one, invisible, God the Creator of the world, who through his mercy saves mankind, asks us to be good. Not that in those days there were only good people. There were just as many cruel, savage, brutal and pitiless warriors in Italy as there were in the lands where the Germans lived, who behaved in a reckless, ruthless and bloodthirsty manner. But now when they did so it was with a worse conscience than in Roman times. They knew they were wicked. And they feared the wrath of God.

Many people wished to live in strict accordance with God's will. They fled the bustling cities and the crowds where the temptation to do wrong is always present and, like the hermits of India, withdrew into the desert for prayer and penitence. These were the earliest Christian monks. They were first seen in the East, in Egypt and in Palestine. To many of them, what was most important was to do penance. They had learnt something about it from those Indian priests who, as you may remember, had special ways of tormenting themselves. Now some of these monks went and sat on the top of tall pillars in the centre of towns, where, barely moving, they spent their lives meditating on the sinfulness of mankind. The little food they needed was pulled up in a basket. There they sat, above all the bustle, and hoped it would bring them nearer to God. People called them Stylites, meaning pillar saints (from *stylos*, the Greek word for pillar).

But in the West, in Italy, there was a holy man who, like the Buddha, could find no inner calm in the solitary life of a penitent. He was a monk named Benedict, meaning the Blessed One. He was convinced that penitence wasn't all that Christ wanted. One must not only *become* good, one must *do* good. And if you want to do good, it's no use sitting on a pillar. You must work. And so his motto was: Pray and work. With a few like-minded monks he formed a community to put his rule into practice. This sort of monastic community is known as an Order, and his is called after him, the Order of the Benedictines. Monks like these lived in monasteries. Anyone wishing to enter a monastery and become a member of that Order for the rest of his life had to make three vows: to possess nothing; to remain unmarried; and to obey the head of the monastery, the abbot, in all things.

Once consecrated as a monk you didn't just pray – though of course prayer was taken very seriously and Mass was celebrated several times a day – you were also expected to do good. But for this you needed some skill or knowledge. And this is how the Benedictine monks became the only people at that time to concern themselves with the thought and discoveries of antiquity. They gathered together all the ancient scrolls and manuscripts they could find so they could study them. And they made copies for others to read. Year in, year out, they filled the pages of thick parchment volumes with their fine, flowing script, copying not only bibles and the lives of saints but ancient Greek and Latin poems as well. We would know very few of these if it hadn't been for the efforts of those monks. Not only that, but they laboriously copied other ancient works on the natural sciences and agriculture, over and over again, taking infinite care not to make mistakes. For, apart from the Bible, what mattered most to them was to be able to cultivate the land properly so that they could grow cereals and bread, not only for themselves but for the poor. In those lawless times wayside inns had all but disappeared, and anyone bold enough to travel had to look for shelter overnight in a monastery. There they were well received. Silence reigned, together with hard work and contemplation. The monks also took it upon themselves to educate the children who lived near their monasteries. They taught them reading and writing, to speak Latin and how to understand the Bible. Those few scattered monasteries were the only places in those days where learning and the handing down of knowledge went on and all memory of Greek and Roman thought was not extinguished.

But it wasn't only in Italy that there were monasteries like these. Monks wanted to build them in wild and out-of-the-way places where they could preach the Gospel, educate people and clear the useless forest for cultivation. Many of the earliest monasteries were built in Ireland and in England which, being islands, had suffered less from the storm of the Migrations. Germanic tribes had settled there too, among whom were the Angles and the Saxons, and Christianity had taken root there very early.

Monks then began to make their way from the British Isles to the kingdoms of the Gauls and the Germans, preaching and teaching as they went. There were still many Germans to convert, though their most powerful leader was a Christian, if only in name. He was called Clovis, and was a member of the Merovingian family. He had become king of the Franks at the age of fifteen, and by a combination of courage, intrigue and murder had brought half of Germania and much of what we now call France – which takes its name from his tribe – together under his rule.

Clovis had himself and his tribe baptised in 496, probably in the belief that the Christian god was a powerful demon who would help him to victory. For he was not devout. There was still much work for the monks to do in Germania. And indeed, they did a great deal. They founded monasteries and taught the Franks and the Alemanni how to grow fruit and vines, proving to the barbarian warriors that there was more to life than brute force and deeds of valour. They frequently acted as advisers to the Christian kings of the Franks at the Merovingian court. And because they were the best at reading and writing they wrote down the laws and did all the king's written work for him. Now the work of writing was also that of ruling: they composed letters to other kings and kept in touch with the pope in Rome. Which meant, in fact, that beneath their plain hooded cloaks those monks were the real masters of the still very disorderly kingdom of the Franks.

Other monks from Britain braved the wild stretches of land and dense forests of northern Germania, and what we know as the Netherlands today. These were very dangerous places to preach the Gospel. The peasants and warriors who lived there weren't even Christian in name and held fast to the beliefs of their ancestors. They prayed to Odin, the god of Battle, whom they worshipped not in temples but in the open air, often beneath ancient trees which they held sacred. One day an English monk and priest called Boniface came and preached under one of these trees. To prove to the northern Germans that Odin was only a fairy-tale figure, he picked up an axe to chop down the sacred tree. Everyone expected him to be struck down on the spot by a bolt of lightning from the heavens. But the tree fell and nothing happened. Lots of people then came to him to be baptised for they no longer believed in the power of Odin or in other gods, but other people were angry and in 754 they killed him.

Nevertheless paganism in Germany was at an end. Before long almost everyone was going to the simple wooden churches which the monks built next to their monasteries, and after the service they would ask the monks' advice on such things as how to cure a sick cow, or how to protect their apple trees against an infestation of caterpillars. The monks were also visited by the mighty, and of these it was often the most brutal and savage who readily gave them large tracts of land, for when they did so they hoped that God would pardon their sins. In this way the monasteries became rich and powerful, but the monks themselves, in their simple, narrow cells, remained poor, praying and working, just as St Benedict had told them.

20

❖

THERE IS NO GOD BUT ALLAH, AND MUHAMMAD IS HIS PROPHET

Can you picture the desert? The real, hot, sandy desert, crossed by long caravans of camels laden with cargoes of rare goods? Sand everywhere. Just occasionally you see one or two palm trees on the skyline. When you get there you find an oasis consisting of a spring with a trickle of greenish water. Then the caravan moves on. Eventually you come to a bigger oasis where there is a whole town of white, cube-shaped houses, inhabited by white-clothed, brown-skinned men with black hair and piercing dark eyes.

You can tell that these men are warriors. On their wonderfully swift horses they gallop across the desert, robbing caravans and fighting each other, oasis against oasis, town against town, tribe against tribe. Arabia probably still looks much as it did thousands of years ago. And yet it was in this strange desert land, with its few, warlike inhabitants, that perhaps the most extraordinary of all the events I have to tell took place.

It happened like this. At the time when the monks were teaching simple peasants and the Merovingian kings were ruling over the Franks – that is to say, around the year 600 – nobody talked about Arabs. They were busy galloping around in the desert, living in tents and fighting each other. They had a simple faith to which they gave little thought. Like the ancient Babylonians, they worshipped the stars, and also a stone which they believed to have fallen from heaven. This stone lay in a shrine called the Shrine of the Kaaba in the oasis town of Mecca, and Arabs often made pilgrimages across the desert to pray there.

Now there was at that time, in Mecca, a man named Muhammad, son of Abdallah. His father was of high birth but not a rich man, a member of a family charged with watching over the Shrine of the Kaaba. He died young, and all he left his son Muhammad were five camels, which didn't amount to much. When Muhammad was six his mother also died, and he had to leave the desert encampment where he lived with the other children of men of high rank and earn his living tending goats for the well-to-do. Later he met a rich widow, much older than himself, and made great journeys in her service as a camel driver leading trading caravans across the desert. He married his employer and they lived happily together and had six children. Muhammad also adopted his young cousin, whose name was Ali.

Strong and vigorous, with black hair and beard, eagle nose and heavy, loping gait, Muhammad was highly respected. He was known as 'the Trustworthy One'. He had shown an early interest in questions of religion and enjoyed talking not just with Arab pilgrims who came to the shrine at Mecca, but also with Christians from nearby Abyssinia, and with Jews, of whom there were large numbers in Arabian oasis towns. In his conversations with Jews and Christians one thing particularly impressed him: both spoke of the doctrine of the One, Invisible and Almighty God.

But in the evenings beside the fountain, he also enjoyed hearing about Abraham and Joseph, and about Jesus Christ and Mary. And one day, when he was on a journey, he suddenly had a vision. Do you know what that is? It is a dream you have when you're awake. It seemed to Muhammad that the Archangel Gabriel appeared before him, and addressed him in thunderous tones: 'Read!' cried the angel. 'But I cannot,' stammered Muhammad. 'Read!' cried the angel a second and again a third time, before commanding him, in the name of the Lord, his God, to pray. Profoundly shaken by this vision, Muhammad returned home. He didn't know what had happened to him.

For three long years, as he journeyed back and forth across the desert, he reflected on his experience, turning it over and over in his mind. And when those three years had gone by he had another vision. Once more the Archangel Gabriel appeared before him in a blaze of heavenly light. Beside himself with fear, he ran home and lay trembling and bewildered on his bed. His wife covered him with his cloak. And as he lay there, he heard the voice again: 'Rise and give warning!' was its command, and: 'Honour thy God!' Muhammad knew then that this was God's message, that he must warn mankind about hell and proclaim the greatness of the One Invisible God. From that moment Muhammad knew he was the Prophet through whose mouth God would make known his wishes to mankind. In Mecca he preached the doctrine of the One Almighty God, the Supreme Judge, who had appointed him, Muhammad, to be his messenger. But most people laughed at him. Only his wife and a few friends and relations had faith in him.

However, it was clear to the priests of the Kaaba, the leading tribesmen who were its guardians, that Muhammad was no fool, but a dangerous enemy. They forbade anyone in Mecca to associate with Muhammad's family or do business with his followers. They hung up this proscription in the Kaaba. It was a terrible blow which must have meant years of hunger and hardship for the Prophet's family and friends. However, in Mecca, Muhammad had met some pilgrims from an oasis town which had long been at enmity with Mecca. In that town there were many Jews, which meant that these Arabs already knew about the doctrine of the One and Only God. And they listened keenly to Muhammad's preaching.

The news that Muhammad was preaching to these hostile tribes, and that his popularity with them was growing, roused the tribe's leaders, the guardians of the Kaaba, to a fury. They resolved to execute the Prophet for high treason. Muhammad had already sent his followers out of Mecca to the desert town that had befriended him, and when the assassins who had been sent to kill him entered his house, he climbed out of a back window and fled to join them. This flight is known as the Emigration – the 'Hegira' in Arabic – and it took place on 16 June 622. Muhammad's followers have counted the years from that date, just as the Greeks did after the Olympiads, the Romans after the founding of Rome and the Christians after the birth of Christ.

In this town that would later be named Medina, 'the City of the Prophet', Muhammad was given a warm welcome. Everyone ran out to meet him and offered him hospitality. Not wishing to offend anybody, Muhammad said he would stay wherever his camel chose to go, which he did. In Medina Muhammad now set about instructing his followers, who listened to him attentively. He explained to them how God had revealed himself to Abraham and to Moses, and how, through the mouth of Christ, he had preached to mankind, and how he had now chosen Muhammad to be his prophet.

He taught them that they should fear nothing and no one but God – or Allah, in Arabic. That it was futile either to fear or to look forward to the future with joy, for their fate had already been ordained by God and written down in a great book. What must be must be, and the hour of our death has been appointed from the day of our birth. We must surrender ourselves to the will of God. The word for 'submission to the will of God' is 'Islam' in Arabic, so Muhammad called his teaching Islam. He told his followers that they must fight for this teaching and be victorious, and that to kill an unbeliever who refuses to recognise him as the Prophet is no sin. That a brave warrior who dies fighting for his faith, for Allah and the Prophet, goes straight to Heaven while infidels (unbelievers) and cowards go to Hell. In his preaching Muhammad told his followers of his visions and revelations (these were later written down and are now known as the Koran), and gave them a most wonderful description of Paradise:

On plump cushions, the Faithful lie, facing one another. Immortal youths go round amongst them bearing goblets

and ewers filled with a pure liquor, and no one who drinks of
it has a headache or is made drunk. All fruits are there, and
the flesh of all fowls, as much as they desire, and doe-eyed
maidens as beautiful as the hidden pearl. Under thorn-free
lotus trees and banana trees laden with fruit, in ample shade
and by running streams, the Blessed take their ease . . . the
fruit hangs low for them to pluck and the silver goblets are
ever made to go round about them. Upon them are garments
of fine green silk and brocade, adorned with silver clasps.

You can imagine the effect of this promise of Paradise on poor
tribespeople living in the scorching desert heat, and how willingly
they would fight and die to be admitted.

And so the inhabitants of Medina attacked Mecca, to avenge
their prophet and loot caravans. At first they triumphed and carried off rich spoils, then they lost it all again. The people of Mecca
advanced on Medina, intending to lay siege to the town, but after
only ten days they were forced to withdraw. The day came when
Muhammad, accompanied by fifteen hundred armed men, made
a pilgrimage to Mecca. The people of Mecca, who had only known
Muhammad when he was poor and derided, now recognised him
as a mighty prophet. Many of them went over to him. And soon
Muhammad and his army had conquered the whole town. But he
spared its inhabitants, only emptying the shrine of its idols. His
power and prestige were now immense and messengers arrived
from encampments and oases far and wide to do him homage.
Shortly before his death, he preached before a gathering of forty
thousand pilgrims, insisting for the last time that there was no
God but Allah and that he, Muhammad, was his Prophet; that the
fight against infidels – or unbelievers – must go on. He also urged
them to pray five times a day, facing Mecca, to drink no wine and
to be brave. Soon afterwards, in 632, he died.

In the Koran it is written: 'Fight the infidel until all resistance is
destroyed.' And in another passage: 'Slay the idolatrous wherever
you shall find them, capture them, besiege them, seek them out in
all places. But if they convert, then let them go in peace.'

The Arabs obeyed their Prophet's words, and when all the infidels in their desert had been either killed or converted they moved on to nearby countries, under the leadership of Muhammad's representatives, or 'caliphs', Abu Bakr and Omar. There, it was as if people were paralysed in the face of such wild religious zeal. Within six years of Muhammad's death the Arab warriors had already made bloody conquests of Palestine and Persia, and amassed vast quantities of loot. Other armies attacked Egypt – still part of the Roman Empire of the East, but by then a worn-out and impoverished land – and in four years it had fallen. The great city of Alexandria met the same fate. It is said that, when asked what should be done with the wonderful library, which at the time held seven hundred thousand scrolls by Greek poets, writers and philosophers, Omar replied: 'If what is in them is already contained in the Koran, they are not needed. And if what is in them is not contained in the Koran, then they are harmful.' Whether this is true or not, we don't know, but certainly there have always been people who think like that. So, in all the fighting and chaos, that most important and precious collection of books was lost to us for ever.

The Arab empire went from strength to strength, the flames, as it were, spreading out from Mecca in all directions. It was as if Muhammad had thrown a glowing spark onto the map. From Persia to India, from Egypt through the whole of North Africa, the fire raged. At this time the Arabs were far from united. Several caliphs were chosen to succeed Omar after his death and they fought bloodily and ferociously against one another. From around the year 670, Arab armies made repeated attempts to conquer Constantinople, the ancient capital of the Roman Empire of the East, but the inhabitants put up a heroic defence, withstanding one siege for seven long years, until the enemy finally withdrew. The Arabs had to content themselves with the islands of Cyprus and Sicily, which they attacked by way of Africa. But they didn't stop there. Returning to Africa, they crossed over into Spain where, as you may remember, the Visigoths had held sway since the time of the Migrations. In a battle that lasted seven days, General Tarik was victorious. Now Spain, too, was under Arab rule.

From there they reached the kingdom of the Franks, ruled by the Merovingians, where they were confronted by bands of Christian-German peasant warriors. The leader of the Franks was Charles Martel, which means Charles the Hammer, because he was so good at knocking people down in battle. And he actually succeeded in defeating the Arabs, in 732, exactly a hundred years after the Prophet's death. If Charles Martel had lost those battles at Tours and Poitiers in the southern kingdom of the Franks, the Arabs would surely have conquered all of what is now France and Germany, and destroyed the monasteries. In which case, we might all be Muslims, like so many of the peoples of the world today.

Not all Arabs continued to be wild desert warriors as they were in Muhammad's time. Far from it! As soon as the heat of battle had reduced a little, they began to learn from the peoples they had defeated and converted in all the conquered lands. From the Persians they learnt about eastern splendour – how to take pleasure in fine rugs and textiles, in sumptuous buildings, wonderful gardens, and precious furnishings and ornaments all beautifully decorated with intricate patterns.

In order to erase all traces of the memory of the worship of idols, Muslims were forbidden to make likenesses of people or animals. So they decorated their palaces and mosques with beautiful, intricate, interlacing patterns of lines of many colours called after the Arabs, 'arabesques'. And from the Greeks who lived in the conquered cities of the Roman Empire of the East, the Arabs learnt even more than they learnt from the Persians. Instead of burning books, they began to collect and read them. They particularly liked the writings of Alexander the Great's famous tutor, Aristotle, and translated them into Arabic. From him they learnt to concern themselves with everything in nature, and to investigate the origins of all things. They took to this readily and with enthusiasm. The names of many of the sciences you learn about at school come from Arabic, names like chemistry and algebra. The book you have in your hand is made of paper, something we also owe to the Arabs, who themselves learnt how to make it from Chinese prisoners of war.

There are two things for which I am especially grateful to the Arabs. First, the wonderful tales they used to tell and then wrote down, which you can read in *A Thousand and One Nights*. The second is even more fabulous than the tales, although you may not think so. Listen! Here is a number: '12'. Now why do you think we say 'twelve' rather than 'one-two' or 'one and two'? 'Because,' you say, 'the one isn't really a one at all, but a ten.' Do you know how the Romans wrote '12' ? Like this: 'XII'. And 112? 'CXII'. And 1,112? 'MCXII'. Just think of trying to multiply and add up with Roman numbers like these! Whereas with our 'Arabic' numbers it's easy. Not just because they are attractive and easy to write, but because they contain something new: place value – the value given to a number on account of its position. A number placed on the left of two others has to be a hundred number. So we write one hundred with a one followed by two zeros.

Could you have come up with such a useful invention? I certainly couldn't. We owe it to the Arabs, who themselves owe it to the Indians. And in my opinion that invention is even more amazing than all the Thousand and One Nights put together. Perhaps it's just as well that Charles Martel defeated the Arabs in 732. And yet it was not such a bad thing that they founded their great empire, because it was through those conquests that the ideas and discoveries of the Persians, the Greeks, the Indians and even the Chinese were all brought together.

21

❖

A Conqueror who Knows
How to Rule

Reading these stories may make you think it's easy to conquer the world or found a great empire, since it happens so often in the history of the world. And in fact it wasn't very difficult in earlier times. Why was that?

Imagine what it must have been like to have no newspapers and no post. Most people didn't even know what was happening in places just a few days' journey from where they lived. They stayed in their valleys and forests and tilled the land, and their knowledge of the world ended where the neighbouring tribes began. Towards these they were generally unfriendly, if not openly hostile. Each tribe harmed the other in whatever way it could, raiding cattle and setting fire to farmsteads. There was a constant tit-for-tat of stealing, feuding and fighting.

All they heard of a world beyond their own small realm were rumours and hearsay. If an army of several thousand men happened to turn up in a valley or clearing, there was little anyone could do. The neighbours thought themselves lucky if their enemies were slaughtered, and it didn't occur to them that their turn might be next. And if they weren't killed, but were merely forced to join that army and attack their nearest neighbours, they were grateful enough. In this way armies grew bigger and a tribe on its own would find it more and more difficult to resist, no matter how bravely it fought. The Arabs often went about their conquests like this, and so did Charlemagne, the famous king of the Franks, whose story you are about to hear.

If conquest was easier than it is today, ruling was much harder. Messengers had to be sent to distant and inaccessible places, warring peoples and tribes had to be pacified and reconciled, and made to look beyond their old enmities and blood-feuds. If you wanted to be a good ruler you had to help the peasants in their misery, and you had to see that people learned something, and that the thoughts and writings of the past weren't lost and forgotten. All in all, a good ruler in those days had to be a sort of father to the vast family of his subjects, and make all their decisions for them.

This was the sort of ruler that Charlemagne was, and it is why he is rightly called 'the Great' (the Latin word *magnus* means 'great'). He was a grandson of Charles Martel, the commander who drove the Arabs out of the Merovingian kingdom of the Franks. The Merovingian kings were not much good at ruling. They had flowing hair and long beards and they did nothing but sit on the throne and parrot the words their advisers had taught them. They moved around in ox-carts, like peasants, not on horseback, and that was how they attended tribal gatherings. The actual governing was done by an able family to which Charles Martel belonged, as did Pepin, the father of Charlemagne. But Pepin wasn't satisfied with being a mere adviser, whispering instructions into his king's ear. He had the power of kingship and he wanted the title as well. So he overthrew the Merovingian king and proclaimed himself king of the Franks. His kingdom covered roughly the western half of what is now Germany, and the eastern part of France.

But you mustn't imagine that this was a settled and well-organised kingdom, a proper state with officials and some sort of police force, or indeed that it was in any way similar to the Roman empire. For at this time the population wasn't united as it had been in the days of the Romans. Instead there were a number of tribes, all speaking different dialects and with different customs, who tolerated each other about as much, or as little, as the Dorians and Ionians of ancient Greece.

The tribal chieftains were known as dukes, from the Latin word *ducere*, to lead, because they marched into battle at the head of their troops. Their lands were known as their duchies. There were a number of these tribal duchies in Germany: the Bavarians, the Swabians and the Alemanni, among others. But the most powerful of all was the duchy of the Franks. It drew its power from the allegiance it was owed by other tribes who had to fight on the side of the Franks in time of war. This supremacy was established in Pepin's time. And like his father, Charlemagne would use it when, in 768, he became king in his turn.

First he conquered all of France. Then he marched over the Alps to Italy where, as you remember, the Lombards had settled at the end of the Migrations. He drove out the king of the Lombards and gave control of those lands to the Pope, whose protector he would be throughout his life. Then he marched on to Spain, where he fought the Arabs, but he didn't stay there long.

Having extended his kingdom to the south and west, Charlemagne turned his attention to the east. New hordes of mounted Asiatic warriors called Avars, similar to the Huns but without a great leader like Attila, had invaded the region where Austria is today. Their camps were always well dug in and protected by rings of dykes which made them hard to capture. Charlemagne and his armies fought the Avars for eight years before defeating them so thoroughly that not a trace of them remains. However, their invasion, like that of the Huns before them, had forced out other tribes. These were the Slavs who had founded a sort of kingdom, albeit one even less stable and more disorderly than that of the Franks. Charlemagne attacked them too, forcing some to join his army and others to pay him annual tribute. Yet in all his campaigns he never lost sight of his goal: to bring all these various Germanic tribes and duchies together under his rule, and forge them into a single people.

Now at that time hardly any of the eastern half of Germany belonged to the kingdom of the Franks. The Saxons lived there, and they were as wild and warlike as the Germanic tribes had been in Roman times. In addition, they were still heathens and would have nothing to do with Christianity. But Charlemagne saw himself as the leader of all Christians and in this he was not unlike the Muslims who thought you could force people to believe. So he fought with the Saxon chieftain, Widukind, for many years. Each time the Saxons surrendered, they would be up in arms again the next day. Charlemagne would then return and lay waste to their land. But he had only to turn his back for the Saxons to free themselves again. They would follow Charlemagne obediently into battle and then turn and attack his troops. In the end they paid a terrible price for their resistance: Charlemagne had more than four thousand of them put to death. The remaining Saxons allowed themselves to be baptised without protest, but it must have been a long time before they were able to feel any affection for the religion of loving kindness.

Charlemagne's power was by now very great indeed. But, as I said, he was not only good at conquering: he knew how to govern and take care of his people too. Schools were especially important to him, and he himself went on learning all his life. He spoke Latin as well as he did German, and he understood Greek. He was an eloquent and ready speaker with a firm clear voice. He was interested in all the arts and sciences of antiquity, taking lessons in rhetoric and astronomy from learned monks from Italy and England. It is said, however, that he found writing diffficult because his hand was more used to grasping a sword than tracing rows of beautifully curved letters with a delicate quill pen.

He loved hunting and swimming. He generally dressed simply. Under a striped silk tunic, he wore a plain linen shirt and long breeches held by gaiters below the knee, and, in winter, a fur doublet over which he flung a blue cloak. A silver- or gold-hilted sword always hung at his belt. Only on special occasions did he wear gold-embroidered robes, shoes decorated with gems, a great gold clasp on his cloak and a gold crown set with precious stones. Try to imagine that towering and imposing figure in all his finery, receiving ambassadors at his favourite palace at Aachen. They came from everywhere: from his own kingdom – that is, from France, Italy and Germany – and from the lands of the Slavs and Austria as well.

Charlemagne kept himself informed about everything that went on in his kingdom and made sure his instructions were faithfully carried out. He appointed judges and had the laws collected and written down. He nominated bishops and even fixed the price of foodstuffs. But what concerned him most was uniting all the Germans. He didn't simply want to rule a handful of tribal duchies. His aim was to weld them all into a single, strong kingdom. Any duke who objected was deposed. And it's worth noting that, from now on, whenever anyone referred to the language spoken by the Germanic tribes, they no longer said Frankish or Bavarian or Alemannish or Saxon. They simply said 'thiudisk', meaning German.

Because Charlemagne was interested in all things German, he made people write down all the ancient songs about heroes, tales which probably came from the time of the wars of the Migrations. These songs were about Theodoric (later called Dietrich of Berne), and Attila, or Etzel, King of the Huns, and Siegfried the Dragon-Slayer who was stabbed by the treacherous Hagen. But they have almost all been lost and we only know them from versions noted down some four hundred years later.

Charlemagne saw himself not only as king of the Germanic peoples and lord of the kingdom of the Franks, but as the defender of all Christians. And it seems that the pope in Rome, who had often enjoyed Charlemagne's protection against the Lombards, agreed with him. On Christmas Eve, in the year 800, when Charlemagne was kneeling in prayer in the great church of St Peter's in Rome, the pope suddenly stepped forward and placed a crown upon his head. Then the pope and all the people fell on their knees before him and proclaimed Charlemagne the new Roman emperor, chosen by God to preserve the peace of the empire. Charlemagne must have been very surprised as it appears that he had no inkling of what was in store for him. But now he wore the crown and was the first German emperor of the Holy Roman Empire, as it later was known.

Charlemagne's mission was to restore the might and grandeur of the old Roman empire. Only this time, instead of heathen Romans, the rulers would be Christian Germans, who would become the leaders of all Christendom. This was Charlemagne's aim and ambition, and it would long be that of German emperors who came after him. But none came as close to achieving it as he did. Envoys from all over the world came to his court to pay him homage. The mighty emperor of the Roman Empire of the East in Constantinople was not the only one anxious to be on good terms with him. So was the great Arab prince, Caliph Harun al-Rashid, in far-off Mesopotamia. From his fabulous palace in Baghdad, near ancient Nineveh, he sent precious gifts to Charlemagne: sumptuous robes, rare spices and an elephant, and a water clock with the most amazing mechanism, unlike anything seen before in the kingdom of the Franks. For Charlemagne's sake, Harun al-Rashid even let Christian pilgrims visit Christ's tomb in Jerusalem, unhindered and unmolested. For Jerusalem was at that time under Arab rule.

All this was due to the intelligence, energy and undoubted superiority of the new emperor, as rapidly became clear after his death in 814 when, sadly, it all fell apart. Soon the empire was shared out among Charlemagne's three grandsons in the form of three separate kingdoms: Germany, France and Italy.

In the lands that had once belonged to the Roman empire, Romance languages continued to be spoken – that is, French and Italian. The three kingdoms would never again be united. Even the German tribal duchies rebelled and won back their independence. On Charlemagne's death, the Slavs proclaimed themselves free, and founded a powerful kingdom under their first great king, Svatopluk. The schools Charlemagne had founded disappeared, and the art of reading and writing was soon lost to all but a handful of far-flung monasteries. Intrepid Germanic tribes from the north, the Danes and the Normans, mercilessly pillaged and plundered coastal cities in their Viking ships. They were almost invincible. They founded kingdoms in the east, among the Slavs, and in the west on the coast of what is now France, where Normandy still bears their name.

Before the century was out, the Holy Roman Empire of the German Nation, Charlemagne's great achievement, was no more. Not even the name remained.

22

❖

A STRUGGLE TO BECOME
LORD OF CHRISTENDOM

The history of the world is, sadly, not a pretty poem. It offers little variety, and it is nearly always the unpleasant things that are repeated, over and over again. And so it was that, barely a hundred years after Charlemagne's death, in times of chaos and misfortune, hordes of mounted warriors from the east invaded yet again, as the Avars and the Huns had before them. Not that there was anything remarkable about that. It was easier, and therefore more tempting, to take the path which led from the Asiatic steppes towards Europe than to launch raids on China. For behind the protection of Shih Huang-ti's great wall, China had now become a powerful and well-organised state, with large and prosperous cities, where life at the imperial court and in the houses of its learned high officials had reached levels of refinement and taste undreamt-of elsewhere.

At the same time as people in Germany were collecting ancient battle songs – only to burn them soon after on the grounds that they were too heathen – and monks in Europe were making timid efforts to turn Bible stories into German rhymes and Latin verse (that is, in about 800), China was home to some of the greatest poets the world has ever known. They wrote on silk, with elegant flourishes of brushes dipped in Indian ink, concise and brief verses which, in the simplest way, express so much that you need only read one once and it is in your head for ever.

Because the Chinese empire was well administered and well protected, the mounted hordes continued to direct their raids towards Europe. This time it was the Magyars' turn. With neither Pope Leo nor Charlemagne to stop them, they made short work of the lands that are now Hungary and Austria, and invaded Germany to loot and kill.

This danger forced the independent tribal duchies to elect a common leader. In 919 they chose Henry, duke of Saxony, to be their king, and he eventually succeeded in driving the Magyars out of Germany and keeping them outside the frontiers. His successor, King Otto (known as Otto the Great), did not destroy them completely, as Charlemagne had the Avars, but after a ferocious battle in 955 he forced them back into Hungary, where they settled and have remained to this day.

Otto the Great didn't keep the land he had taken from the Magyars for himself, but bestowed it on a prince, as was then the custom. His son, Otto II, did likewise when, in 976, he bestowed part of present-day Lower Austria (the district around Wachau) on a German nobleman called Leopold, a member of the Babenberg family. Like all noblemen granted land by the king, Leopold built himself a castle and ruled over his land like a prince, for while the royal grant endured he was no longer merely a royal official but the lord of his domain.

Most of the peasants who lived on these lands were no longer freemen, as German peasants had been in earlier times. They belonged to the land the king bestowed, or to land owned by a nobleman. Like the sheep or the goats that grazed there, like the deer, the bears and the wild boar in the forest, like the streams and the woodland, the meadows, the pastures and the fields, the people belonged to the land they tilled. They were known as serfs, or bondsmen, because they were bound to the land. Nor were they free citizens of the kingdom. They had neither the right to go where they wished nor the right to decide to till or not to till their fields.

'Were they slaves, then, like in antiquity?' Well, not exactly. For as you remember, the coming of Christianity had put an end to slavery in our lands. Serfs weren't slaves, because they went with the land, and the land still belonged to the king even after he had bestowed it on a nobleman. A nobleman or prince was not allowed to sell or kill serfs as masters once could their slaves. But he could make them carry out his orders. The serfs had to cultivate his land and work for him, when he told them to. They had to send regular supplies of bread and meat up to the castle for him to eat, because a nobleman didn't work in the fields. Most of his time was spent hunting, whenever he felt like it. The land the king had bestowed on him, known as his fief, was his land, and would be inherited by his son, as long as he did nothing to offend the king. In return for his fief all a prince had to do was to take his lords of the manor and his peasants with him into battle to fight for the king, if there was a war. And of course, there often was.

At this time virtually the whole of Germany had been granted in this way to different lords. The king kept little for himself, and the same went for France and England. In France, in 987, a powerful duke called Hugh Capet became king, while in 1016 England was conquered by a Danish seafarer called Cnut, or Canute, who also ruled over Norway and part of Sweden, and he, too, granted his lands as fiefs to powerful princes.

The power of the German kings was greatly increased by their victory over the Magyars. Otto the Great, having defeated the Hungarians, made the Slavic, Bohemian and Polish princes recognise him as their feudal overlord as well. This meant that they had to look on their own lands as being held in trust for the German king, and were obliged to bring their armies to his aid in time of war.

Confident in his might, Otto the Great marched on Italy, where, amidst fearful confusion, savage fighting had broken out among the Lombards. Otto declared Italy a German fief too, and bestowed it on a Lombard prince. Greatly relieved that Otto had been able to use his power to bring the Lombard nobility to heel, the pope crowned him Roman emperor in 962, just like Charlemagne in 800.

So once again, German kings became Roman emperors, and by that title the protectors of Christendom. They owned the land the peasants ploughed from Italy to the North Sea, and from the Rhine to far beyond the Elbe, where Slav peasants became serfs of German noblemen. The emperor didn't grant these lands only to noblemen. He frequently bestowed them on priests, bishops and archbishops. And they too, being no longer mere ministers of the Church, ruled like noblemen over great estates and rode into battle at the head of their peasant armies.

At first this suited the pope very well. He was on good terms with the German emperors who protected and defended him and were all very pious men.

However, the situation soon changed. The pope didn't want the emperor to decide which of his priests should become bishop of Mainz, or Trier, or Cologne, or Passau. 'These are religious appointments,' said the pope, 'and I, as head of the Church, must decide them.' But the fact remained, they weren't just religious appointments. Take the archbishop of Cologne, for example: he was both guardian of the souls of that district and its prince and lord. Therefore the emperor maintained that it was for him to decide who was to be a prince or a lord in his land. And if you think about it for a moment, you will see that each, from his own stand-point, was right. Bestowing land on priests had created a dilemma, for the lord of all priests is the pope, but the lord of all lands is the emperor. This could only lead to trouble, and it soon did. This trouble became known as the Investiture Controversy.

In Rome, in 1073, an exceptionally pious and zealous monk, who had already devoted his life to defending the purity and power of the Church, became pope. He was called Hildebrand, and as pope took the name of Gregory VII.

Meanwhile in Germany a Frankish king was on the throne. His name was Henry IV. Now it is important to realise that the pope saw himself not only as head of the Church, but also as the divinely appointed ruler of all Christians on earth. At the same time, the German emperor and successor to the ancient Roman emperors and Charlemagne saw *himself* as protector and supreme commander of the entire Christian world. And even though Henry IV had not yet been crowned emperor, he still believed, that, as German king, it was his right. Which of the two should yield?

When the struggle between them began, the world was in an uproar. Some were for King Henry IV, others sided with Pope Gregory VII. So many people were involved in this contest that we know of 155 arguments written for and against the king by his supporters and opponents. A number of these portray King Henry as being a wicked and hot-tempered man, while in others it is the pope who is accused of being heartless and power-hungry.

I think we should believe neither. Once we have decided that each, from his own standpoint, was right, whether King Henry behaved badly towards his wife (as his opponents said), or pope Gregory was elected pope without following the usual formalities (as his opponents said), matters little to us. We can't go back into the past and see exactly what did happen, and find out whether these accusations against the pope and the king had any truth in them. They probably didn't, for when people take sides they are usually unfair. However, I'm now going to show you just how hard it is to get at the truth, after more than nine hundred years.

We can be sure of one thing: King Henry was in a difficult situation. The nobles on whom he had bestowed lands (that is, the German princes) were against him. They didn't want their king to become too powerful in case he started ordering them around. Pope Gregory opened hostilities by shutting King Henry out of the Church – by which I mean that he forbade any priest to give him Holy Communion. This was known as excommunication. Then the princes let it be known that they would have nothing to do with an excommunicated king, and that they were going to choose someone else to take his place. Somehow Henry had to get the pope to lift this terrible ban. His fate depended on it. If he failed, he would lose his throne. So, all alone and without his army, he set out for Italy to try to persuade the pope to lift the ban.

It was winter, and the German princes who wanted to prevent King Henry's reconciliation with the pope occupied all the roads and paths. So Henry, accompanied by his wife, had to make a great detour, and in the freezing winter's cold they made their way over the Alps, probably by the same pass that Hannibal had used when he invaded Italy.

Meanwhile the pope was on his way to Germany to negotiate with Henry's enemies. When he heard of Henry's approach, he fled and took refuge in a fortress in northern Italy called Canossa, convinced that Henry was arriving with an army. But when Henry appeared alone, only wishing to have the excommunication lifted, he was amazed and overjoyed. Some say the king came dressed as a penitent, wearing a rough, hooded cloak, and that the pope made him wait three days in the castle courtyard, barefoot in the snow, before he took pity on him and lifted the ban. Contemporaries describe the king as whimpering and begging the pope for mercy, which the pope, in his compassion, finally granted.

Today people still talk of 'going to Canossa' when somebody has to humble himself before his adversary. But now let's see how one of the king's friends tells the same story. This is his version: 'When Henry saw how badly things were going for him, he secretly thought up a very cunning plan. Giving no warning whatsoever, he set out to see the pope. His intention was to kill two birds with one stone: on the one hand he would have the excommunication lifted, and on the other, by going in person, he would prevent the pope from meeting his enemies, and so avert a great danger.'

So the pope's friends saw Henry's going to Canossa as an outstanding success for the pope, and the king's supporters saw it as a great triumph for their leader.

From this you can see how careful one must be in judging a dispute between two rival powers. But the struggle did not end at Canossa, or with the death of King Henry – who had actually become emperor meanwhile – or with the death of Pope Gregory. For although Henry later managed to have Gregory deposed, the will of that great pope prevailed. Bishops were chosen by the Church, and the emperor was only allowed to say if he agreed with the choice. The pope, not the emperor, became lord of Christendom.

You remember those Nordic seafarers, the Normans, who conquered a stretch of land along the northern coast of France still known as Normandy today? They quickly learnt to speak French, like their neighbours, but they didn't lose their appetite for adventurous sea voyages and conquest. Some of them went as far as Sicily, where they fought the Arabs, then conquered southern Italy and went on, under their great leader Robert Guiscard, to defend Pope Gregory against Henry IV's attacks. Others crossed the narrow stretch of sea that lies between France and England, known as the English Channel, and under their king, William (afterwards named 'the Conqueror'), defeated the English king (a descendant of the Danish King Canute) at the Battle of Hastings. This was in 1066, a date which all the English know, because it was the last time an enemy army succeeded in setting foot on English soil.

William had his officials draw up a list naming every village and property in the land, many of which he bestowed on his fellow soldiers as fiefs. The English nobility were now Normans. And because the Normans who came from Normandy spoke French, the English language is still a mixture of words from Old German and Romance languages.

23

❖

Chivalrous Knights

I am sure you have heard of knights of old from the Age of Chivalry. And you have probably read books about knights and their squires who set out in search of adventure; stories full of shining armour, plumed helmets and noble steeds, blazoned escutcheons and impregnable fortresses, jousting and tournaments where fair ladies give prizes to the victors, wandering minstrels, forsaken damsels and departures for the Holy Land. The best thing is that all of it really existed. All that glitter and romance is no invention. Once upon a time the world really was full of colour and adventure, and people joyfully took part in that strange and wonderful game called chivalry, which was often played in deadly earnest.

But when exactly was the Age of Chivalry, and what was it really like? The word chivalry comes from the French word *chevalier* meaning horseman, and it was with horsemen that chivalry began. Anyone who could afford a good charger on which to ride into battle was a knight. If he couldn't, he went on foot and wasn't a knight. Noblemen whose lands had been bestowed on them by the king were also knights and their serfs had to provide hay for the horses. A nobleman might, in his turn, bestow part of his fief on his agent or steward, who would also be rich enough to own a fine horse even if, in other respects, he had little power. When his lord was summoned to war by the king he had to ride with him. So stewards were also knights. Only peasants and poor servants, farm-lads and labourers who went to war on foot weren't knights.

It all began around the time of the emperor Henry IV – that is to say, after the year 1000 – and went on for several centuries, in Germany and in England, but above all in France.

However, these knights weren't yet knights as you or I would imagine them. That only happened gradually. First the princes and nobles set about building themselves great fortresses, fortresses that were intended to be secure against all assault. These can still be seen today in hilly places, or standing, proud and defiant, on sheer cliffs, with only one approach along a tiny, narrow track.

Before you reached the castle gate there was usually a wide ditch or moat, sometimes full of water. Over the moat was a drawbridge, with chains on either side to haul it up at any moment. When the bridge was raised, the castle was secure and no one could get in. On the other side of the ditch were thick, strong walls with loop-holes to shoot arrows through and holes for pouring boiling pitch down on the enemy. The walls themselves were topped by tooth-like battlements, behind which you could hide to spy on the enemy. Within this thick wall there was often another one, and sometimes even a third, before you reached the castle courtyard. The court-yard then gave access to the rooms where the knight lived. A hall with a fireplace and a fire was reserved for the women, who were not as hardened to discomfort as the men.

For there was nothing comfortable about life in a castle. The kitchen was a soot-blackened room where meat was roasted on a great spit over a crackling log fire. Apart from the rooms for the knights and their valets there were two others: the chapel, where the chaplain held divine service, and the keep. The keep was a massive tower, generally in the heart of the castle, where stores were usually kept, and in which the knights took refuge once their enemies had overcome . . . the mountain, the moat, the drawbridge, the boiling pitch and the three walls. At which point, they were confronted by this mighty tower, where the knights were often able to hold out until help arrived.

And of course, we mustn't forget the dungeons! These were cramped and freezing cells in the depths of the castle into which knights threw their prisoners. There they were left to languish in the dark until they died or were ransomed for a vast sum.

You may have seen one of these castles. But the next time you do, don't just think of the knights in chain mail who lived there. Instead, take a look at the walls and towers and spare a thought for the people who built them. Towers perched high on tops of mountain crags, walls hung between precipices. All made by peasant serfs, men deprived of liberty – bondsmen, as they were called. For it was they who had to split and carry the rocks, haul them up and pile them on top of each other. And when their strength gave out, their wives and their children had to take over. A knight could command them to do anything. Better a knight than a serf any day.

Sons of serfs became serfs and the sons of knights, knights. It wasn't so very different from ancient India and its castes.

At the age of seven a knight's son was sent away to another castle, to learn about life. He was called a page, and had to serve the ladies – carry their trains and perhaps read to them aloud – for women were rarely taught to read or write whereas pages usually were. On reaching the age of fourteen, a page became a squire. He didn't have to stay in the castle and sit beside the fire any more. Instead, he was allowed to accompany his knight when he went hunting, or to war. A squire had to carry his knight's shield and spear and hand him his second lance on the battlefield when the first one shattered. He had to obey his master in all things and be true to him. If he proved a brave and loyal squire, he in his turn would be dubbed a knight at the age of twenty-one. The ceremony of dubbing was a very solemn one. The squire first had to fast and pray in the castle chapel. He also received Communion from the priest. Then, in full armour, but without his helmet, sword or shield, he knelt between two witnesses. His lord, who was to dub

him a knight, tapped him on each shoulder and on the neck with
the flat blade of his sword, while reciting the following words:

> In the name of God and of Mary his mother
> Accept this blow and never another.
> Be upright, true and brave.
> Better a knight than a slave.

Only then was the squire allowed to rise. He was a squire no longer.
He was a knight who might now dub others knights, whose shield
now bore his coat of arms – a lion, a leopard or a flower – and who
would usually choose a fine motto or device to live by. He was
solemnly presented with his sword and helmet, golden spurs were
fitted to his boots and his shield was set on his arm. Off he rode in
his bright plumed helmet, with his mighty lance and a scarlet cloak
over his chain mail, accompanied by his own squire, to prove
himself worthy of his knighthood.

From all this solemn ceremony you can see that a knight was by
now something more than just a soldier on horseback. He was
almost a member of an order, like a monk. For to be a good knight,
bravery was not enough. A monk served God through prayers and
good works and a knight served God through his strength. It was
his duty to protect the weak and defenceless, women and the poor,
widows and orphans. He was only allowed to draw his sword in a
just cause, and must serve God in each and every deed. To his
master – his liegelord – he owed absolute obedience. For him he
must risk all. He must be neither brutal nor cowardly, and in battle
must only fight man to man, never two against one. A vanquished
opponent must never be humiliated. We still call this sort of
behaviour chivalrous, because it conforms to the knights' ideal.

When a knight loved a lady, he did battle in her honour, and
went in search of adventures to win fame for his beloved. He
pronounced her name with reverence and did everything she
asked. That, too, is part of chivalry. And if it seems natural to you
today to let a lady go through a door first, or to bend down and
pick up something she has dropped, it's because inside you there
is a remnant of the thinking of those knights of old who believed

that it is a gentleman's duty to protect the weak and honour women.

In peacetime, too, a knight would demonstrate his courage and his skill in games of chivalry known as tournaments. Knights from many countries gathered to test their strength at these war games. Dressed in full armour they galloped towards one another at full tilt, each doing his best to unhorse the other with his blunted lance. The lady of the castle presented the winner with a prize – usually a garland of flowers. To please the ladies a knight had to do more than shine at feats of arms. He had to behave in a moderate and noble manner, not curse or swear as soldiers usually did, and master chess-playing and poetry and other arts of peace.

In fact, knights were often great poets, who wrote songs praising the women they loved, telling of their beauty and their virtue. They also sang of the deeds of other knights of the past. There were long stories in verse, telling of King Arthur and the Knights of the Round Table, of Perceval (or Parsifal) and Lohengrin and the Quest for the Holy Grail (the cup Christ drank from at the Last Supper), of the unhappy love of Tristan and Isolde, and even stories about Alexander the Great and the Trojan War.

Minstrels wandered from castle to castle, singing of Siegfried the Dragon-slayer and Theodoric, King of the Goths (who became Dietrich of Berne). These songs, sung in Austria on the Danube at that time, are among the earliest we know, because those transcribed under Charlemagne have all been lost. And if you read the story of Siegfried in the *Song of the Nibelungen,* you will find all the ancient Germanic peasant warriors behaving like true knights. Even the terrifying Attila the Hun, solemnly celebrating his marriage to Siegfried's widow, Kriemhild, in Vienna, is portrayed as a noble and chivalrous king.

As you know, a knight's first duty was to fight for God and for Christendom. And it wasn't long before they found a wonderful opportunity to do so. Christ's tomb in Jerusalem was, as was the whole of Palestine, in the hands of Arab unbelievers. So when reminded of their duty to help liberate the tomb by a great preacher in France, and by the pope – whose victory over the

German kings had made him the mightiest ruler of Christendom – Christian knights in their tens of thousands cried out enthusiastically: 'It is God's will! It is God's will!'

Under the leadership of a French knight, Godfrey of Bouillon, a great army set off along the Danube in 1096, first to Constantinople and then on through Asia Minor towards Palestine. These knights and their followers had crosses of red material stitched to their shoulders and were called 'crusaders'. Their aim was to liberate the land in which Christ's cross had once stood. When, after long years of battles and unimaginable hardships, they finally reached the walls of Jerusalem, it is said that they were so moved by the sight of the Holy City, which they knew from the Bible, that they wept and kissed the soil. Then they besieged the town. It was valiantly defended by Arab soldiers, but eventually they took it.

Once inside Jerusalem, however, they behaved neither like knights nor like Christians. They massacred all the Muslims and committed hideous atrocities. Then they did penance, and, singing psalms, proceeded barefoot to Christ's tomb.

The crusaders founded the Christian kingdom of Jerusalem, with Godfrey of Bouillon as its Protector. But because it was small and weak, far from Europe and in the midst of Muslim kingdoms, the little state was forever under attack from Arab warriors. This meant that, back in England, France and Germany, priests were forever urging knights to go on new crusades. Not all of these were successful.

However, one good thing came of the Crusades, although it wouldn't have pleased the knights at all. In the distant Orient the Christians discovered Arab culture – their buildings, their sense of beauty and their learning. And within a hundred years of the First Crusade, the writings of Alexander the Great's teacher, the books of Aristotle, were translated from Arabic into Latin and eagerly read and studied in Italy, France, Germany and England. People were surprised to find how similar many of his teachings were to those of the Church and filled heavy Latin tomes with complicated thoughts on the subject. All that the Arabs had learnt and experienced in the course of their conquests around the world was now brought back to Europe by the crusaders. In a number of ways it was the example of those they looked on as their enemies that transformed the barbaric warriors of Europe into truly chivalrous knights.

24

❖

EMPERORS IN THE AGE
OF CHIVALRY

In these fairy-tale times, full of colour and adventure, there was a new family of knights ruling in Germany. They took their name, Hohenstaufen, from their castle. One of them was the emperor Frederick I, nicknamed Barbarossa by the Italians on account of his magnificent fiery-red beard. Now you may wonder why history should choose to remember him by his Italian name – after all, Frederick I was a German emperor. It is simply because he spent much of his time in Italy and the deeds that made him famous happened there. It wasn't just the pope and his power to bestow the imperial crown of Rome on German kings that attracted Barbarossa to Italy. He was also determined to rule the whole of Italy, because he needed money. 'Couldn't he get money from Germany?' I can hear you asking. No, he couldn't. Because in those days in Germany there was almost none at all.

Have you ever wondered why people actually need money? 'To live on, of course!' you say. But that isn't strictly true. Try eating a coin. People live on bread and other foods, and someone who grows grain and makes his own bread doesn't need money, any more than Robinson Crusoe did. Nor does anyone who is given his bread for nothing. And that's how it was in Germany. The serfs cultivated their fields and gave a tenth of their harvest to the knights and monks who owned the land.

'But where did the peasants get their ploughs from? And their smocks and their yokes and the things they needed for their animals?' Well, mostly by exchange. If, for example, a peasant had an ox, but would rather have six sheep to give him wool to make a jacket, he would exchange them for something with his neighbour. And if he had slaughtered an ox, and spent the long winter evenings turning the two horns into fine drinking cups, he could exchange one of the cups for some flax grown by his neighbour, which his wife could weave and make into a coat. This is known as barter. So in Germany people managed perfectly well in those days without money, since most of them were either peasants or landowners. Nor did the monasteries need money, for they too owned a lot of land which pious people either gave them or left to them when they died.

Apart from vast forests, small fields and a few villages, castles and monasteries, there was almost nothing else in the whole great German kingdom – that is to say, there were hardly any towns. And it was only in towns that people needed money. Shoemakers, cloth merchants and scribes can hardly satisfy their hunger and thirst with leather, cloth and ink. They need bread. But can you see yourself going to the shoemaker and paying for your shoes with bread for him to live on? And in any case, if you aren't a baker, where will you find the bread? 'From a baker!' Yes, but what will you give the baker in return? 'Perhaps I can lend him a hand.' And if he doesn't need your help? Or if you have already promised to help the lady who sells fruit? You see, it would be unimaginably complicated if people who live in towns were to barter.

This is why people agreed to decide on something to exchange which everyone would want and therefore accept, something easy to share out and carry around, which wouldn't go bad or lose its value if you put it away. It was decided that the best thing would be metal – that is, gold or silver. All money was once made of metal, and rich people went around with purses stuffed with gold coins on their belts. That meant you could give the shoemaker money for shoes, and he could use it to buy bread from the baker, who could give it to the peasant in exchange for flour, and the peasant might then use your money to buy a new plough. He wouldn't find that for barter in his neighbour's garden.

However, there were very few towns in Germany in the days of chivalry, so people there had little need of money, whereas in Italy money had been in use since Roman times. Italy had always had great cities and many merchants with bags of money on their belts and even more stowed away in great chests.

Some of these towns were by the sea, like Venice, which is actually in the sea on a cluster of little islands where the inhabitants had taken refuge from the Huns. Then there were other great harbour towns such as Genoa and Pisa, whose ships sailed far across the seas and came back from the Orient with fine cloth, rare spices and weapons of great value. These goods were sold off in the ports, to be sold again inland in cities like Florence, Verona or Milan, where the cloth might be made into clothes, or perhaps banners or tents. These then went to France, whose capital city, Paris, already contained almost a hundred thousand inhabitants – or to England, or even to Germany. But not much went to Germany because there was very little money there to pay for such things.

People who lived in towns grew richer and richer, and no one could give them orders because they weren't peasants and didn't belong to anyone's fief. On the other hand, since no one had granted them land, they weren't lords either. They governed themselves, much as people did in antiquity. They had their own courts of law and were as free and independent in their cities as the monks and the knights. Such citizens (called burghers in Germany or the bourgeoisie in France) were known as the Third Estate. Of course, peasants didn't count.

This brings us back at last to the Emperor Barbarossa, who needed money. As Holy Roman Emperor he wanted to be the actual ruler of Italy, and to receive tribute and taxes from Italian citizens. But the citizens would have none of it. They were used to their freedom and didn't wish to give it up. So Barbarossa took an army over the Alps to Italy, where he summoned a number of famous jurists in 1158, who solemnly and publicly declared that as Holy Roman emperor and successor to the Roman Caesars, he had all the rights his predecessors had had a thousand years before.

The Italian cities took no notice. They still refused to pay. So the emperor led his army against them, and in particular against Milan, the town at the heart of the rebellion. It is said that he was so incensed by their refusal that he swore not to wear his crown until he had forced the town into submission. And he kept his oath. Only when Milan had fallen, and was utterly destroyed, did he hold a banquet at which he and his wife appeared with their crowns once more on their heads.

But no matter how many great and successful campaigns he led, Barbarossa had only to turn his back and head for home for the rumblings of revolt to start up again. The Milanese rebuilt their town and refused to recognise a German ruler. In all, Barbarossa led six campaigns against Italy, but his fame was always greater than his success.

He was seen to be the very model of a knight. He was extremely strong – mentally as well as physically. And he was generous and knew how to hold a feast. Today we have forgotten what a real feast is like. Everyday life, compared to ours, may have been mean and monotonous, but a feast in those days was unlike anything you could imagine. It was indescribably lavish and magnificent, like something out of a fairy-tale. Barbarossa held one in Mainz when his sons were dubbed knights, in 1181, to which forty thousand knights with all their squires and attendants were invited. They stayed in brightly coloured tents and the emperor and his sons had the grandest one of all, which was made of silk and stood in the centre of the encampment. Fires blazed all around with whole oxen, wild boar and innumerable chickens roasting over them on spits. People came from far and wide dressed in all sorts of costumes – jugglers and acrobats and wandering minstrels who sang all the great songs of old in the evening while they feasted. What a sight it must have been! The emperor himself displayed his skills, jousting with his sons, while all the nobles in the land looked on. A feast like this went on for days. Long after it was over the minstrels continued to sing about it.

As a true knight, Barbarossa eventually went on a crusade. This was the Third Crusade, in 1189. King Richard the Lionheart of England and the French King Philip also took part. They went by sea. But Barbarossa chose to go by land and was drowned in a river in Asia Minor.

His grandson Frederick II of Hohenstaufen was even more remarkable, even greater and altogether more admirable than Barbarossa. He was brought up in Sicily, and while he was still a child and unable to rule himself there was a lot of trouble in Germany between the great rival families over who was to be the new sovereign. Some favoured Philip, Barbarossa's youngest son, while others had elected Otto, whose family was called Welf. This gave people who already couldn't endure each other yet another reason to squabble. If one was for Philip then his neighbour would side with Otto, and the happy custom of these rival factions – known in Italy as the Guelphs and the Ghibellines – persisted for many years. Even after Philip and Otto were long gone.

Meanwhile Frederick had grown up in Sicily. And I mean grown up. Both in body and in mind. His guardian, Pope Innocent III, was one of the most important men there has ever been. What Gregory VII – the German king Henry IV's great adversary – had fought so hard for, and had failed to achieve, Innocent III had accomplished. He really was lord of all Christendom. A man of exceptional intelligence and culture, he ruled them all – not just the spiritual leaders of the Church, but all the princes of Europe. His power even reached as far as England. When, one day, King John refused to carry out his orders, he excommunicated him and forbade any priest to celebrate Mass in England. The English nobility became so angry with their king that they took away almost all his power. In 1215 he had to solemnly swear that he would never again oppose their will. This was the famous Magna Carta, the Great Charter to which King John put his seal, in which he granted his barons a whole host of rights which English citizens hold to this day. But England still had to pay taxes and tribute to Pope Innocent III, so great was his power.

Frederick II of Hohenstaufen wasn't only highly intelligent: he was an attractive and likeable young man as well. In order to claim his crown as king of the Germans, he set out from Sicily, virtually on his own, on an adventurous ride which took him through Italy and over the Swiss mountains to Constance. However, when he arrived he found that his rival Otto was marching towards him at the head of an army. There seemed little hope for Frederick. But the burghers of Constance, like all those who met him and came to know him, were so charmed by him that they rallied round and hastily closed the city gates. When Otto arrived exactly one hour later, all he could do was turn round and go away.

Having similarly won over all the German princes, Frederick suddenly found he had become a mighty ruler, lord of all the vassals of Germany and Italy. So again the two powers were in conflict, just as in the days of Pope Gregory VII and Henry IV. But Frederick was no Henry. He did not go to Canossa, and he didn't intend to beg the pope for mercy. Like Pope Innocent III, he was convinced that he had been called to rule the world. Frederick knew everything that Innocent had known – after all, Innocent had been his guardian. He knew everything the Germans knew, for they were his family. And finally, he knew everything the Arabs knew, for he had grown up in Sicily. He was to spend much of his life there and in Sicily there was more for him to learn than anywhere else in the world.

Sicily had been ruled by everyone: the Phoenicians, Greeks, Carthaginians, Romans, Arabs, Normans, Italians and Germans. Soon it would be the turn of the French. It must have been just like the Tower of Babel, except that there people had ended up understanding almost nothing, whereas Frederick ended up by understanding nearly everything there was to know. Not just every language, but many whole branches of knowledge. He wrote poetry, and he was a superb huntsman. He even wrote a book on falconry, for people hunted with hawks in those days.

Above all, he knew about religions. But there was one thing he could never understand: why people were always fighting. He liked to have discussions with learned Muslims, even though he was a devout Christian. When the pope got wind of this he was angrier than ever. And in particular a pope whose name was Gregory. He was just as powerful, but perhaps not as wise as his predecessor, Pope Innocent III. He wanted Frederick to undertake a crusade at all costs, and threatened to excommunicate him if he didn't. So in the end he did. But what all other crusades had achieved only through great sacrifices and loss of life, Frederick did without any fighting at all: Christian pilgrims were allowed to visit the Holy Sepulchre without fear of being attacked and all the land around Jerusalem was held to belong to them. And how did he do that? He just sat down with the sultan who ruled there and they came to an agreement.

Both sides were happy that things had gone so well, and that war had been averted, but the bishop of Jerusalem was not content, for no one had consulted him. So he complained to the pope that the emperor was too friendly with the Arabs, and the pope became convinced that Frederick had become a Muslim. But Emperor Frederick II didn't care. He just rejoiced that he had achieved more for Christians than anyone else had ever done and crowned himself king of Jerusalem, for no priest could be found who was willing to crown him against the pope's wishes.

Then he set sail for home, taking with him presents given to him by the sultan: hunting leopards and camels, rare stones and many other curiosities. And he made a collection of these in Sicily and engaged great artists to work for him, and took pleasure in beaut-iful things whenever he was tired of ruling. But he certainly did rule. He disliked the custom of granting land as fiefs. Instead, he appointed officials and, rather than give them land, he paid them a monthly salary. For this being Italy, they already used money. And he ruled justly but also with great severity.

Frederick was so different from everyone else around him that nobody understood what he was trying to achieve. Least of all Pope Gregory, who called him the Antichrist, while others called him *stupor mundi*, which means the wonder of the world. In far-off Germany few people paid any attention to their strange emperor with his odd ideas. And because people didn't understand him, he had a hard life. Even his own son turned against him and stirred up trouble among the Germans, and his best-loved adviser went over to the pope, leaving Frederick entirely alone. Of all the ingenious and practical schemes he had hoped to show the world, very few saw the light of day. Unable to carry them out, he became increasingly bitter and ill-tempered. And so he died, in the year 1250.

His son Manfred died in the struggle for power when he was still a young man, and his grandson Conradin was taken prisoner by his enemies and beheaded in Naples at the age of twenty-four. Such was the sad end of that great ruling family of knights, the Hohenstaufens.

But while Frederick was still reigning in Sicily and quarrelling with the pope, a dreadful misfortune overtook the world which neither could prevent. New hordes of mounted warriors arrived from Asia. This time it was the Mongols, the most fearsome of them all. Even Shih Huang-ti's great wall could not restrain them. Under their leader, Ghengis Khan, they first conquered China, looting and sacking with appalling savagery. Then came Persia's turn, after which they took the path of the Huns, the Avars and the Magyars towards Europe. Sowing terror and destruction, they raged first through Hungary and on through Poland. Finally, in 1241, they reached the German frontier town of Breslau, which they seized and burned to the ground. Everywhere they went there

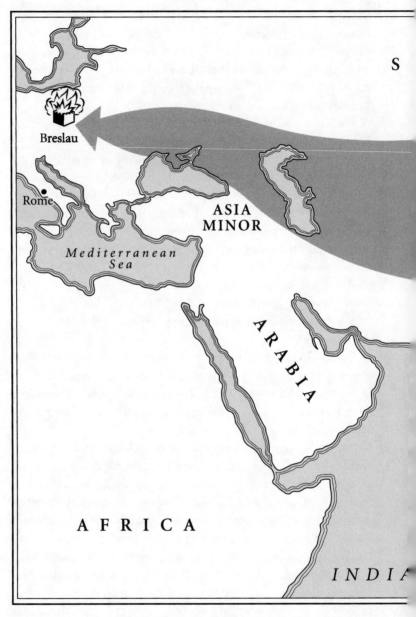

This was the size of the warlike Mongols' mighty empire when they threatened the whole of Europe after the destruction of Breslau.

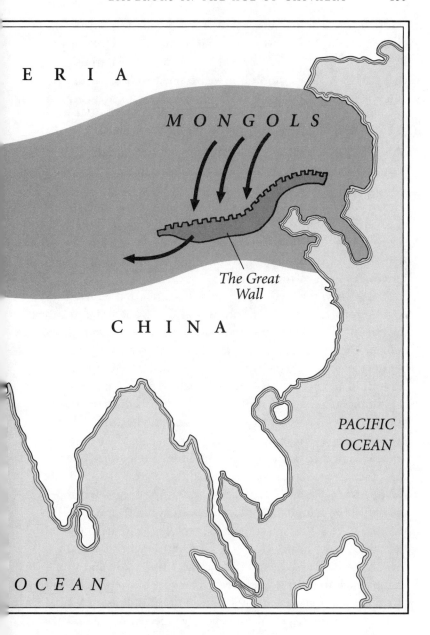

MONGOLS

The Great
Wall

CHINA

ERIA

PACIFIC
OCEAN

OCEAN

was slaughter. No one was spared. Their empire was already the greatest the world had ever known. Just imagine: from Peking to Breslau! Moreover, in the course of their invasions their troops had changed from savage hordes to well-trained warriors with very cunning leaders. Christendom could do nothing to stop them. A great army of knights fell before them. And then, when the danger was at its height, their emperor died somewhere in Siberia, and the Mongols turned back, leaving nothing but wasteland behind.

In Germany the death of the last Hohenstaufen led to greater confusion than ever. No one could agree on a new king so none was chosen. And because there was neither a king nor an emperor, nor anyone else in control, everything went to the dogs. The strong simply robbed the weak of everything they had. People called it the right of might, or 'fist-law'. Of course, might is never *a* right, nor is it right. It's simply wrong.

People knew this well enough and despaired, and wished they could return to the old days. Now you can wish, and you can dream. But if you keep on wishing and dreaming you sometimes end up believing that what you want has come true. And so people began to persuade themselves that the Emperor Frederick wasn't really dead, but under a spell in an enchanted mountain, where he was sitting and waiting. And this in its turn had a remarkable effect. I don't know whether you have ever found yourself dreaming of someone who appears first as one person and then as someone else, and then, somehow, as both at the same time? Because this is what happened. People dreamed that a great, wise and just ruler (this was Frederick II of Sicily) was sitting deep down under the Kyffhäuser mountains and would one day return and make his purpose known. And yet, at the same time, they also dreamed that he had a great beard (this was now Frederick's grandfather, Frederick I Barbarossa), and that he was all-powerful and would vanquish all his enemies and create a kingdom as wonderful and magnificent as it had been at the time of the great Feast of Mainz.

The worse things got, the more people expected a miracle. They pictured the king asleep inside the mountain, where he had slept so long that his fiery red beard had grown right through the stone table on which he leant. Once in every hundred years, he would wake and ask his page if the ravens were still circling the mountain. Not until his page replied 'No, Sir, I can't see them' would he rise and split the table with his sword and shatter the mountain in which the spell had imprisoned him and ride out in shining armour with all his men. You can imagine what people would make of that today!

But in the end no miraculous apparition came to set the world to rights, just an energetic, able and far-sighted knight, whose castle, the Habsburg – or Hawk's Castle – was in Switzerland. His name was Rudolf. The princes had elected him king of the Germans in 1273, hoping that a knight so poor and obscure as he would be biddable and weak. But they hadn't reckoned on his intelligence and shrewdness. He may have started out with little land – and therefore little power – but he knew of a very simple way to obtain more, and with it more power.

He went to war against the rebellious King Otakar of Bohemia, defeated him and confiscated part of his kingdom. As king he was entitled to do this. Then, in 1282, he bestowed the same lands – which happened to be Austria – on his own sons. This formed the basis of his family's power. The Habsburgs were able to increase this power with a succession of new fiefs, and by marriage and in-heritance, until they had become one of the most esteemed and influential noble families of Europe. It must be said that they ruled more over their vast family fief (by which I mean Austria) than they did over the German empire, despite their title of German king and emperor. Those lands were ruled by other lords – dukes and bishops and counts – all of whom lived like princes, enjoying almost unlimited power over their domains. Nevertheless, with the last of the Hohenstaufens the real Age of Chivalry had ended.

25

❖

CITIES AND CITIZENS

In the course of the hundred years that passed between the deaths of Frederick Barbarossa in 1190 and Rudolf I of Habsburg in 1291, Europe changed in more ways than it is possible to imagine. As I have already said, at the time of Barbarossa there were powerful cities, mainly in Italy, whose citizens were bold enough to oppose and even take up arms against the emperor, while at that time Germany was largely a land of knights, monks and peasants. But over the following hundred years the situation in Germany changed beyond recognition. Many eastward crusades had already taken Germans far from home and they had established trading relationships in distant countries. They no longer exchanged oxen for sheep, or drinking horns for cloth, because they, too, were using money. And where there was money there were markets where all sorts of goods could be bought. These markets could not be held just anywhere. They had to be in fixed places protected by walls and towers, usually near a castle. Anyone who set up a stall in one and traded, as a burgher was no longer bound in serfdom to a landowner. People liked to say 'city air brings freedom',

because burghers in the bigger towns answered to no one but
the king.

But you mustn't imagine that life in a town in the Middle Ages
was anything like it is today. Most towns were small, crooked mazes
of tiny alleys and narrow houses with high, pointed gables.
Merchants and craftsmen lived there with their families, crowded
together in little space. When a merchant went on his travels he was
usually accompanied by armed guards. This was because many
knights in those days had forgotten all about chivalry and were
little more than brigands. High up in their castles they sat, waiting
for merchants to rob. However, the burghers didn't put up with
this for long: they had money and they were able to hire soldiers.
As a result there were frequent fights between burghers and robber
knights, and quite often it was the burghers who won.

Craftsmen such as tailors, shoemakers, drapers, bakers, lock-
smiths, painters, joiners, stonemasons and master builders all
belonged to groups or associations known as guilds. A guild such
as that of the tailors was almost as hard to enter and had rules that
were almost as strict as those of the knights. Not just anyone could
become a master-tailor. First you had to serve your time as an
apprentice. Then you became a journeyman and went on your
travels in order to get to know other towns and other ways of
working. Young men like these went on foot, and often spent years
wandering through many countries before they returned home, or
found a city which had a place for a master-tailor. Small towns
didn't need many tailors, and the guilds made sure there were no
more masters of any trade than there was work for them to do. A
journeyman had to demonstrate his skill by completing a master-
piece (perhaps a fine coat) and only then would he be ceremoniously declared a Master and admitted to the guild.

Each guild had its own rules and entertainments, its banners
and fine mottos, just like the knights. And of course their mottos,
too, were not always respected. But at least they had them. A
member of a guild was bound to support his fellow members
and not steal their trade, nor must he cheat his own customers
with poor goods. He was expected to treat his apprentices and

journeymen well and do his best to uphold the good name of his trade and his town. He was, so to speak, one of God's craftsmen, just as a knight was a warrior fighting for God.

Indeed, while knights gave their lives in crusades to liberate Christ's tomb, burghers and craftsmen would often sacrifice their wealth, their strength and their well-being when it came to building a church in their town. The new church or cathedral had to be bigger, more beautiful and more magnificent than any building the neighbouring towns could boast of. The whole town shared this ambition and all the inhabitants devoted themselves to the project. The best-known master-builder was summoned to draw up the plans, stonemasons were engaged to cut stone and carve statues, painters to paint pictures for the altar and make windows that would shine like jewels within the church. But more important than whose idea it had been, or who had designed or built it, was the fact that the church was the work of the whole town, a communal offering to God. You only need look at one to see it. For these churches are no longer the massive fortresses that were still being built in Germany in Barbarossa's time, but glorious, high-vaulted halls with slim pillars and slender bell towers, and room inside for the whole town to gather when they came to hear the preachers. For by now new monastic orders had sprung up whose monks were less concerned with tilling the soil around their monasteries and copying manuscripts, but chose instead to roam the land as beggars, preaching repentance to the people and explaining the Holy Scriptures. Everyone flocked to the churches to hear them and wept over their sins, promising to mend their ways and live according to Christ's teachings of loving kindness.

But like the crusaders, who in the name of piety had carried out that dreadful massacre in Jerusalem, there were many citizens who failed to hear in those penitential sermons a call to mend their ways, and instead learnt to hate all those who didn't share their faith. Jews, above all, were their targets, and the more pious they felt themselves to be, the more they abused them. You must bear in mind that the Jews were the only tribe from antiquity left in Europe. The Babylonians, the Egyptians, the Phoenicians, the

Greeks, the Romans, the Gauls and the Goths had all either per-ished or merged with other peoples. Only the Jews, whose state had been repeatedly destroyed and who had endured all those terrible times when they had been persecuted and hounded from one country to the next, had survived. After two thousand years, they were still patiently awaiting the coming of their Saviour, the Messiah. Forbidden to own fields, they couldn't be peasants, let alone become knights. Nor were they allowed to practise any craft. The only occupation open to them was trade. So that is what they did. Even then they were only permitted to live in specified parts of the town and only allowed to wear certain clothes. Yet, in time, some of them were able to earn a lot of money which knights and burghers borrowed and were often unable to repay. This only made the Jews more hated and they were repeatedly attacked and robbed. Having neither the power nor the right to defend them-selves, they were helpless, unless the king or a priest chose to take their side – but this was rarely the case.

Bad enough then to be a Jew, but worse still if you were some-one who, having pored long over the Bible, began to doubt some aspect of its teaching. Such people were called heretics and the persecutions they suffered were terrible. Anyone perceived to be a heretic was publicly burned alive, just like the Christians in Nero's time. Whole cities were razed to combat heresy and entire regions laid waste. Crusades were waged against them, just as they were against Muslims. And all this was done by the very people who, for the God of mercy and his Good News, were building those magnificent cathedrals. Buildings which, with their soaring towers and great decorated porches, with their stained glass windows gleaming like jewels in the darkness and their thousands of statues, seemed to offer a glorious vision of the Kingdom of Heaven.

France had cities and churches before there were any in Germany. France was richer, and had had a less turbulent history. Moreover, the kings of France had been quick to find a use for the citizens of the new Third Estate. After about 1300 they rarely assigned land to the nobility, but kept it instead for themselves and paid burghers to manage it (just as Frederick II had done in Sicily).

As a result French kings held more and more land. And land in those days, as you know, meant serfs, soldiers and power. By 1300, the French kings were the most powerful sovereigns, for it was only now that the German king, Rudolf of Habsburg, was beginning to establish his power by bestowing land on his relatives. Besides which, the French did not only rule France, but southern Italy as well. It wasn't long before their power had become so great that, in 1309, they were able to force the pope to leave Rome and take up residence in France where they could keep a close eye on him. The popes lived in a great palace in Avignon surrounded by wonderful works of art, but they were, in effect, prisoners. And this is why, remembering the Babylonian captivity of the Jews (which lasted, as you know, from 597 to 538 BC), this period from 1305 to 1376 is known as the Babylonian Captivity of the Popes.

But the kings of France were still not satisfied. As you remember, a Norman family had conquered England in 1066, and they had been ruling England ever since. This made them nominally French and, as such, subjects of the kings of France, who could therefore claim sovereignty over England as well as France. However, when no heir was born to the French royal family, the kings of England claimed that, both as relatives and as vassals of the French kings, they should now rule France as well as England. The dispute that followed turned into a terrible struggle. It began in 1337 and lasted for more than a hundred years. What had started as a chivalrous contest between a few knights became a war in which great armies of soldiers were paid to fight each other. These were not members of a grand, communal order for whom battle was a noble pursuit, but ordinary Englishmen and Frenchmen, fighting one another for the independence of their lands. The English won more and more land for themselves, conquering ever greater parts of France – not least because the French king who was in power towards the end of this war was thick-witted and incompetent.

But the French people did not want to be ruled by foreigners. And it was then that the miracle happened. A simple seventeen-year-old shepherdess called Joan of Arc, who felt herself called by God to the task, succeeded in persuading the French to put her at the head of an army, dressed in full armour, and the English were driven from the land. 'Only when the English are in England will there be peace,' she said. But the English took their revenge. They captured her and sentenced her to death for witchcraft. And in 1431 Joan of Arc was burned at the stake. But perhaps it isn't so surprising that they thought she was a witch. For doesn't it seem like magic that a simple, uneducated peasant girl, all on her own, armed with nothing but courage and a passionate conviction, should be able to wipe out the accumulated defeats of almost a century in just two years, and bring about the crowning of her king?

And yet this time of the Hundred Years War was also a time of unimaginable brilliance and excitement, a time when towns were expanding and proud knights no longer sat in grim seclusion in their lonely strongholds, but chose instead to inhabit the courts of rich and powerful kings and princes. In Flanders and Brabant (now Belgium), but, above all, in Italy, life was truly magnificent. Here there were prosperous towns, trading in precious cloth such as silks and brocades, and offering every conceivable comfort and luxury. Knights and noblemen feasted at court in splendid, richly embroidered robes. And when they danced in rings with their ladies, in great halls and in flower gardens, to the music of lutes and viols, I, too, should have liked to be there. The dresses worn by the ladies were even richer and more elaborate than the clothes of the men. And they had head-dresses that were tall and pointed like church steeples, to which long, fine veils were attached. In their pointed shoes and sumptuous robes glittering with thread-of-gold they looked like delicate and graceful dolls. How unhappy they must have been in the smoke-filled halls of those ancient fortresses! Now they lived in castles that were spacious and airy, with turrets and battlements and thousands of windows, in rooms hung with brightly coloured tapestries, where the conversation was elegant and refined. And when a nobleman led his lady into the banqueting hall, to the feast laid out in all its splendour, he would hold her hand lightly with just two fingers, spreading the others as widely as he could. By now, reading and writing was common in towns. It was a necessity for tradesmen and artisans, and many knights liked to address artful and elegant poems to their elegant ladies.

Nor was knowledge any longer the preserve of a handful of monks in their cells. Soon after 1200, students from countries far and wide were flocking in their thousands to the famous University of Paris, where they studied and argued a great deal over the opinions of Aristotle, and how these might or might not agree with what was written in the Bible.

This way of life, both at court and in the city, finally reached Germany, and in particular the court of the German emperor. His court, at that time, was in Prague. For after the death of Rudolf of Habsburg, other families of kings and emperors had been elected. And since 1310 it had been the Luxembourg family who ruled from their seat in Prague. But the fact was that by now this rule hardly included any German lands at all. Power was once more in the hands of individual princes who ruled independently in areas such as Bavaria, Swabia, Württemberg and Austria. The only real difference between the German emperor and these princes was that he was the most powerful among them. The Luxembourgs' land was Bohemia, and Charles IV, a just sovereign and lover of splendour, had been ruling there from Prague since 1347. The knights at his court were no less noble than those of Flanders and the paintings in his palaces were just as fine as those at Avignon. In 1348 he, too, founded a university, in Prague. It was the German empire's first university.

Hardly less splendid than the court of Charles IV was that of his son-in-law in Vienna, Rudolf IV, known as 'the Founder'. As you can see, none of these rulers lived in lonely fortresses any more, nor did they set out across the world on adventurous military campaigns. Their castles were built in the centres of towns. This alone tells you how important towns had become. But it was only the beginning.

26

❖

A New Age

Have you ever come across an old school exercise book, or something else you once wrote and, on leafing through it, been amazed at how much you have changed in such a short time? Amazed by your mistakes, but also by the good things you had written? Yet at the time you hadn't noticed that you were changing. Well, the history of the world is just the same.

How nice it would be if, suddenly, heralds were to ride through the streets crying: 'Attention please! A new age is beginning!' But things aren't like that: people change their opinions without even noticing. And then all of a sudden they become aware of it, as you do when you look at your old school books. Then they announce with pride: 'We are the new age.' And they often add: 'People used to be so stupid!'

Something of the sort happened after 1400 in the cities of Italy. Especially in the large and prosperous cities of central Italy, and in Florence in particular. They had guilds there too, and had built a great cathedral. But Florence had none of the noble knights that were to be found in France and Germany. For a long time

Florentine burghers had ignored the commands of their German emperors, and by now they were as free and independent as the citizens of ancient Athens. And as the years went by these free and prosperous burghers, shopkeepers and craftsmen had come to care about entirely different things from those that had mattered to the knights and craftsmen of the Middle Ages.

To be a warrior or a craftsman and dedicate one's life to the service and glory of God was no longer every man's aim. What mattered was to be someone in your own right, to have a head on your shoulders and know how to use it. To think and judge for yourself. To act on your own authority, without the need to consult others. And, rather than resorting to old books to find out how things were done in the past, to use your own eyes and act accordingly. That's what it really came down to: using your eyes and acting accordingly. Independence, ability, intellect, knowledge and skill were what counted. People no longer asked first about your rank, your profession, your religion or what country you came from. They said: tell us what you can do.

And suddenly, in about 1420, the Florentines noticed that they were no longer the people they had been in the Middle Ages. They had different concerns. They found different things beautiful. To them the old cathedrals and paintings seemed gloomy and rigid, the old traditions irksome. And, in their search for something more to their liking, something free, independent and unconstrained, they discovered antiquity. And I mean literally discovered. It mattered little to them that the people of those times had been heathens. What astonished them was what those people could do. How they had freely and openly debated and discussed, with arguments and counter-arguments, everything in nature and the world. How everything interested them. These people were to serve as their models.

A great search for books written in Latin began, and people strove to write Latin that was as clear and as precise as that of the ancient Romans. They also learnt Greek and so discovered the wonderful works of the Athenians of the time of Pericles. Soon people were more interested in Themistocles and Alexander, in

Caesar and in Augustus than in Charlemagne or Barbarossa. It was as if the entire period since antiquity had been nothing but a dream, as if the free city of Florence were about to become an Athens or a Rome. People suddenly felt they were witnessing a re-birth of the ancient, long-gone era of Greek and Roman culture. They themselves felt born again through the discovery of these ancient works. And this is why this period in history came to be known in Italy as the *Rinascimento*, or as we know it from the French, the *Renaissance* – the re-birth. Everything that had happened in between they blamed on the barbarian Germanic tribes who had destroyed the empire. The Florentines were determined to do all they could to revive the spirit of antiquity.

They were enthusiasts for everything Roman, for the superb statues and the magnificent and imposing buildings whose ruins lay all over Italy. Previously dismissed as 'heathen ruins', these had been shunned and feared. Now people suddenly rediscovered their beauty. And the Florentines once more began to build with columns.

But people didn't just seek out old things. They looked at nature again, this time with the fresh and unprejudiced eyes of the Athenians, two thousand years before them. And when they did so they discovered a new beauty in the world, in the sky and trees, in human beings, flowers and animals. They painted these things as they saw them. The solemn grandeur and spirituality of the illus-trations to sacred texts in monks' books and cathedral windows now gave way to a style that was natural and spontaneous, full of colour and vitality, yet accurate and true to life as they intended. Using your eyes and acting accordingly also made for the best art. Which might explain why the greatest painters and sculptors were to be found in Florence at this time.

Nor did these painters merely sit down before their paintings like good craftsmen and represent what they saw. They wanted to understand what it was that they were painting. In Florence there was one artist in particular for whom painting good paintings was not enough, no matter how beautiful they might be. And his were far and away the finest. He wanted to have a perfect understanding of all the things he painted and how they related to each other. This painter's name was Leonardo da Vinci. He lived from 1452 to 1519 and was the son of a farm servant-girl. He wanted to know how a person looked when they cried and when they laughed, and also what the inside of a human body was like – the muscles, bones and sinews. So he asked hospitals to give him the bodies of people who had died, which he then dissected and explored. This was something quite unheard of at the time. And he did not stop there. He also looked at plants and animals in a new way and puzzled over what makes birds able to fly. This led him to think about whether people, too, might not be able to fly. He was the first person to carry out an accurate and precise investigation into the possibility of constructing an artificial bird or flying machine. And he was convinced that one day it would be done. He was interested in everything in nature. Nor did he limit himself to the writings of Aristotle and the Arab thinkers. He always wanted to know if what he read was really true. So, above all, he used his eyes, and with those eyes he saw more than anyone had ever seen before, because he was always asking himself questions about what he observed. Whenever he wanted to know about something – for example, why whirlpools happen or why hot air rises – he did an experiment. He had little time for the learned writings of his contemporaries and was the first person to investigate the secrets of nature by means of experiments. He made sketches and noted down his observations on scraps of paper and in a vast accumulation of notebooks. Leafing through his jottings today, one is constantly amazed that a single human being could investigate and analyse so many different things, things about which nothing was known at the time and few cared to know about.

Yet few of his contemporaries had any inkling of the many discoveries that this famous painter was making, or knew of his novel ideas. He was left-handed and wrote in minuscule mirror-writing, a reversed script, which is far from easy to read. This was probably intentional, for in those days it was not always safe to hold independent opinions. Among his notes we find the sentence: 'The sun does not move.' No more than that. But enough to tell us that Leonardo knew that the earth goes round the sun, and that the sun does not circle the earth each day, as had been believed for thousands of years. Perhaps Leonardo limited himself to this one sentence because he knew it didn't say so in the Bible, and that many people believed that what the Bible had to say about nature must never be contradicted, even though the ideas it contained were those of Jews who had lived two thousand years earlier, when the Bible was first written down.

But it wasn't only the fear of being thought a heretic that led Leonardo to keep all his wonderful discoveries to himself. He understood human nature all too well and knew that people would only use them to kill each other. Elsewhere there is a note in Leonardo's handwriting which reads: 'I know how one can stay under water and survive a long time without food. But I will not publish this or reveal it to anyone. For men are wicked and would use it to kill, even at the bottom of the sea. They would make holes in the hulls of ships and sink them with all the people in them.' Sadly, the inventors who came after him were not all great men like Leonardo da Vinci, and people have long known what he was unwilling to show them.

In Leonardo's time there lived in Florence a family that was exceptionally rich and powerful. They were wool merchants and bankers, and their name was Medici. Like Pericles in ancient Athens, it was they who, through their advice and influence, dictated the course of the history of Florence throughout virtually the whole period between 1400 and 1500. Foremost among them was Lorenzo de' Medici, known as 'the Magnificent' because he made such wonderful use of his great wealth, and gave his support and protection to so many artists and scholars. Whenever he came across a gifted young man he instantly took him into his household and had him educated. A description of the customs of Lorenzo's household gives you an idea of how people thought at the time. There was no seating order at table. Instead of the eldest and most respected sitting at the top of the table above the rest, it was the first to arrive who sat with Lorenzo de' Medici, even if he were no more than a young painter's apprentice. And even an ambassador, if he came last, took his place at the foot of the table.

This entirely new delight in the world, in talented people and beautiful things, in the ruins and books of the Greeks and Romans, soon spread out from Florence in all directions, for people are always quick to learn about new discoveries. Great artists were summoned to the pope's court – which was by now once more in Rome – to build palaces and churches in the new style and to adorn them with paintings and statues. This was especially the case when rich prelates from the Medici family became pope. They then brought Italy's greatest artists to Rome, where they created their most important works. To be sure, this totally new way of looking at things did not always sit comfortably with the old piety. Popes of this period were not so much priests and guardians of the souls of Christendom as magnificent princes, intent on the conquest of the whole of Italy, who meanwhile lavished colossal sums of money on glorious works of art for their capital city.

This sense of a rebirth of pagan antiquity gradually spread to the cities of Germany, France and England. There, too, people began to take an interest in the new ideas and forms, and to read the new Latin books. This had become much easier and cheaper since 1450. For in that year a German made a great invention, one no less extraordinary than the invention of letters by the Phoenicians. This was the art of printing. It had long been known in China and for some decades in Europe that you could rub black ink on carved wood and then press it on paper. But Gutenberg's invention was different. Instead of printing from whole blocks of wood, he made single letters out of metal, which could be lined up and held in a frame and then printed from as many times as one wished. When the desired number of copies of a page had been made, the frame could be undone and the letters used again in a different order. It was simple and it was cheap. And of course much simpler and much cheaper than when people spent long years laboriously copying books by hand, as Roman and Greek slaves and the monks had had to do. Soon a whole host of printers had sprung up in Germany, Italy and elsewhere, and printed books, Bibles and other writings were eagerly bought and read, not just in Europe's cities, but in the countryside as well.

However, another invention of the time was to have an even greater impact on the world. This was gunpowder. Once again, the Chinese had probably known about it for a long time, but they mostly used it to make fireworks. It was in Europe, from 1300 onwards, that people began to use it in cannons for shooting at fortresses and men. And before long, soldiers were carrying massive and cumbersome guns in their hands. Bows and arrows were still much faster and more effective. A good English bowman could release 180 arrows in fifteen minutes, which was roughly the time it took for a soldier to load his thunderbox, set a slow-match to the charge and fire it once. Despite this, guns and cannons were already in evidence during the Hundred Years War, and after 1400 their use became widespread.

But such weapons were not for knights. There was nothing chivalrous about firing a bullet into a man's body from a distance. As you know, what knights did was to gallop towards one another and try to knock each other out of the saddle. Now, to protect themselves against the bullets, they had to abandon their chain mail in favour of increasingly heavy and solid armour. Dressed in this from top to toe they looked like iron men and must have been a fearsome sight. But the armour was unbearably hot and impractical and the knights could hardly move. For this reason, no matter how bravely they fought, they were no longer so intimidating. In 1476 a famous, warlike knight and prince of the Duchy of Burgundy – known as Charles the Bold on account of his fearlessness – led an army of knights in armour to conquer Switzerland. But when they got there the free peasants and burghers of Murten surprised them and, fighting on foot, simply knocked all the knights off their horses and clubbed them to death. They then made off with all the magnificent and valuable tents and rugs that the knights had brought with them on their campaign of conquest. You can see these today in Bern, the capital of Switzerland. Switzerland remained free, and the knights had had their day.

This is why the German emperor who was ruling around 1500 is known as the Last Knight. His name was Maximilian, and he was a member of the Habsburg family, whose might and wealth had grown steadily since the time of King Rudolf. Since 1438 their power had spread beyond their own country of Austria, and such was their influence that all the German emperors who had been elected since then had been Habsburgs. Nevertheless, the German noblemen and princes gave most of them a good deal of trouble, and Maximilian the Last Knight was no exception. They exercised almost unlimited power over their fiefdoms and had become increasingly reluctant to accompany their emperor into battle when he commanded them to do so.

With the arrival of money and cities and gunpowder, the granting of land with bonded peasants in return for military service had become as outdated as chivalry. Which is why, when Maximilian went to fight the French king for his Italian possessions, he took paid soldiers instead of his vassals. Soldiers like these were called mercenaries. They were rough, rapacious brutes who strutted about in outlandish costumes and thought of little but plunder. And since they fought for money rather than for their country, they went to the person who paid them most. This cost the emperor a great deal of money that he didn't have, so he was forced to borrow from rich merchants in the towns. And this in its turn meant that he had to keep on good terms with the towns, which upset the knights who felt increasingly unwanted and unneeded.

Such problems gave Maximilian a headache. Like the knights of old he would far rather have ridden in tournaments and composed fine verses about his adventures to present to his beloved. He was a strange mixture of the old and the new. For he was very taken with the new art, and was always asking the great German painter, Albrecht Dürer – who had learnt a lot from the Italians, but had taught himself even more – to make paintings and engravings in his honour. Through these wonderful portrait paintings by the first of the new German artists, we can actually see what the Last Knight looked like. These works, together with the paintings and buildings of the great Italian artists, are in fact the 'heralds' who cried: 'Attention please! A new age has begun!'

And if we called the Middle Ages a starry night, we should look upon this new, wide-awake time, which began in Florence, as a bright, new dawn.

27

❖

A NEW WORLD

What until now we have called the history of the world is in fact the history of no more than half the world. Most of the events took place around the Mediterranean – in Egypt, Mesopotamia, Palestine, Asia Minor, Greece, Italy, Spain and North Africa. Or not far from there: in Germany, France and England. We have cast the odd glance eastwards, towards China's well-defended empire, and towards India, which, during the period that now concerns us, was ruled by a Muslim royal family. But we haven't bothered with what lies to the west of old Europe, beyond Britain. No one bothered with it. A handful of northern seafarers on their raids once glimpsed an inhospitable land, far out in the west, but they soon turned back, for there was nothing there worth taking. Intrepid mariners like the Vikings were few, and in any case, who would dare set out across the unknown, and possibly never-ending ocean, leaving behind them the coasts of England, France and Spain?

This hazardous enterprise only became possible with a new invention. This, too – and I nearly added 'of course'! – came from

China. It was the discovery that a piece of magnetised iron hanging freely always turns towards the north. You will have guessed what it is: a compass. The Chinese had long used compasses in their journeys across deserts, and now news of this magical instrument leaked out via the Arabs and eventually reached Europe during the Crusades, in about 1200. But at that time the compass was rarely used. People were puzzled and frightened by it. But gradually their fear gave way to curiosity – and something more than curiosity. For in those far-off lands there might be treasures, undiscovered riches there for the taking. Yet no one dared set out across the western ocean. It was too immense and too unknown. And what might lie on the other side?

It so happened that a penniless but adventurous and ambitious Italian from Genoa, called Columbus, who had spent much time poring over ancient books of geography, was obsessed with this idea. Where indeed might you end up if you kept on sailing westwards? Why, you would end up in the east! For wasn't the earth round, shaped like a sphere? It said so in several of the writings of antiquity. And if by sailing westwards you went half way round the world and then landed in the east, you would be in China, in the fabulous Indies, lands rich in gold and ivory and rare spices. And, with the help of a compass, how much simpler it would be to sail across the ocean than to make a long and arduous journey across deserts and over fearsome mountain ranges as Alexander had once done, and as the trading caravans still did when they brought silks from China to Europe. With this new route, thought Columbus, the Indies were only days away, rather than months by land. Everywhere he went he told people about his plan, but they just laughed and called him a fool. Still he persisted: 'Give me ships! Give me just *one* ship and I'll bring you gold from the fabulous east!'

He turned to Spain. There, in 1479, the rulers of two Christian kingdoms had been united by marriage and were engaged in a merciless campaign to expel the Arabs – who, as you know, had ruled in Spain for more than seven hundred years – not only from their wonderful capital, Granada, but from their kingdom altogether. Neither the royal court of Portugal nor that of Spain showed much enthusiasm for Columbus's plan, but it was put to the learned men and mariners of the famous University of Salamanca for their consideration. After four more years of desperate waiting and pleading, Columbus learned that the university had rejected his plan. He resolved to leave Spain and try his luck in France. On the way he chanced to meet a monk who was none other than the confessor of Queen Isabella of Castile. Fired with enthusiasm for Columbus's project, the monk persuaded the queen to grant him a second audience. But Columbus nearly spoiled it all again. The reward he demanded, if his plan were to succeed, was no small thing: he was to be knighted, appointed Grand Admiral and Viceroy (king's representative) of all the lands he discovered, and he would keep a tenth of all taxes levied there, and more besides. When the monarchs turned down his request he left Spain immediately for France. If he discovered any lands, these would now belong to the French king. This frightened Spain. The monarchs gave in and Columbus was recalled. All his demands were met. He was given two sailing ships in poor condition – it would be no great loss if they sank. And he rented a third himself.

And so he set sail across the ocean towards the west, on and on, always westwards, determined to reach the East Indies. He had left Spain on 3 August 1492 and was delayed for a long time on an island repairing one of his ships. Then on they went again, further and further towards the west. But still no sight of the Indies! His men grew restless. Their impatience turned to despair and they wanted to turn back. Rather than tell them how far they were from home, Columbus lied to them. At last, on 11 October 1492, at two o'clock in the morning, a cannon fired from one of the ships signalled 'Land ahoy!'

Columbus was filled with pride and joy. The Indies at last! The friendly people on the shore must be Indians, or, as the Spanish sailors called them, 'Indios!' Now, of course, you know that he was wrong. Columbus was nowhere near India, but on an island off America. Thanks to his mistake we still call the original inhabitants of America 'Indians' and the islands where Columbus landed the 'West Indies'. The real India (or East Indies) was still an

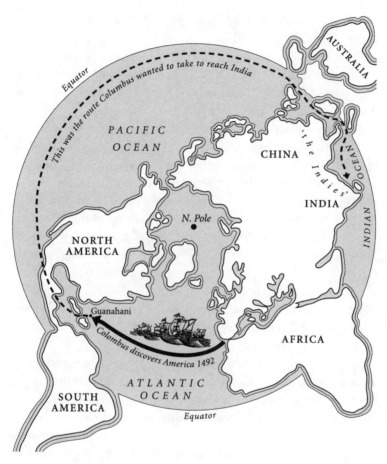

*The great sea voyage that Columbus undertook was rather short if you com-
pare it with the journey he had intended to make. The best way to compare
the two is by looking at the globe from the north pole outwards.*

interminable distance away. Much further than Spain was behind
them. Columbus would have needed to sail on for at least another
two months, and it is likely that he would have perished miserably
with all his men and never reached his goal. But at the time he
thought he was in the Indies, so he took possession of the island
in the name of the Spanish Crown. During his later voyages he

continued to maintain that the lands he had discovered were the Indies. He couldn't bring himself to admit that his grand idea was a mistake, that the earth was much bigger than he had imagined. The land route to the Indies was far shorter than the voyage across the whole of the Atlantic and Indian Ocean. He could only think of being Viceroy of the Indies, the lands of his dreams.

You may know that it is from this date, 1492 – the year in which that fanciful adventurer Christopher Columbus accidentally discovered America only because it was in his way, as it were – that the Modern Age is said to begin. The date chosen to mark the beginning of the Middle Ages, 467, might seem a more obvious choice. For that was the year when the Roman Empire of the West fell, together with its last emperor – the one with the curious name: Romulus Augustulus. But in 1492 absolutely no one, not even Columbus, had any idea that this voyage might mean more than a new source of gold from unknown lands.

Of course, on his return Columbus was given a hero's welcome, but during his later voyages his pride and his ambition, his greed and his wild imaginings made him so unpopular that the king had his own viceroy and admiral arrested and brought home from the West Indies in chains. Columbus kept those chains for the rest of his life, even after he was returned to royal favour, honour and riches. It was an insult he could neither forget nor forgive.

The first Spanish ships carrying Columbus and his companions had discovered only islands, whose simple and good-natured inhabitants had little to offer them. All that interested the Spanish adventurers was the source of the gold rings that some of them wore through their noses. The islanders gestured towards the west, and so America was discovered. For the Spaniards were actually in search of the fabled land of Eldorado. Convinced of its existence, they had visions of whole cities roofed with gold. These conquistadores, as they were called, who left Spain in search of new lands to conquer for their king and to enrich themselves with loot, were rough fellows, little better than pirates. Driven by their insatiable greed into ever more crazy adventures, they exploited and deceived the natives at every turn. Nothing could deter them and no means

were too foul wherever gold was concerned. They were indescribably brave and indescribably cruel. And the saddest thing of all is
that, not only did these men call themselves Christians, but they
always maintained that all the atrocities they committed against
heathens were done for Christendom.

One conqueror in particular, a former student of law named
Hernando Cortez, was possessed by the wildest ambition. He
wanted to march deep into the heart of the country and seize all
its legendary treasures. In 1519 he left the coast at the head of
150 Spanish soldiers, thirteen horsemen and a few cannons. The
Indians had never seen a white man before. Nor had they seen a
horse. Horrified by the cannons, they were convinced that the
Spanish bandits were powerful magicians, or even gods. Still, they
made many brave attempts to defend themselves, attacking the soldiers by day as they marched and in their camp at night. But from
the outset Cortez took terrible revenge, setting fire to villages and
killing Indians in their thousands.

Before long, messengers came from a mighty king whose country lay further inland. They begged him to turn back and gave him
magnificent gifts of gold and feathers of many colours. But the gifts
only served to increase his curiosity and his greed. So on he
marched, enduring unimaginable hardships, and forcing many
Indians into his army as great conquerors had always done. At last
he came to the kingdom of the mighty king who had sent the
messengers with their gifts. The king's name was Montezuma, and
his land was called Mexico, as was its capital city. Montezuma
waited respectfully for Cortez and his small force outside the city,
which stood on an island at the centre of a great chain of lakes.
The Spaniards were astonished when they were led across a long
causeway into the city and saw the splendour, beauty and might of
this great capital that was as big as any city in Europe. It had wide,
straight streets and a great number of canals and bridges. And
there were many squares and great marketplaces to which tens of
thousands of people came each day to buy and sell.

In his report to the king of Spain Cortez wrote: 'Here they trade
in all kinds of merchandise: in foodstuffs and in jewellery made of

gold, silver, pewter, brass, bone, mussel and lobster shell and feathers, in cut and uncut gems, in lime and brick, in timber, both rough and prepared . . .' In some streets, he says, they sell nothing but birds and animals of all kinds, while in others they sell infinite varieties of plants. He talks of pharmacies and barbers' shops, bakeries and inns, merchants selling rare garden plants and fruits, utensils and pigments for painting, and how, in the marketplace, three judges always sat, ready to settle any dispute as it arose. And he describes the city's monumental temples, each in itself as big as a town, with their tall towers and brightly decorated rooms covered in huge and terrifying depictions of gods to whom dreadful human sacrifices were made.

He was particularly impressed by Montezuma's royal palace. Spain, he said, had nothing to compare with it. This palace was several storeys high, raised on pillars faced with jasper, its vast halls enjoying views as far as the eye could see. Beneath it stretched a fine park, with bird-ponds and a great zoo in which all sorts of wild animals were caged. Montezuma was attended by a sumptuous court of high-ranking officials who showed him the greatest deference. He changed his dress four times a day, always appearing in new and different robes never to be worn again. One approached him with one's head bowed, and when he was carried through the streets of Mexico in a sedan chair, the people had to throw themselves to the ground before him and must never be seen to look upon his face.

Cortez used guile to trap this mighty sovereign. As if paralysed by their disrespect and insolence, Montezuma didn't lift a finger against the white intruders. For according to an ancient saying, white gods, sons of the sun, would one day come from the east to take possession of Mexico, and Montezuma believed the Spaniards to be these gods. In fact they behaved more like white devils. They took advantage of a ceremony in a temple to attack and kill all the Mexican nobility, knowing that they would be unarmed. In the ensuing revolt Cortez forced Montezuma to appeal to the angry crowds from the palace roof. But the people ignored him. They hurled stones at their own king, and Montezuma fell, mortally wounded. In the carnage that followed, Cortez demonstrated his true courage. For, by some miracle, his little band of Spaniards fled the town in all its uproar and, carrying the sick and wounded, made their way back to the coast through that hostile land. Of course he soon returned with fresh troops and they burned and destroyed the whole of that magnificent city. And that was only the beginning. There and in other parts of America the Spaniards proceeded to exterminate the ancient, cultivated Indian peoples in the most horrendous way. This chapter in the history of mankind is so appalling and so shameful to us Europeans that I would rather not say anything more about it.

Meanwhile the Portuguese had discovered the true sea route to the Indies, where their behaviour was little better than that of the Spaniards. All the wisdom of ancient India meant nothing to them. They too wanted gold, and nothing else would do. In the end, so much gold reached Europe from India and America that burghers grew richer and richer as knights and landowners grew poorer and poorer. And because all the ships sailed out westwards and returned from the west, it was Europe's western ports that benefited most and grew in power and importance. Not only those of Spain and Portugal, but the ports of France and England and Holland as well. However, Germany played no part in these overseas conquests. For they had far too many problems to deal with at home.

28

❖

A New Faith

As you will remember, there were popes ruling in Rome after 1400 who cared more for might and magnificence than for their role as priests, and it was they who commissioned the most famous artists to build beautiful churches. This was especially true of two Medici popes, members of the family that had already done so much for the prestige and adornment of Florence. During their reigns the grandest and most magnificent buildings rose into the skies above Rome. Old St Peter's – a church thought to have been founded by Constantine the Great and in which Charlemagne had been crowned emperor – was too plain for their taste. They planned to build a new church, far bigger and more beautiful than any seen before. But it would cost a great deal of money. Where this money came from mattered less to the popes of the day than getting hold of it and completing their wonderful church. And in their desire to please the pope, priests and monks collected money in a way which did not conform with the teachings of the Church. They made the faithful pay for the forgiveness of their sins, and called it 'selling indulgences'. They did this in spite of the Church's own teaching, according to which only sinners who repented might be forgiven.

Now there was at that time in Wittenberg, in Germany, a monk who belonged to the order of the Augustinians. His name was Martin Luther. When, in 1517, one of these sellers of indulgences came to Wittenberg to collect money for the new St Peter's, whose construction that year was under the supervision of Raphael, the most famous painter in the world, Luther was determined to draw attention to the irreligious nature of this way of raising funds. He nailed a kind of poster to the doors of the church, on which he had written ninety-five theses – or points for discussion – denouncing this trade in divine forgiveness. What shocked Luther most was that people might think that they could atone for their sins with money, that God's free, forgiving mercy could be bought. He had always seen himself as a sinner living, like all sinners, in fear of God's wrath. Only one thing could save him from God's punishment and that was God's infinite mercy which, as Luther believed, could not be bought, for if it could, it would no longer be mercy. Before God, who sees all and knows all, even a good person is a sinner who deserves to be punished. Only faith in God's freely given mercy can save him, and nothing else.

In the bitter arguments that now broke out on the subject of indulgences and their abuse, Luther's opinions took on an increasingly insistent and forceful tone, both in his teaching and his writings. Nothing but faith matters, said Luther. All else is superfluous. And that also goes for the Church and the priests who, when they celebrate Mass, intercede on behalf of the faithful so that they, too, may share in God's mercy. God's mercy needs no intercessors. All an individual needs to be saved is his own unshakable belief and faith in his God. Faith means believing in the great mysteries of the Gospel, believing that we are eating Christ's body and drinking his blood from the chalice when we take Holy Communion. No one can help another person to obtain God's grace. Every believer is, as it were, his own priest. A priest of the Church is no more than a teacher and helper, and as such may live like other men, and even marry. A believer must not be content to accept the teaching of the

Church. He must look to the Bible for God's purpose and seek it out for himself. For, in Luther's opinion, the truth was only to be found in the Bible.

Luther was not the first to have such thoughts. A hundred years earlier a priest called Jan Hus had taught much the same in Prague. In 1415 he was brought before a council of Church dignitaries in Constance, and despite the promise of an imperial safe conduct, was burned as a heretic. Many of his followers were persecuted and killed in a succession of long and bloody battles that devastated half Bohemia.

The same fate might have befallen Luther and his followers, but times had changed. Thanks largely to the invention of the art of printing, Luther's writings were bought and read throughout Germany. They were written in a style that was vigorous and rousing – and often very coarse. Many people were won over by his arguments. When the pope came to hear of it, he threatened to excommunicate Luther. But Luther's following was by now so great that he no longer cared. He burned the pope's letter in public, and then he really was excommunicated. Next he announced that he and his followers had left the Church altogether. Germany was in an uproar, and many people sided with him, for the luxury-loving pope, with all his wealth, was not at all popular in Germany. Nor was there much opposition from the German princes, for if the bishops and archbishops were to lose their power, the Church's vast estates would fall to them. So they, too, joined the Reformation, which was the name that was given to Luther's attempt to re-awaken the Christian piety of old.

Now at about this time – that is, in 1519 – the emperor Maximilian, the 'Last Knight', died. His grandson, the Habsburg Charles V, who was also a grandson of the Spanish queen, Isabella of Castile, became the new German emperor. He was just nineteen years old and had never set foot in Germany, having only lived in Belgium, Holland and Spain, which also formed part of his inheritance. As king of Spain he also ruled over newly discovered America, where Cortez had recently made his conquests. And so anyone who wished to flatter him could say that over his kingdom the sun never set (it being daytime in America when it is night-time here). His vast realm – comprising as it did the ancient hereditary Habsburg lands of Austria, the Low Countries inherited from Charles the Bold of Burgundy, Spain and the German empire – had only one rival in Europe, and this was France. However, the French kingdom, under its able king, Francis I, though far smaller than Charles V's empire, was more united, richer and more stable. These two kings now embarked on a fearfully complicated and long drawn-out war over Italy, the richest country in Europe. Successive popes backed first one, then the other, until finally, in 1527, Rome was sacked and pillaged by the emperor's German troops and Italy's wealth destroyed.

But in 1519, when Charles V first came to power, he was a very devout young man, still on excellent terms with the Pope, and anxious, once his coronation at Aachen was over, to settle the case of the heretic Luther. It would have been simplest to have him arrested, but Frederick, Duke of Saxony, the Prince of Wittenberg, where Luther was living, would not allow it. Known as Frederick the Wise, he was to be Luther's great protector and would one day save his life.

So instead Charles V ordered the rebellious monk to present himself before the first parliament that Charles was to hold in Germany. This was in Worms, in 1521. All the princes and great men of the empire were there, in a solemn and splendid assembly. Luther came before them dressed in his monk's cowl. He had already made it known that he was ready to renounce his teaching if it could be shown from the Bible to be wrong – for as you know, Luther would accept only what was written in the Bible as the word of God. The assembled princes and noblemen had no wish to become trapped in a war of words with this ardent and learned Doctor of Theology. The emperor ordered him to renounce his teaching. Luther asked for a day to think. He was determined to hold fast to his convictions, and wrote at the time to a friend: 'Truly, I shall not renounce even one letter of it, and put my trust in Christ.' The next day he appeared again before the assembled princes and noblemen of the parliament and made a long speech in Latin and German, in which he set out his beliefs. He said he was sorry if, in his zeal to defend himself, he had given offence, but recant he could not. The young emperor, who had probably not understood a word, told him to answer the questions clearly and come to the point. To this Luther replied heatedly that only arguments drawn from the Bible would compel him to recant: 'My conscience is bound by the word of God, and for that reason I can and will renounce nothing, for it is dangerous to act against one's conscience . . . So help me God. Amen.'

The parliament then passed an edict declaring Luther an outlaw, which meant that nobody was allowed to give him food, aid or shelter. If anyone did, they too would be outlawed, as would anyone caught buying or in possession of his books. Nor would anyone be punished for his murder. He was, as they put it, 'free as a bird'. But his protector, Frederick the Wise, had him kidnapped and taken in secret to his castle, the Wartburg. There Luther lived in disguise and under a false name. He took advantage of his voluntary captivity to work on a German translation of the Bible so everyone could read it and think about its meaning. However, this was not as easy as it sounds. Luther was determined that all Germans should read his Bible, but in those days there was no language that all Germans could read: Bavarians wrote in Bavarian, Saxons in Saxon. So Luther had to invent a language that everyone could understand. And in his translation of the Bible he actually succeeded in creating one that, even after nearly five hundred years, is not all that different from the German that people write today.

Luther stayed in the Wartburg until one day he heard that his speeches and writings were having an effect which did not please him at all. His Lutheran followers had become considerably more violent in their zeal than Luther himself. They were throwing paintings out of churches and teaching that it was wrong to baptise children, because everyone had to decide for themselves whether they wished to be baptised. People called them Iconoclasts and Anabaptists (destroyers of images and re-baptisers). Moreover, there was one aspect of Luther's teaching that had had a

profound effect on the peasants, and which they had taken very
much to heart: Luther had taught that each individual should obey
the voice of his own conscience and no one else and that, subject
to no man, should freely and independently strive for God's mercy.
The feudal peasant serfs understood this to mean that they should
be free men. Armed with scythes and flails they banded together,
killing their landlords and attacking monasteries and cities. Against
all these Iconoclasts, Anabaptists and peasants, Luther now turned
the full force of his preaching and writings, just as he had previously used them in his attacks on the Church, and so he helped
crush and punish the rebel bands. This lack of unity among Protestants, as Luther's followers were called, was to prove very useful to
the great, united, Catholic Church.

For Luther wasn't alone in thinking and preaching as he did
during those years. In Zurich a priest called Zwingli had taken a
similar path, and in Geneva another learned man named Calvin
had distanced himself from the Church. Yet despite the similarities
of their teachings, their followers could never bring themselves to
tolerate, let alone live with, one another.

But now there came a new and even greater loss for the papacy.
In England, King Henry VIII was on the throne. He had married
Catherine of Aragon, an aunt of the emperor Charles V. But he
didn't like her. He wanted to marry her lady-in-waiting, Anne
Boleyn, instead. When he asked the pope, as head of the Church, to
grant him a divorce, the pope refused. So, in 1533, Henry VIII
withdrew his country from the Roman Church and set up a
Church of his own, one that allowed him his divorce. He continued to persecute Luther's followers, but England was lost to the
Roman Catholic Church for ever. It wasn't long before Henry was
tired of Anne Boleyn as well, so he had her beheaded. Eleven days
later he remarried, but that wife died before he could have her executed. He divorced the fourth and married a fifth, whom he also
had beheaded. The sixth outlived him.

As for the emperor Charles V, he had grown weary of his vast
empire, with all its troubles and confusion, and the increasingly
savage battles fought in the name of religion. He had spent his life

fighting: against German princes who were followers of Luther, against the pope, against the kings of both England and France, and against the Turks, who had come from the east in 1453 and had conquered Constantinople, capital of the Roman Empire of the East. They had then gone on to lay waste to Hungary and in 1529 had reached the gates of Vienna, the capital of Austria which they besieged without success.

And having grown tired of his empire, along with its sun that never set, Charles V installed his brother Ferdinand as ruler of Austria and emperor of Germany, and gave Spain and the Netherlands to his son Philip. He then withdrew, in 1556, an old and broken man, to the Spanish monastery of San Geronimo de Yuste. It is said that he spent his time there repairing and regulating all the clocks. He wanted them to chime at the same time. When he didn't succeed, he is reported to have said: 'How did I ever presume to try to unite all the peoples of my empire when I cannot, even once, persuade a few clocks to chime together.' He died lonely and embittered. And as for the clocks of his former empire, whenever they struck the hour, their chimes were further and further apart.

29

❖

THE CHURCH AT WAR

In one of the battles between the emperor Charles V and the French king Francis I, a young Spanish knight was gravely wounded. His name was Ignatius of Loyola. During his long and painful convalescence he thought hard about his past life as a young nobleman, and immersed himself in readings from the Bible and the lives of the saints. And as he did so, the idea came to him that he would change his life. He would continue to be a warrior as he always had been, but he would serve a very different cause: that of the Catholic Church, now so imperilled by Luther, Zwingli, Calvin and Henry VIII.

But when he was finally restored to health, he didn't simply go off and fight in one of the many wars that had broken out between Lutherans and Catholics. He took himself to university. There he studied and reflected, and reflected and studied, to prepare himself for the battle he had chosen to undertake. For it seemed clear to him that if you want to conquer others you must first conquer yourself. So with unbelievable severity he worked at mastering himself. Somewhat like the Buddha, but with a different aim in mind. Like the Buddha, Ignatius wished to rid himself of all desires. But rather than seeking release from human suffering here on earth, he wanted to devote himself, body and soul, to the service of the Church. After many years of practice he reached a point at which he could successfully prevent himself from having certain thoughts, or, if he wished, picture something so clearly in his mind that it was as if he saw it there in front of him. His preparation was complete. He demanded no less of his friends. And when they had all achieved the same iron control over their thoughts, they founded an order together called the Society of Jesus. Its members were known as Jesuits.

This little company of select and highly educated men offered itself to the Pope to campaign for the Church, and in 1540 their offer was accepted. Their battle began immediately, with all the strategy and force of a military campaign. The first thing they did was to tackle the abuses that had brought about the conflict with Luther. In a great gathering of the Church held in Trent in the Southern Tirol, which lasted from 1545 to 1563, changes and reforms were agreed that enhanced the power and dignity of the Church. Priests would return to being priests, and not just princes living in splendour. The Church would take better care of the poor. Above all, it would take steps to educate the people. And here the Jesuits, as learned, disciplined and loyal servants of the Church, came into their own. For as teachers they could make their ideas known, not only to the common people, but to the nobility as well through their teaching at universities. Nor was it only through their work as teachers and preachers of the faith in distant lands that their influence spread. In the courts of kings they were frequently employed as confessors. And because they were men of great intelligence and understanding, trained to see into the souls of men, they were well placed to guide and influence the mighty in their decisions.

This movement to re-awaken the piety of old, not through a separation from the Catholic Church, but through the renewal of that Church, and thus to actively challenge the Reformation, is known as the Counter-Reformation. People became very austere and strict during this period of religious warfare. Almost as austere and strict as Ignatius of Loyola himself. The delight Florentines took in their leaders' magnificence and splendour was over. And once again, what was looked for in a man was piety and readiness to serve the Church. Noblemen stopped wearing bright and ample robes and now looked more like monks in severe, black, close-cut gowns and white ruffs, over which their sombre, unsmiling faces tapered away into little pointed beards. Every nobleman wore a sword on his belt and challenged anyone who insulted his honour to a duel.

These men, with their careful, measured gestures and their rigid formality, were mostly seasoned warriors, and never more implacable than when fighting for their beliefs. Germany was not the only land riven by strife between Protestant and Catholic princes. The most ferocious wars were fought in France, where Protestants were known as Huguenots. In 1572 the French queen invited all the Huguenot nobility to a wedding at court, and on the eve of St Bartholomew, she had them assassinated. That's what wars were like in those days.

No one was more stern, more inflexible or more ruthless than the leader of all the Catholics. King Philip II of Spain was the son of the emperor Charles V. His court was formal and austere. Every act was regulated: who had to kneel at the sight of the king and who might wear a hat in his presence. In what order those who dined were to be served at the high table, and in what order the nobles were to enter the church for Mass.

King Philip himself was an unusually conscientious sovereign, who insisted on handling every decision and every letter himself. He worked from dawn to dusk with his advisers, many of whom were monks. His purpose in life as he saw it was to root out all forms of unbelief. In his own country he had thousands of people burned at the stake for heresy – not just Protestants, but Jews and Muslims who had lived there since the time when Spain was under Arab rule. And because he saw himself as Protector and Defender of the Faith, just as the German emperor had before him, he joined forces with a Venetian fleet and attacked the Turks, whose sea power hadn't stopped growing since their conquest of Constantinople. The allied Christians were victorious, and the Turkish fleet was completely destroyed at Lepanto, in 1571.

His war against the Protestants went less well. He may have succeeded in exterminating them at home in Spain, but this was not the case elsewhere. As in his father's time, the Low Countries (meaning Belgium and Holland) were also part of his empire. And many of the burghers who lived there were Protestants, especially in the rich northern towns. He did all he could to make them renounce their faith, but they wouldn't give in. So he sent a Spanish nobleman to be their governor, and he was even more fanatical and inflexible than Philip himself. The Duke of Alba, with his thin, pale face, his narrow pointed beard and icy gaze, was just the sort of warrior that Philip favoured. In cold blood the Duke of Alba sentenced a great number of burghers and noblemen to be hanged. Finally, people could stand it no longer. There was a fierce and bloody battle which ended in 1579 with the liberation of the Protestant towns of the Low Countries and the expulsion of the Spanish troops. Now, as free, rich, independent and enterprising trading cities, they too could try their luck across the seas, in India and America.

But King Philip II of Spain's most cruel defeat was yet to come. In England, Queen Elizabeth I, the daughter of King Henry VIII, was on the throne. Elizabeth was very clever, strong-willed and determined, but she was also vain and cruel. She was determined to defend England against the many Catholics still present in the country whom she persecuted relentlessly. Her cousin, Mary Stuart, the Catholic queen of Scotland, was a woman of great beauty and charm, and she, too, believed she had a right to the English throne. Elizabeth had her imprisoned and executed. Elizabeth also helped the Protestant burghers of the Low Countries in their war against Philip of Spain. Philip was furious. He resolved to conquer England for Catholicism or destroy it.

At immense cost he raised a huge fleet of 130 great sailing ships with around two thousand cannon, and more than twenty thousand men. It takes no time to read, but just try to imagine 130 sailing ships at sea. This was the Invincible Armada. When it set sail from Spain in 1588, loaded with heavy cannon and weaponry and food and supplies for six months, it seemed inconceivable that England's small island might ever succeed in resisting such a mighty force. However, the heavily laden warships were cumbersome and hard to manoeuvre. The English avoided confrontation and darted in and out in their nimbler vessels, attacking the Spanish ships. One night they launched fireships into the midst of the Spanish fleet, creating panic and confusion and sending them in all directions. Many ships drifted along the English coast and went down in severe gales. Barely half the Armada reached home and not one ship succeeded in landing on an English shore. Philip betrayed no sign of his disappointment. It is said that he greeted the commander of the fleet warmly and thanked him, saying: 'After all, I sent you to fight men, not the wind and waves.'

But the English didn't only chase the Spaniards from their own waters. They attacked Spanish merchant ships off America and India and, together with the Dutch, had soon supplanted the Spanish in many of their rich trading ports. Starting in North America, to the north of the Spanish colonies, they established trading posts much as the Phoenicians had once done. And many Englishmen and women who had been persecuted or banished during the conflicts of religion went there to find freedom.

The Indian ports and trading posts were not actually under English and Dutch rule, but were governed by merchants from those two countries who grouped together to do business and bring treasures from the Indies to Europe. These societies of merchants were known as East India Companies. They hired soldiers whom they sent inland, where they punished unfriendly natives and any who refused to part with their goods at a sufficiently low price. This treatment of India's Indians was little better than that shown by the Spanish conquistadores towards the Indians of America. In India, too, the conquest of coastal regions by English and Dutch merchants was made easier by the lack of unity among India's princes. Soon the peoples of North America and India were using the language of a small island off the north-west coast of

France. That island was England. A new world empire was taking shape. At the time of the Roman empire, Latin was the language of the world. Now the world would have to learn English.

30

❖

Terrible Times

If I wished, I could write many more chapters on the wars
between Catholics and Protestants. But I won't. It was a dreadful
era. Events soon became so confused that people no longer knew
why or against whom they were fighting. The Habsburg emperors
of Germany – ruling now from Prague, now from Vienna – had no
real power outside Austria and part of Hungary. They were pious
men who wished to re-establish the sovereignty of the Catholic
Church throughout their empire. Nevertheless, they did for a while
allow Protestants to hold religious services. Until one day a revolt
broke out in Bohemia.

In 1618, discontented Protestants threw three of the emperor's
Catholic councillors out of a window at Prague castle. They landed
in a pile of manure, and so came to little harm. Nevertheless, this
event – known as the Defenestration of Prague – gave the signal for
a dreadful war to begin which lasted for thirty years. Thirty years.
Just imagine! If someone heard about the Defenestration at the age
of ten, they would have had to wait until they were forty to experience peace. *If* they experienced it! For in no time the war had

turned into a dreadful massacre as hordes of ill-paid soldiers from countries far and wide rampaged through the land, looting and killing. The expectation of plunder was what drew the vilest and most brutal men of all nations into the ranks of these armies. Religious faith was long forgotten. Protestants fought in Catholic armies, Catholics in Protestant ones. Friend and foe suffered alike from their rapacity. Wherever they pitched their tents they demanded food and, above all, drink from the local peasants. And if a peasant refused to give them what they wanted, they took it by force, or they killed him. In their improbable patch-work of rags and their great plumed hats, swords dangling from their belts and pistols at the ready, they rode around burning, killing and tormenting the defenceless peasantry out of sheer wickedness and depravity. Nothing could stop them. The only person they would obey was their commander. And if he won their affection, they followed him with blind devotion.

One such commander on the emperor's side was Wallenstein, a poor country nobleman of immense ambition and ability. He led his armies up into north Germany to capture the Protestant towns. Thanks to his skill and strategy, the war was nearly decided in favour of the emperor and the Catholic Church. However, a new country entered the conflict. This was Sweden, under its powerful, pious and Protestant ruler, Gustavus Adolphus. His aim was to rescue the Protestant faith and found a mighty Protestant empire under Sweden's leadership. The Swedes had retaken north Germany and were marching on Austria when, in 1632 (the fourteenth year of this dreadful war), Gustavus Adolphus fell in battle. Neverthe-less, many of his battalions reached the outskirts of Vienna and wrought havoc there.

France also joined the war. Now you might think that the French, being Catholics, would have sided with the emperor against the Protestants of north Germany and Sweden. But the war had long stopped being about religion. Each country was out to get what it could from the general confusion. And because the two Habsburg rulers, the emperor of Germany and the king of Spain, were the dominant powers in Europe, the French, under the guidance of their exceptionally intelligent minister, Cardinal Richelieu, hoped to exploit the situation to make France Europe's greatest power. So that's why France's soldiers fought *against* those of the emperor.

Meanwhile, Wallenstein, as the emperor's general, was at the height of his power. His army worshipped him, and his fierce soldiers fought for him and for the fulfilment of his aims, rather than for the emperor or the Catholic faith, being indifferent to both. The effect of this was that Wallenstein increasingly saw himself as the rightful sovereign. Without him and his troops the emperor was powerless. So he took it upon himself to hold talks with the enemy about a possible peace agreement, and ignored all the emperor's commands. The emperor decided to arrest him. But in 1634, before he could do so, Wallenstein was murdered by an English captain who had once been his friend.

However, the war continued for fourteen more years, becoming increasingly wild and confused. Whole villages were burned, towns plundered, women and children murdered, robbed and abducted. There seemed to be no end to it. The soldiers seized the peasants' livestock and trampled their crops. Famine, disease and roaming packs of wolves made wastelands of great stretches of Germany. And after all these years of appalling suffering, the envoys of the various rulers finally met in 1648 and, after interminable and complicated discussions, agreed on a peace which left things more or less as they had been in the first place, before the Thirty Years War had begun. What had been Protestant would remain Protestant. The lands the emperor controlled – Austria, Hungary and Bohemia – would remain Catholic. With the death of Gustavus Adolphus, Sweden had lost most of the influence it had gained and only held onto a few strips of conquered land in north Germany and on the Baltic coast. Cardinal Richelieu's envoys were alone in succeeding to secure a number of German fortresses and towns near the Rhine for France. Which made the wily French minister the only true victor in a war which hadn't even concerned him.

Germany was devastated. Barely half the population had survived, and those who had were destitute. Many left and made their way to America, while others tried to enlist in foreign armies, since they didn't know about anything but fighting.

On top of all this misery and despair a terrible madness began to infect a growing number of people: the fear of evil spells, of sorcery and witchcraft. People had also been superstitious in the Middle Ages and had believed in all sorts of ghouls and ghosts, as you remember. But it was never as bad as this.

Things had begun to get worse during the time of the power- and splendour-loving popes, the time we know as the Renaissance, when the new St Peter's church was being built and indulgences were sold. Those popes weren't pious, but that only made them all the more superstitious. They were afraid of the Devil and every conceivable form of magic. And each of the popes of the period around 1500, whose names we associate with the most wonderful works of art, was also responsible for chilling decrees calling for witches and sorcerers to be hunted down without mercy, especially in Germany.

You may ask how it is possible to hunt down something that isn't there and never was. And that is precisely why it was so terrible. If a woman wasn't liked in her village – perhaps because she was a little odd, or made people feel uncomfortable – anyone could suddenly say 'That woman's a witch! She's the cause of those hailstorms we've been having!' or 'She gave the mayor his bad back!' (and in fact, both in Italian and in German, people still use the expression 'witch-hurt' when talking about backache). Then the woman would be arrested and interrogated. They would ask her if she was in league with the Devil. Naturally, she would be horrified and deny it. But then they would torture and torment her for so long and in such a dreadful way that, half dead with pain, she would admit to anything in her despair. And that was it. Now that she had confessed to being a witch she would be burned alive. Often while she was being tortured they would ask if there were other witches in the village making magic with her. And in her weakness she might blurt out any name that came into her head, in the hope that the torture would stop. Then others in their turn would be arrested and tortured until they confessed and were burned. Fear of the Devil and witchcraft were rife during the dreadful period after the Thirty Years War. In Catholic and Protestant districts alike, thousands and thousands of people were burned. The few Jesuit priests who protested against this madness were powerless to stop it. People in those days lived in a state of constant fear of the unknown, of magical powers and the works of the Devil. Only this fear can begin to explain the atrocities inflicted on so many thousands of innocent people.

What is most remarkable, however, is that at a time when people were at their most superstitious there were still some who had not forgotten the ideas of Leonardo da Vinci and the other great Florentines, people who went on using their eyes in order to see and make sense of the world. And it was they who discovered the real magic, magic that lets us look into the past and into the future and enables us to work out what a star billions of miles away is made of, and to predict precisely when an eclipse of the sun is due and from what part of the earth it will be visible.

This magic was arithmetic. Of course these people didn't invent it, for merchants had always been able to add and subtract. But they became increasingly aware of the number of things in nature that are governed by mathematical laws. How a clock with a pendulum 981 millimetres long needs exactly one second per swing, and why this is so. They called these the laws of nature. Leonardo da Vinci had already said that 'Nature doesn't break her own laws.' And so it was known with certainty that if you take any natural event and measure and record it precisely, you will discover that, given the same circumstances, the result will always be the same, no matter how often it is repeated – indeed, it *cannot* be different. This was an extraordinary discovery, and a far greater magic than anything the poor witches were accused of. For now the whole of nature – the stars and drops of water, falling stones and vibrating violin strings – was no longer just one incomprehensible tangle that made people fearful and uneasy. If you knew the correct mathematical formula you had a magic spell for everything. You could say to a violin string: 'To make an A, you must be this long and this tight and move backwards and forwards 435 times in a second.' And the note the string made would prove it.

The first man to understand the extraordinary magical power of applying mathematical calculation to things in nature was an Italian called Galileo Galilei. He had devoted many years to observing, analysing and describing such things when, one day, someone denounced him for writing exactly what Leonardo had observed but not explained. What he had written was this: the sun does not move – on the contrary, it is the earth which moves round the sun, together with the planets. This discovery had already been made by a Polish scholar named Copernicus, after many years of calculation. It had been published in 1543, not long after Leonardo's death and shortly before his own, but the theory had been denounced as un-Christian and heretical by Catholic and Protestant priests alike. They pointed to a passage in the Old Testament in which Joshua, the great warrior, asks God not to let dusk fall until his enemy is destroyed. In answer to his prayer, we read: 'The sun stood still and the moon stayed, until the people had avenged themselves on their enemies.' If the Bible says the sun stood still, people argued, then the sun must normally be in motion. And to suggest that the sun did not move was therefore heretical, and contradicted what was written in the Bible. So in 1632, when he was nearly seventy years old, Galileo, who had devoted his whole life to scholarship, was brought before the religious tribunal known as the Inquisition, and made to choose between being burned as a heretic or renouncing his theory about the movement of the earth around the sun. He signed a declaration saying that he was but a poor sinner, for he had taught that the earth moved round the sun. In this way he avoided being burned, the fate of so many of his predecessors. Nevertheless, when he had signed the declaration, he is said to have muttered under his breath: 'And yet it moves.'

None of these fixed ideas was in the end able to prevent Galileo's ideas and methods and all the discoveries he made from influencing and inspiring people in ever-increasing numbers. And if today, thanks to mathematical formulas, we can make nature do whatever we want, so that we have telephones, aeroplanes and computers, and all the rest of our modern technology, we should be grateful to all those who, like Galileo, investigated nature's mathematical laws at a time when it was almost as dangerous a thing to do as it was to be a Christian in Nero's day.

31

❖

An Unlucky King
and a Lucky King

The only important country not to join in the fighting of the Thirty Years War was England. Lucky English, you may say. But they too were going through troubled times even if the end, when it came, was not as devastating as it was in Germany. Now you may remember that in 1215 King John of England signed a great Charter of Liberties – the Magna Carta – in which he made a solemn promise that he and his successors would never act without first consulting the barons and the nobility. For nearly four hundred years English monarchs kept this promise, until one day a new king, Charles I, the grandson of the beheaded Mary Stuart, came to the throne, and he didn't wish to abide by the agreement. He disliked having to consult the nobility and the elected members of his parliament. He preferred to govern as he pleased, and this cost the country a great deal of money.

The English didn't like it at all. Many of them were strict and zealous Protestants, called Puritans, who had a deep loathing for all forms of wealth and display. A farmer and member of parliament named Oliver Cromwell was their leader in the conflict that eventually broke out between Parliament's supporters and those of the king which split the country in two. (People called Cromwell's supporters Roundheads because they wore their hair close-cropped, unlike the long-haired royalists who were known as Cavaliers.) Cromwell was a deeply religious man and a brave, determined and ruthless commander. His soldiers were well trained and no less ardent than he was. After many battles the king was taken prisoner and brought to trial at Westminster, where he was charged with high treason. He refused to recognise the court and made no effort to defend himself, for he believed that only God could be the judge of the king of England. Charles was sentenced to death, and in 1649 he was beheaded. Oliver Cromwell then ruled England, not as king, but as 'Lord Protector of the Commonwealth', as he described himself. And this wasn't just a title, because it is exactly what he did. Following in Elizabeth's footsteps he devoted himself to increasing England's power – through her colonies in America and trading settlements in India, and by building a strong fleet and expanding sea trade – and did his utmost to weaken England's Dutch neighbours. After his death, however, kings soon ruled England once again. But government was now less difficult than it had been before and went on becoming easier. And since that time no other English monarch has ever dared break the ancient promises laid down in the Magna Carta.

It was easier for the kings of France. There they had no great charter. Moreover, they ruled over a prosperous, well-populated country which was in no danger of collapse, even after the terrible wars of religion. But above all, at the time of the Thirty Years War the real ruler of France had been that formidably gifted minister, Cardinal Richelieu. He achieved at least as much for France as Cromwell did for England – if not more. Richelieu had been especially good at winning over the knights and the nobility. Through skill and cunning – like a good chess-player who knows how to exploit every move and turn a small advantage into a greater one – he gradually reduced their powers until he was able to assume them all himself, including, as you saw, the power of France in Europe. And because he had helped weaken the German emperor in the Thirty Years War, and because Spain had been reduced to poverty and Italy dismembered, and because England wasn't yet very powerful, by the time Richelieu died France was the dominant country in Europe. A year after the cardinal's death, in 1643, King Louis XIV ascended the throne. He was then four years old and still holds the world record for the length of his reign. He ruled until 1715: that is, for seventy-two years. And what's more, he really did rule. Not, of course, when he was a child, but as soon as his guardian, Cardinal Mazarin, had died (Mazarin had been Cardinal Richelieu's successor), he was determined to rule himself. He gave orders that no passport was to be issued to any Frenchman unless he himself had granted it. The court was highly amused, imagining his interest to be no more than a young king's whim. He would soon tire of ruling. But he didn't. For to Louis, kingship was no mere accident of birth. It was as if he had been given the leading role in a play which he would have to perform for the rest of his life. No one before or since has ever learnt that role so well, or played it with such dignity and ceremony to the end.

All the powers that Richelieu, and later Mazarin, had held, Louis XIV now took upon himself. The nobility had few rights other than that of watching him perform his role. This solemn performance – the so-called *lever* – began early, at eight o'clock in the morning, when he deigned to rise. First to enter the bedchamber were the royal princes of the blood together with the chamberlain and the doctor. Then two great curled and powdered wigs, like flowing manes, were ceremoniously extended to him on bended knee. Depending on his inclination, he chose one, and then inserted himself into a magnificent dressing gown, before seating himself beside the bed. Only at this point were the noblemen of highest rank, the dukes, permitted to enter the bedchamber, and while the king was shaved his secretaries, officers and various officials all entered in their turn. After which the doors were thrown wide to admit a host of splendid dignitaries – marshals, governors, princes of the Church and royal favourites – all there to gaze with admiration upon the solemn spectacle of His Majesty the King getting dressed.

Everything was regulated down to the last detail. The greatest honour was to be permitted to offer the king his shirt, which had first been carefully warmed. This honour belonged to the king's brother or, in his absence, to the person next in rank. The chamberlain held one sleeve, a duke the other and the king inserted himself. And so it went on, until the king was fully dressed, in brightly coloured silk stockings, silk knee-breeches, a satin brocade doublet and a sky-blue sash, with his sword at his side, and an embroidered coat and a lace collar which a high official with the title of Guardian of the King's Collars held out to him on a silver tray. The king then left his bedchamber, plumed hat on his head and cane in hand, smiling and elegant, to make his entry into the Great Hall with a well-turned and courteous greeting for each, while all those around gaped at him with awestruck expressions and declared that today he was more beautiful than the sun god Apollo, stronger than Hercules, hero of the ancient Greeks. He was the God-given sun itself, *le Roi Soleil* – the Sun King – on whose warmth and light all life depended. Just like the pharaoh, you might think, for he had been called the Son of the Sun. But there was one big difference. The ancient Egyptians really believed it, while for Louis XIV it was only a sort of game which he and everyone present knew was no more than a ceremonious, well-rehearsed and magnificent performance.

In his antechamber after morning prayers the king announced the programme for the day. There then followed many hours of real work which he undertook in order to have personal control over all affairs of state. Apart from this there was a lot of hunting, and there were balls and theatrical productions by great poets and actors which the court enjoyed and which he, too, always attended. Every meal involved a ceremony no less wearisome and solemn than the *lever*, and even his going to bed was a complicated ballet-like production that gave rise to some comical moments. For example, everyone had to bow to the king's bed, like the faithful before the altar in church, even when the king wasn't in it. And whenever the king played cards and made conversation there was always a swarm of people standing around him at a respectful distance, hanging on his every word.

To dress like the king, to carry one's cane as he did, to wear one's hat as he did, to sit and move as he did, was the aim of all men at court. And that of the women was to please him. They wore lace collars and ample, rustling robes made of the richest fabrics and were adorned with precious jewels. Life revolved around court and was staged in the most magnificent palaces anyone had ever seen. For palaces were Louis XIV's great passion. He had one called Versailles built for himself outside Paris. It was almost as big as a town, with an infinite number of rooms covered in gold and damask, and crystal chandeliers, mirrors in their thousands, and furniture that was all gilded curves, upholstered in velvets and silks. The walls were hung with splendid paintings where people could see Louis in many guises. There is one that shows him dressed as Apollo, receiving homage from all the peoples of Europe. Grander still than the palace was its park. Everything about it was magnificent, elaborate and theatrical. No tree might grow as it pleased, no bush retain its natural form. Everything green was clipped, trimmed and shaped into walls of green foliage, curved hedges, vast lawns and spiralling flowerbeds, avenues and circuses, set with statues, lakes and fountains. Forced to live out their lives at court, once-mighty dukes and their ladies strolled up and down white gravel paths, exchanging witty and well-turned phrases on the way the Swedish ambassador had recently performed his bow, and things of that sort.

Just think what such a palace and such a way of life must have cost! The king had two hundred servants for himself alone, and that was only the start of it. But Louis XIV had clever ministers, mainly men of humble origin chosen for their outstanding ability. These men were all experts at extracting money from the country. They kept tight control of foreign trade and encouraged France's own crafts and industry as much as they could. But the true cost fell on the peasants, who were burdened with crippling taxes and duties of all kinds. And while at court people ate off gold and silver dishes, piled high with the choicest delicacies, the peasants ate scraps and weeds.

But it wasn't life at court which cost the most. Far more expensive were the wars that Louis XIV kept waging, often with no other purpose than to increase his own power at the expense of the neighbouring states. With his immense and well-equipped army he invaded both Holland and Germany, seizing, for example, Strasbourg from the Germans, without offering any real pretext for his actions. He saw himself as the master of all Europe which, in a sense, he was. All the great men of Europe imitated him. Soon every German prince – even those who owned no more than a miserable patch of land – had his own gigantic castle in the style of Versailles, with all the gold and damask, the clipped hedges, the men in great wigs, the powdered ladies in voluminous gowns, the courtiers and the flatterers.

They tried to imitate him in every way, but there was always something missing. They *were* what Louis XIV only played at being: somewhat comical puppet-kings, with pompous airs and glittering fancy dress. Louis XIV himself was more than that. And in case you don't believe me, I'm going to quote something from a letter he wrote to his grandson, when his grandson was leaving to become king of Spain: 'Never favour those who flatter you most, but hold rather to those who risk your displeasure for your own good. Never neglect business for pleasure, organise your life so that there is time in it for relaxation and entertainment. Give the business of government your full attention. Inform yourself as much as you can before taking any decision. Make every effort to get to know men of distinction, so that you may call on them when you need them. Be courteous to all, speak hurtfully to no man.' These really were the guiding principles of King Louis XIV of France, that remarkable mixture of vanity, charm, extravagance, dignity, indifference, frivolity and sheer hard work.

32

❖

MEANWHILE,
LOOKING EASTWARDS …

Wile Louis XIV was holding court in Paris and Versailles, Germany suffered a new misfortune: the Turks. As you know, more than two hundred years earlier (in 1453), they had conquered Constantinople and established a great Muslim empire, known as the Ottoman empire, incorporating Egypt, Palestine, Mesopotamia, Asia Minor and Greece – in other words, the whole of the ancient Roman Empire of the East, of whose magnificence and splendour, it must be said, not much remained. Under their great leader, Suleiman the Magnificent, they had then pushed onwards beyond the Danube and defeated the Hungarian army in 1526. Almost every Hungarian nobleman, including the king, had been killed. Having conquered the better part of Hungary, the Turks had tried to take Vienna, but they soon turned back. As you remember, their fleet had been destroyed in 1571 by King Philip II of Spain and his Venetian allies. But they were still a powerful state and a Turkish pasha – or governor – was ruling in Budapest. Now many Hungarians were Protestants, and when their king had been killed they had become unwilling subjects of the Catholic emperor

and had fought against him during the religious wars. After the
Thirty Years War these uprisings continued, until one day the
Hungarian nobility asked their Turkish neighbours for help.

The sultan, as the Turkish ruler was called, was only too happy
to respond to this request. For a long while he had been wanting a
war because his soldiers and warriors had become too powerful at
home. He was afraid that he would lose control of them and was
delighted to be able to send them off to fight. If they won, so much
the better, and if they lost he would be rid of them. You can see
what sort of a person he was! So in 1683 he mobilised a huge army
from all four corners of his empire. The pashas of Mesopotamia
and Egypt brought their soldiers, and Tatars, Arabs, Greeks, Hungarians and Romanians all assembled in Constantinople under the
leadership of the Grand Vizier – or prime minister – Kara Mustafa,
and prepared to march on Austria. There were more than two
hundred thousand of them, armed to the teeth and dressed in
exotic and colourful costumes and turbans with banners bearing
their sign: the crescent moon.

The emperor's armies stationed in Hungary were in no position
to withstand such an assault. They retreated and left the way to
Vienna open to the Turks. Like all towns at that time, Vienna had
fortifications at the ready. These were now hastily put in place, and
cannon and supplies brought in. Twenty thousand soldiers were to
hold the city until the emperor and his allies came to their aid. But
the emperor and his court had fled, first to Linz and then to Passau.
And when the Viennese saw smoke rising from distant villages and
suburbs set on fire by the Turks, some sixty thousand people abandoned the city, in an unending stream of carts and carriages.

Now the Turkish cavalry arrived. Their gigantic army ringed
Vienna and began firing cannon balls at the walls and undermining
them with explosives. The Viennese fought back with all their
might. A month went by. With each day the danger increased as
more and more breaches appeared in the walls, and still no help
came. Terrible outbreaks of disease began to sweep through the
town, far more deadly than the Turkish bullets. Supplies of food
were running low, despite daring sorties by soldiers who sometimes

returned with an ox or two. As time went on, people found themselves paying twenty or thirty crowns for a cat – no small sum in those days for such unappetising fare! The walls were on the verge of collapse when the imperial troops finally reached Vienna. The Viennese could breathe at last! However, the imperial troops from Austria and Germany hadn't come on their own. The Polish king, Jan Sobieski, who had previously signed an alliance with the emperor against the Turks, had declared himself willing to help in return for significant concessions. These included the honour of supreme command which the emperor wanted himself, so precious time was lost in negotiation. In the end Sobieski's army took up position on the heights above Vienna and from there charged down upon the Turks. After fierce fighting, the Turks fled without even taking the time to decamp, leaving rich pickings for the imperial soldiers. The camp, consisting of forty thousand tents, set out in neat, straight lines separated by narrow lanes, was just like a small town, and a truly magnificent sight.

The Turks continued to retreat. Had they succeeded in taking Vienna, the situation would have been almost as bad as if the Muslim Arabs had defeated Charles Martel at Tours and Poitiers a thousand years earlier.

However, the imperial troops pushed them further and further back, while Sobieski's men went home. A distinguished French general was to lead the Austrian army in this triumphant pursuit. This was Prince Eugene of Savoy, a man whom Louis XIV wouldn't have in his army on account of his plain appearance. In the years that followed he took country after country from the Turks. The sultan was forced to give up all of Hungary, which then became part of Austria. These victories brought much wealth and power to the imperial court at Vienna, and now Austria too began to build magnificent castles and many fine monasteries in a sparkling new style which they called Baroque. Meanwhile, Turkish power continued to decline, not least because a new and mighty enemy had appeared behind them. This was Russia.

Until now we have heard nothing about Russia. It was a vast wilderness of forests, with great steppes in the north. The landowners ruled the poor peasants with terrible cruelty and the sovereign ruled the landowners with, if anything, greater cruelty. One of Russia's tsars, around 1580, was known as Ivan the Terrible, and rightly so. Beside him Nero was mild. In those days Russians took little notice of Europe and what went on there. They were too busy fighting among themselves and killing each other. Although they were Christians they didn't come under the pope's authority. Their spiritual leader was the bishop or patriarch of the Roman empire of the East in Constantinople. So they didn't have a great deal to do with the West.

In 1689 – that is, six years after the Turkish siege of Vienna – a new tsar came to the throne. This was Peter, known as Peter the Great. He was no less barbarous or cruel than many of his predecessors. Nor was he any less fond of drinking or less violent. But he was determined to model his empire on western states, like France, England or the German empire. He knew what was needed: money, trade and cities. But how had other countries acquired these? So he went to find out. In Holland he saw great seaports with mighty ships that sailed as far as India and America to do business. He wanted ships like these, and he needed to know how they were made. Without a second thought, he took a job as a ship's carpenter, first in a Dutch shipyard and later in the dockyard of the Royal Navy in England, to learn the art himself. Then he went home, taking with him a team of skilled craftsmen to build his ships.

All he needed now was a seaport. So he gave orders for one to be built. A city on the sea, just like those he'd seen in Holland. The coast to the north of Russia, however, was nothing but barren marshland and actually belonged to Sweden, with which Peter the Great was at war. This didn't deter him. Peasants were rounded up from the surrounding countryside and made to drain the swamps and drive piles into the ground. He had eighty thousand labourers toiling there, and soon a real seaport rose up out of the marshes.

He named it St Petersburg. Next, Russians had to be made into true Europeans. They had to stop wearing their traditional long-skirted kaftans and weren't allowed to grow their hair and beards long. From now on they were to dress like Frenchmen or Germans. Anyone who protested or disagreed with Peter's innovations was flogged and then executed. Even his own son. He was not a nice man, but he achieved what he wanted. The Russians may not have become Europeans overnight, but they were now ready to enter the field as players in Europe's bloody contest for power.

Peter the Great made the first move. He attacked Sweden which, following the victories of Gustavus Adolphus in the Thirty Years War, had become the mightiest state in northern Europe. Sweden's ruler in Peter's time may not have had the piety or the perspicacity of Gustavus Adolphus, but he was one of the most extraordinary adventurers the world has ever known. The young King Charles XII came to power in 1697. He might have leapt straight out of the pages of the popular adventure books that left me spellbound as a boy in Vienna. His exploits can hardly be believed. He was as foolhardy as he was brave – and that's saying something! He and his army fought Peter the Great and defeated an army five times as strong as his own. Then he conquered Poland and pushed straight on into Russia without bothering to wait for another Swedish army, which was on its way to assist him. On he went, deeper and deeper into Russia, always at the head of his troops, wading through rivers and trudging through swamps, without ever meeting any resistance from the Russian army. Autumn came, and then winter – the bitter, biting-cold Russian winter – and still Charles XII had had no chance to prove his courage against the enemy. Only when his men were half-dead with hunger, cold and exhaustion did the Russians finally appear and inflict a massive defeat on them. This was in 1709. Forced to flee, Charles made for Turkey. And there he remained for five years, vainly trying to persuade the Turks to go to war with Russia. Eventually, in 1714, news reached him from Sweden that his subjects had had enough of their king's adventures in Turkey. The nobility were about to elect a new ruler.

This shows you the route taken by Charles XII, King of Sweden, the daring young adventurer who marched through Poland and into Russia, and later raced back to Stralsund from Turkey and met his death besieging a fortress in Norway.

Disguised as a German officer and with only one attendant, Charles crossed the Turkish frontier without delay and, riding as fast as he could by day and sleeping in mail coaches by night, raced back to Stralsund in north Germany – in those days part of Sweden – in a mad sixteen-day journey that involved all sorts of perilous adventures as they passed through enemy territory. Roused from his bed, the governor of the fortress could scarcely believe his eyes when he saw his king standing before him, for like everyone else he thought he was somewhere in Turkey. The town was delighted with Charles XII's dramatic appearance, but Charles simply fell into bed and slept for a very long time. His feet were so swollen from his long ride that his boots had to be cut off him. But there was no more talk of electing a new king. Charles hadn't been back in Sweden long before he embarked on a new military adventure. He made enemies of England, Germany, Norway and Denmark. Norway was first on his list. He died while besieging a Norwegian fortress in 1718, shot, some say, by someone on his own side because the country simply would not tolerate any more wars.

With this enemy out of the way Peter the Great, who now called himself Emperor of All the Russias, was able to increase his empire's might, expanding in all directions: into Europe, into Turkey, into Persia and into the countries of Asia.

33

❖

A Truly New Age

If you could talk to a gentleman from the time of the Turkish siege, there would be many things about him that would surprise you. The way he spoke and the many Latin and French words he used. His elaborate and convoluted turns of phrase and habit of slipping in Latin quotations that neither you nor I could place, and his grand and solemn bows. You would, I think, suspect that beneath that venerable wig was someone with a large appetite for good food and fine wines. And – if you will forgive me for mentioning it – you could hardly fail to notice that beneath the fancy lace, the embroidery and the silk, this prinked, perfumed and powdered gentleman stank, because he hardly ever washed.

But nothing could prepare you for the shock you would have if he were to begin to air his views. All children should be thrashed. Young girls (no more than children) should be married (and to men they barely know). A peasant's lot is to toil and not complain. Beggars and tramps should be whipped and put in chains in the marketplace for everyone to mock. Thieves should be hanged and murderers publicly chopped into pieces. Witches and the other harmful sorcerers that infest the country should be burnt. People of different beliefs should be persecuted, treated as outcasts or thrown into dark dungeons. A comet seen recently in the sky must mean bad times ahead. As protection against the coming plague, which has already claimed many victims in Venice, it would be sensible to wear a red armband. And finally, a Mr So-and-so – an English friend – has an excellent and well-established business selling negroes from Africa to America as slaves: a brainwave of that most worthy gentleman since, as we all know, American Indian convicts don't take well to manual labour.

And you would hear these opinions not only from the mouth of some coarse or uncouth fellow, but from the most intelligent and pious people in all walks of life and from all nations. Only after 1700 did things gradually change. The widespread and terrible suffering that Europeans endured during the wretched wars of religion had made some people wonder if it was really right to judge someone by his or her religious belief. Was it not more important to be a good and honest human being? Would it not be better if people got on with one another regardless of any differences of opinion or belief that they might have? Better if they respected one another and tolerated each other's convictions? This was the first and most important idea that the people who thought about such things now voiced: the principle of tolerance. Only in matters of religion could there be differences of opinion. No rational person disputes the fact that two plus two makes four. Therefore reason – or sound common sense, as they also termed it – is what can and should unite all men. In the realm of reason you can use arguments to convince others of the rightness of your opinions, whereas another's religious beliefs, being beyond rational argument, should be respected and tolerated.

And so reason was the second most important thing to these people. Clear and reasoned thinking about mankind and nature was rediscovered in the works of the ancient Greeks and Romans and in those of the Florentines during the time of the Renaissance. But, more than anywhere else, it was to be found in the works of men like Galileo, who had boldly set out to investigate the magic of nature's mathematical formulas. Differences of belief played no part in these things: there was only experiment and proof. Reason alone could explain the appearance of nature and the workings of the universe. Reason, which is given in equal measure to all mankind the world over.

Now if reason is given to all, it must follow that all people are of equal worth, and as you remember, that was just what Christianity had ˈtaught: that all men are equal before God. But those who preached tolerance and reason took this argument one step further: they didn't only teach that all people were essentially equal; they demanded that they be treated equally as well. That every human being, as God's creature, endowed by Him with reason, had rights that no one might or should deny him. The right to choose his own calling and to choose how he lived: and the freedom to act or not to act as his reason and his conscience dictated. Children, too, should not be taught with the cane but with reason, so that they might come to understand the difference between right and wrong. And criminals were human beings too – no doubt, they had done wrong, but they could still be helped to mend their ways. It was dreadful, they argued, to brand a man's cheek or forehead with a red-hot iron for one wrongdoing, leaving a mark he would bear for the rest of his life so that all might say 'That man is a criminal'. There was something, they said, which forbade a person to be publicly humiliated. It was called human dignity.

All these ideas, which from 1700 onwards were debated first in England and later in France, came to be called the Enlightenment, because the people who held them wanted to combat the darkness of superstition with the pure light of reason.

Many people today think that the Enlightenment only taught what was obvious, and that people in those days had a rather simple view of the great mysteries of nature and the world. This is true. But you must realise that what seems obvious to us wasn't in the least so then, and that it took a great deal of courage, self-sacrifice and perseverance for people to keep on repeating them so that they seem obvious to us today. And of course you must also realise that reason cannot, and never will, give us the key to all mysteries, although it has often put us on the right track.

In the two hundred years that followed the Enlightenment, more mysteries of nature were studied and explained than in the preceding two thousand years. But what you must never forget is the importance for our own lives of tolerance, reason and humanity – the three fundamental principles of the Enlightenment. Because of them we no longer take someone suspected of having committed a crime and torture them inhumanly on the rack until, half out of their wits, they confess to anything we want. Reason has taught us that there's no such thing as witchcraft, so no more witches are burnt at the stake. (The last time a woman was convicted of witchcraft in England was in 1712.) Diseases are no longer fought by superstitious means, but mainly through cleanliness and the scientific investigation of their causes. We don't have slaves or peasant serfs any more. All citizens are subject to the same laws and women have the same rights as men. All this we owe to the brave citizens and writers who dared stand up for these ideas. And it was daring. They may have lacked understanding and behaved unjustly in their struggle with ancient and long-held traditions, but they fought a long and hard battle to win tolerance, reason and humanity.

The battle would have taken much longer, and involved far greater sacrifices, if some of Europe's rulers hadn't fought in the front line for the ideas of the Enlightenment. One of the first to do so was Frederick the Great, king of Prussia.

As you know, the title of emperor, passed down through several generations of Habsburgs, was by this time not much more than a venerable title. The Habsburgs' only real power was over Austria, Hungary and Bohemia, whereas in Germany power was in the hands of numerous princes who ruled over Bavaria, Saxony and many other big and small states. The Protestant lands in the north were among those which had paid the least attention to the Catholic emperor in Vienna since the Thirty Years War, and the most powerful of these princedoms was Prussia. Since the reign of its great sovereign Frederick William I, who ruled from 1640 to 1688, Prussia had taken more and more land from Sweden, until finally, in 1701, its princes had declared themselves kings. Prussia was a severe warrior state, whose nobility knew no greater honour than to serve as officers in the distinguished army of their king.

Now, since 1740, Prussia had been under the rule of its third king, Frederick II, who was a member of the Hohenzollern family. Known as Frederick the Great, he was without doubt one of the most cultivated men of his age. He was on friendly terms with a number of Frenchmen who preached the ideas of the Enlightenment in their writings, and he himself wrote much on the subject in French. For although he was king of Prussia he scorned the German language and customs, which, as a result of the Thirty Years War, were in a very poor state. His aim and his duty, as he saw it, was to make Prussia a model state and in so doing demonstrate the value of the thinking of his friends in France. He liked to say that he saw himself as the first servant of the state: the butler, as it were, rather than the owner. And in that role he concerned himself with every detail of his project of put-ting the new ideas into practice. One of the first things he did was to abolish the barbaric practice of torture. He also relieved the peasants of some of the heavier duties to their landlords. And he was always particularly concerned that all his subjects, from the poorest to the mightiest, should receive equal justice. A rare thing in those days.

But, above all, Frederick wanted to make Prussia the mightiest of all the German states, and destroy Austria's imperial power. He didn't foresee any difficulty in this. Austria was ruled by a woman, the Empress Maria Theresa. When she came to the throne in 1740, aged only twenty-three, Frederick thought it a suitable moment to remove one of the empire's possessions. So he took his well-trained army to the province of Silesia and seized it. From that time on he would spend most of the rest of his life fighting the empress of Austria. The state of his army was always of the utmost importance to him. He drilled his troops unremittingly until he had the best army in the world.

But Maria Theresa was a far more formidable opponent than he had first thought, although no warmonger at heart. She was deeply religious, and first and foremost a mother. She had sixteen children

in all. Although Frederick was her enemy, she followed his example in introducing many of his reforms in Austria as well. Like him,
she abolished torture, made the peasants' lives easier, and took a
special interest in establishing good education throughout the
land. She genuinely saw herself as a mother to her people, and
never pretended to know all the answers herself. She chose the
ablest people to be her advisers, among them men quite capable of
holding their own against Frederick during the long wars, not only
on the battlefield, but also as envoys to all the courts of Europe,
where they won sympathy for her cause. Even France, which for
centuries had taken sides against the empire, was eventually won
over, after which Maria Theresa gave her daughter Marie
Antoinette in marriage to the future King Louis XVI of France, as
a pledge of their new friendship.

Frederick now found himself surrounded by enemies on all
sides: Austria, France, Sweden and Russia, now a vast and mighty
empire. Without waiting for them to declare war on him, he occupied Saxony, which was also hostile. He then went on to wage a
bitter war that lasted seven long years, in which his only support
came from the British. But his perseverance paid off, for despite the
superior strength of his enemies, not only did he not lose the war,
he even managed to hold on to Silesia.

From 1765 Maria Theresa ceased to rule Austria alone. Her son
Joseph ruled with her and succeeded her after her death as
Emperor Joseph II. He was an even more zealous fighter for the
ideas of the Enlightenment than either Frederick or his mother.
Tolerance, reason and humanity were all that mattered to him. He
abolished the death sentence and peasant serfdom. Protestants
were once again allowed to worship freely, and although a good
Catholic himself, he confiscated some of the lands and wealth of
the Catholic Church. He was an invalid and, knowing that he
might not have long to rule, he did everything with such zeal, such
impatience and such haste that it was often all too quick, too
unexpected and altogether too much for his subordinates to
endure. He had many admirers, but his people loved him less than
they loved his more cautious and pious mother.

At the same time as Austria and Germany were witnessing the triumph of the ideas of the Enlightenment, in America the inhabitants of many British colonies were refusing to be British subjects any longer, or to pay taxes to Britain. In their fight for independence they were led by Benjamin Franklin, an ordinary citizen who spent much of his time studying the natural sciences, in the course of which he invented the lightning conductor. He was a plain and upright man, energetic and hard-working. Under his leadership and that of another American, George Washington, the British colonies and trading ports organised themselves into a confederation and, after a long struggle, drove the British soldiers from their shores. Now they too could adopt the principles of the new way of thinking. In 1776 they declared the sacred rights of all men to liberty and equality to be the founding principles of their new state. But for the negro slaves on their plantations, life simply went on as before.

34

❖

A Very Violent Revolution

All countries felt the ideas of the Enlightenment to be just and fair, and ruled accordingly. Even the empress of Russia, Catherine the Great, regularly exchanged letters with the French thinkers of the Enlightenment. The only exceptions were the kings of France, who behaved as if they neither knew nor cared about the new ideas. Louis XV and Louis XVI, the Sun King's successors, were incompetent, and content merely to imitate their great predecessor's outward show of power. The pomp and magnificence remained. Vast sums were spent on entertainments and operatic productions, on a succession of new chateaux and great parks with clipped hedges, on swarms of servants and court officials dressed in lace and silk. Where the money came from didn't concern them. Finance ministers soon became expert swindlers, cheating and extorting on a grand scale. The peasants worked till they dropped, and citizens were forced to pay huge taxes. Meanwhile at court, amid exchanges that were not always light-hearted and witty, the nobility dissipated and gambled the money away.

But if a noble landowner happened to leave the palace and go home to his estate, it was even worse for the peasants. For he and his attendants would rampage across the land after hares and foxes, their horses' hooves trampling the carefully tended fields. And woe betide the peasant who protested! He would be lucky to escape with a few blows across the face from his lord's riding whip, for a noble landowner was also his peasant's judge and could punish him as he pleased. A landowner who enjoyed the king's favour could obtain a note from him which simply said: 'Mr ____ is to be imprisoned. Signed: King Louis XV.' The nobleman wrote in the name himself, so that anyone who displeased him for any reason whatsoever was simply made to disappear.

But at court these lords were elegant, prinked, powdered and perfumed, rustling in their robes of silk and lace. Weary of the heavy pomp and splendour of Louis XIV's time, they favoured a lighter, less formal way of speaking. Instead of their full-bottomed wigs they now wore light, white-powdered ones with a little plait at the back. No one could dance and bow better than they – unless it was their ladies, tight-laced in their corsets, the skirts of their crinolines billowing and round like giant bells. And while all these fine lords and ladies strolled in the gardens of the royal palaces, their estates decayed and the peasants starved. Yet even they some-times tired of such an unnatural life that was all elegance and sophistication, so they invented a new pastime. They played at Simplicity and Nature. This consisted of living in charming shep-herds' huts which they had built in the grounds of their chateaux, and giving themselves the names of shepherds and shepherdesses taken from Greek poems. What could be more natural or more simple?!

Into this bright confusion of elegance, gracefulness and over-refinement came Maria Theresa's daughter, Marie Antoinette. She was a very young girl, barely fourteen years old, when she became the wife of the future king of France. And, of course, she thought everything was as it should be. She threw herself delightedly into all the fairy-tale masked balls and operas, she acted in plays, she was an enchanting shepherdess and thought life in the French royal palaces was altogether wonderful. Nevertheless, her elder brother, the emperor Joseph II, and her mother repeatedly warned her to live simply and to avoid stirring up further resentment among the poor with foolish extravagance and frivolity. In 1777, the emperor Joseph wrote her a long and serious letter saying: 'Things cannot go on like this, there will be a terrible revolution if you do not do something to prevent it.'

Yet things did go on like that, for twelve more years. And the revolution when it came was all the more terrible for it. By then the court had squandered all the country's wealth. Nothing was left with which to pay for the monstrous daily extravagances. In 1789, King Louis XVI finally decided to summon a meeting of the three estates – the nobility, the clergy and the bourgeoisie – to advise him on how to restore the country's finances.

However, their proposals and requests did not please the king, and he told his master of ceremonies to give the order for the representatives of the estates to leave the chamber. But when he attempted to do so, the impassioned voice of a very clever man named Mirabeau was heard to call out: 'Go and tell his majesty that we are here through the will of the people, and will not leave except at the point of a bayonet!'

No one had ever spoken to the king of France like this before. The court officials had no idea what to do. While they consulted one another, the assembled representatives of the nobility, clergy and the bougeoisie went on discussing what was to be done about the economic crisis. It was no one's intention to overthrow the king. All they wanted to do was to introduce the sorts of reform that other states had already adopted. But although the king was a weak and indecisive man who liked nothing better than pottering about and making things – locks, in particular – he was not accustomed to taking orders, and it never occurred to him that anyone would dare to oppose him. So he called out troops to disperse the assembly of the three estates by force. The people of Paris were enraged, for they had pinned their hopes on this assembly. Crowds gathered and everyone rushed to the state prison, the Bastille, where many Enlightenment thinkers had been confined, and where a whole host of innocent people were now thought to be held. The king did not dare fire on his own subjects for fear of further increasing the fury of the mob. So the mighty fortress was stormed and its garrison killed. The mob surged through the streets of Paris in triumph, parading the liberated prisoners, although it turned out that the only people in the prison at the time were common criminals.

Meanwhile the assembled representatives had made some extraordinary decisions. They wanted the principles of the Enlightenment to be put into effect in their entirety – in particular the one which said that reason, being common to all men, meant that all men were equal and must be treated as such under the law. The assembled nobility led the way by grandly renouncing all their privileges, to everyone's delight. Any citizen of France would have the right to any job, and each would have the same rights and the same duties in relation to the state – human rights, as these were called. Henceforth the people, it was proclaimed, would be the true rulers, and the king merely their representative.

As you can imagine, what the assembly of the estates actually meant was that the ruler was there to serve the people rather than vice versa, and that he would no longer be allowed to abuse his power. But the Parisians who read it in the press took the doctrine of the sovereignty of the people to mean something entirely different. They thought it meant that people in the streets and marketplaces, communally known as 'the people', would be the rulers. And when the king still refused to see reason and entered into secret negotiations with foreign courts, asking for help against his own people, a procession led by market women went out to the Palace of Versailles. They killed the guards, burst into the magnificent rooms with the wonderful chandeliers, mirrors and damask hangings, and forced the king and his wife, Marie Antoinette, together with their children and their entourage, to return to Paris where they were under the people's control.

The king and his family made one attempt to flee abroad. But because they did it with all the ceremony and formality of someone setting out to a masked ball at court, they were recognised and brought back, and placed under close guard. The National Assembly had meanwhile decided to introduce many more changes. All the possessions of the Catholic Church were confiscated, as were those of noblemen who had fled abroad in fear of the revolution. Then the Assembly decreed that the people must elect new representatives, to vote on the laws.

And so in 1791 a great number of young people came to Paris from all over France to give their advice. But the other kings and rulers of Europe had had enough. It was not as if they felt Louis deserved their support, for they had little respect for his behaviour, nor were they altogether sorry to see the might of France reduced. But they could not sit back and watch while a fellow monarch was stripped of his powers. So Prussia and Austria sent a few troops to France to protect the king. This threw the people into a frenzy. The whole country was up in arms at the uninvited interference. Every nobleman or supporter of the king was now deemed to be a traitor, in league with foreign accomplices of the court. Noblemen were dragged from their beds at night by raging mobs, thrown into prison and murdered. Things grew worse by the minute. Soon everything that had to do with the past had to be rooted out and destroyed.

It began with dress. Supporters of the Revolution gave up wearing wigs, knee breeches and silk stockings, and wore red nightcaps on their heads and long trousers as we still do today. This was both simpler and cheaper. Dressed in this way they took to the streets shouting: 'Death to all aristocrats! Liberty! Equality! Fraternity!' As far as fraternity was concerned, the Jacobins – as the most violent party was called – had a rather odd understanding of the word. They were not only against aristocrats: they were against anybody who disagreed with them, and anyone who crossed them lost his head. A special machine called a guillotine was invented, which did the job quickly and efficiently. A special court was set up, known as the Revolutionary Tribunal, and day in, day out, it sentenced people to death, upon which they were guillotined in the squares of Paris.

The leaders of these frenzied mobs were remarkable people. One of them, Danton, was an impassioned orator, a bold and unscrupulous man whose powerful speeches incited the people to ever new attacks upon the king's supporters. Robespierre was the opposite of Danton. He was a stiff, sober and dry lawyer who made interminable speeches in which he never failed to mention the heroes of Greece and Rome. Always impeccably dressed, he would climb the steps of the pulpit of the National Assembly and speak about nothing but virtue – the virtue of Cato and the virtue of Themistocles, the virtue of the human heart in general, and the heart's hatred of vice. And because vice had to be hated, the heads of France's enemies had to be chopped off, so that virtue could triumph! And who exactly were these enemies of France? Why, all those who did not share his opinions. So Robespierre had hundreds of his opponents killed in the name of the virtue of the human heart. But you mustn't think he was a hypocrite. He was probably convinced that he was right. No one could bribe him with gifts, or move him with tears. He was terrifying. And his aim was to spread terror. Terror among the enemies of Reason, as he called them.

Even King Louis XVI was brought before the People's Tribunal and condemned to death because he had appealed to foreigners for help against his own people. Soon afterwards Marie Antoinette was beheaded. In dying they both displayed more dignity and greatness than they had during their lives. There was genuine outrage abroad over the executions, and many troops marched on Paris. But the people had no intention of giving up their newfound freedom. Men were called up to fight from all over France, and the German armies were beaten back, while in Paris, and above all, in provincial towns where opposition to the Jacobins was greatest, the Reign of Terror intensified.

Robespierre and the representatives had declared Christianity to be an ancient superstition and abolished God by decree. Instead, people were to worship Reason. And a printer's young bride wearing a white dress and a blue cloak, representing the goddess of Reason, was led through the city amid festive music. Soon even this was not virtuous enough for Robespierre. A new decree was issued announcing that God *did* exist and man's soul was immortal. Robespierre himself appeared as priest of the Supreme Being – as

God was now called – wearing a hat decorated with feathers, and with a bunch of flowers in his hand. He must have looked quite ridiculous, and many people must have laughed when they saw him. However, his power was almost at an end. Danton had had enough of the daily beheadings and asked for mercy and compassion. Robespierre's reaction to this was to say: 'Only criminals ask for mercy on behalf of criminals.' So Danton, too, was beheaded and Robespierre had his final victory. But soon, after yet another of his interminable speeches, in which he insisted that the executions had barely begun, that freedom's enemies were still all around, that vice was triumphant and the country in peril, it so happened that, for the first time, nobody clapped. Instead there was just a deathly hush. A few days later, he, too, was beheaded.

France's enemies had been defeated. The nobility had either been killed, driven out of France, or had opted to become common citizens. Equality before the law had been achieved. The possessions of the Church and the ruling class had been shared out among the peasants, who had been liberated from feudal serfdom. Every Frenchman was free to choose his profession and aspire to any office. The people were tired of fighting and wanted to enjoy the fruits of this tremendous victory in peace and stability. The Revolutionary Tribunal was abolished, and in 1795 five men were elected to form a Directorate, which was to rule the country according to its new constitution.

Meanwhile the ideas of the French Revolution had reached out beyond the frontiers and been met with great enthusiasm in neighbouring countries. Belgium and Switzerland also formed republics based on the principles of human rights and equality, and these republics were given military support by the French government. And it so happened that, in the ranks of France's armies, there was a young officer who would one day prove stronger than the whole Revolution.

35

❖

The Last Conqueror

What I have always loved best about the history of the world is that it is true. That all the extraordinary things we read were no less real than you and I are today. What is more, what did happen is often far more exciting and amazing than anything we could invent. I am now going to tell you the story of one of the most astonishing of all those adventures, which was nevertheless as real as your life or mine. It took place not so long ago. My own grandfather was alive then, and he would have been about your age.

It begins like this. Near Italy there is an island, mountainous, sunny and poor, called Corsica. On that island there lived a lawyer, together with his wife and their eight children. His name was Buonaparte. At the time when his second son, Napoleon, was born, in 1769, the island had just been sold to France by the Genoese. This did not go down well with the Corsicans and there were many battles with the French governors. The young Napoleon was to become an officer, so his father sent him, at the age of ten, to a military school in France. He was poor – his father could barely support him, and this made him withdrawn and unhappy and he didn't play with his fellow students. 'I sought out a corner of the school,' he was to say later, 'where I could sit and dream to my heart's content. When my companions tried to take over my corner, I defended it with all my might. I already knew instinctively that my will could triumph over the will of others, and that anything I wanted could be mine.'

He learnt a lot and had a wonderful memory. At seventeen he became a second lieutenant in the French army, and it was there that he was given the nickname 'the little corporal', because he was so short. He almost starved. He read widely and missed nothing. When the Revolution broke out three years later in 1789, Corsica wanted to free itself from French rule. Napoleon returned home to fight the French. But he was soon back in Paris, for, as he wrote in a letter at the time, 'only in Paris can one do anything.' He was right. In Paris he did succeed in doing something. It so happened that one of Napoleon's fellow countrymen was serving as a senior officer in an army sent by the revolutionaries to crush resistance in the provincial town of Toulon. He took the twenty-five-year-old lieutenant with him, and didn't regret it. Napoleon gave such sound advice, on where to place the cannons and where to aim them, that the city was quickly taken. For this he was made a general. But in those troubled times this was no sure sign of a great career. If you were the friend of one party, you were the enemy of another. When the government, which was made up of Robespierre's friends, was overthrown, Napoleon was arrested too. True, he was soon released, but in punishment for his friendship with the Jacobins he lost his command and was dismissed from the army. He was desperately poor and the future looked grim. However, once again, thanks to someone he knew, his name was put forward to the five men of the Paris Directorate, and they gave him the task of crushing a violent demonstration of young noblemen. Napoleon didn't hesitate to fire into the crowd and so dispersed the demonstrators. In recognition, he was reinstated to the rank of general and given command of a small army sent to Italy to spread the ideas of the French Revolution.

It seemed a hopeless task. The army lacked everything. France was destitute and in chaos. In 1796, at the outset of the campaign, General Napoleon (who now signed himself 'Bonaparte', in the French manner) spoke briefly to his troops: 'Soldiers! You are almost naked and ill-fed. The government owes you much and cannot pay you. But I will lead you to the most fertile plain in the world. Rich provinces and great towns will fall into your hands, and in them you will find honour, glory and riches. Soldiers! Do you lack courage and steadfastness?' With these words he inspired his soldiers, and so great was his skill in the face of the far greater strength of his enemies that he won victories everywhere he went. Within a few weeks of the start of the campaign he was able to write in a letter of command to his troops: 'Soldiers! In fourteen days you have won six victories, captured twenty-one banners and fifty-five pieces of cannon. You have won battles without cannon, crossed rivers without bridges, marched great distances without boots, slept in the open without brandy and often without bread. I rejoice that each of you, upon returning home, will be able to say with pride: I too was of that army that conquered Italy!'

And, true to his words, it wasn't long before his army had conquered the whole of northern Italy and made it a republic along the lines of France or Belgium. Wherever he went, if a beautiful work of art caught his eye, he had it sent to Paris. Then he turned north towards Austria, because the emperor had attacked him in Italy. Messengers from the emperor in Vienna came to meet him in the town of Leoben in Styria. A raised seat had been prepared for the emperor's envoy in the council chamber. 'Take away that chair,' said Napoleon, 'I can never see a throne without feeling the urge to sit on it.' He then demanded that the emperor cede to France all the parts of Germany that lay to the west of the Rhine. After that he returned to Paris. But in Paris there was nothing for him to do. So he put forward a proposal to the government for an adventurous undertaking. France's greatest enemy at this time was Britain, and, thanks to their many colonial possessions in America, Africa, India and Australia, the British had become very powerful. The French couldn't attack Britain directly because their army was too weak and, besides, they didn't have enough good ships. But on the other hand, if Napoleon were to occupy Egypt, he could strike at the sources of Britain's wealth by threatening the route to its colonial possessions in India.

So Napoleon took an army to Egypt. Like Alexander the Great, he wanted to conquer the whole of the Orient. He took scholars with him too, to observe and study the remnants of antiquity. On reaching Egypt he spoke to the Muslim Egyptians as if he were a prophet, like Muhammad. In solemn tones he told them that he could read the innermost secrets of their hearts. His coming, he said, had been prophesied centuries before, and they would find it written in the Koran. 'All efforts to resist me are doomed, for I am destined to succeed in all I undertake.'

And at first events seemed to prove him right. He defeated the Egyptian armies in a great battle beside the pyramids in 1798, and on other occasions too, for no one was better than he at fighting battles on dry land. But at sea the British had the upper hand, and their famous admiral Nelson destroyed the French fleet off Aboukir on the Egyptian coast. When plague broke out among his troops and news came that the government in Paris was in disarray, Napoleon abandoned his soldiers and secretly took ship for France. There he received a hero's welcome. Everyone hoped that the famous general would prove as capable at home as he had been in hostile lands. Encouraged by their support, in 1799 he boldly turned his guns on the seat of government in Paris. His grenadiers threw the elected representatives of the people out of the council chambers, and he assumed supreme command. Following the example of ancient Rome, he proclaimed himself consul.

In that role Napoleon held court in splendour in the former residence of the kings of France, and brought back many noblemen from exile. But mostly he worked night and day at establishing order in France. To him, this meant that nothing should happen at any time or in any place unless he wished it. And he succeeded. He established a collection of laws in accordance with the new basic principles and named it after himself: the Napoleonic Code. In a new campaign in Italy he defeated Austria once again. He was idolised by his soldiers and all of France worshipped him because he had brought the country glory and conquests. They made him consul for life. But this still did not satisfy Napoleon. In 1804 he proclaimed himself emperor. Emperor of the French! The pope himself made the journey to France to crown him. Soon afterwards he had himself proclaimed king of Italy as well. The other countries grew fearful of this mighty newcomer, and Britain, Prussia, Austria, Russia and Sweden formed an alliance against him. Napoleon didn't let this worry him. He wasn't afraid of enemy armies, however large they were. In the winter of 1805 he attacked and inflicted a crushing defeat on an alliance of enemy troops at Austerlitz. Now Napoleon was lord of almost all of Europe. He gave each of his relatives a kingdom – a little souvenir, as it were. His stepson became viceroy of Italy, his elder brother was given Naples, his younger brother Holland, his brother-in-law part of Germany and his sisters duchies in Italy. Which was not bad going for a Corsican lawyer's family who, hardly twenty years before, had been sitting round a table on their distant island, sharing a simple meal.

In Germany, too, all the power was in Napoleon's hands, because the German princes who had turned their backs on the emperor in Vienna long ago had now become allies of the mighty Napoleon. The emperor Francis gave up the title of German emperor, and that was the end of the Holy Roman Empire of the German Nation which had begun with the coronation of Charlemagne in Rome a thousand years before. The year was 1806. From now on, Francis of Habsburg was merely emperor of Austria.

Next Napoleon attacked the Hohenzollerns, and in a matter of days the Prussian armies had been soundly defeated. In the same year he entered Berlin, and from there he imposed his laws on Europe. First and foremost, he forbade anyone in the whole of Europe to have any business dealings with France's enemies, the British. This was known as the Continental System. Having lost his entire fleet to Admiral Nelson at the Battle of Trafalgar the previous year, Napoleon could not invade that powerful country. Instead he planned to bring the British to their knees with an economic blockade. When the other states refused to agree to this, he returned to Germany and attacked the Russians, now allied with the Prussians. And, in 1807, he was able to present his youngest brother with part of Germany as his kingdom.

Now it was Spain's turn. He conquered that country and gave its crown to his brother Joseph, previously king of Naples, and gave Naples to one of his brothers-in-law. But the day came when the inhabitants of all these countries had had enough of being passed around the Bonaparte family as presents. The Spaniards were the first to resist French rule, from 1808 onwards. They didn't fight any battles as such, but the entire population was in a constant state of rebellion which the French soldiers were unable to crush, despite their brutal efforts. The emperor of Austria had also had enough of being bossed around by Napoleon. In 1809 a new war broke out. Napoleon's army was approaching Vienna and had reached the outskirts, at Aspern. There, for the first time in his life, Napoleon experienced defeat, at the hands of the valiant general Archduke Charles. However, only a few days later he soundly defeated the Austrian army at Wagram. He marched into Vienna, installed himself in the imperial palace at Schönbrunn and forced the emperor Francis to give him the hand of his daughter Marie-Louise in marriage. For a member of the imperial house of Habsburg, whose family had reigned from Vienna for more than 500 years, this was no easy thing to do. Napoleon had no princely ancestry. He was just a jumped-up little lieutenant who, through his extraordinary ability and nothing else, was now lord and master of Europe.

In 1810 Marie-Louise gave birth to a son, to whom Napoleon gave the title King of Rome. Napoleon's empire was by now considerably larger than that of Charlemagne, if we include all the kingdoms of his brothers and sisters and generals, which were theirs only in name. If he didn't like their conduct he used to write them insulting letters. For example, to his brother, the king of Westphalia, he wrote: 'I've seen one of your orders of the day to the soldiers that will make you the laughing stock of Germany, Austria and France. Have you no friend to tell you a few home truths? You are a king and the emperor's brother – titles worth nothing on the battlefield. There, you have to be a soldier and nothing but a soldier. Forget your ministers, your ambassadors and your finery. You have to sleep out in the vanguard with your men, sit on your horse, day and night. March in the vanguard, so you know what's going on.' The letter ends: 'And for God's sake have the wit to write and speak correctly!' This was how the emperor treated his brothers, the kings of Europe. But he treated the people even worse. He cared nothing for what they thought or what they felt. To him they were merely a source of money or, better still, soldiers. But as time went on they became less and less willing to obey him. After the Spaniards, the peasants in the Tirol were the next to rebel against the French and Bavarian soldiers. The Tirol was a region that Napoleon had taken away from the emperor of Austria and given to the kingdom of Bavaria. Their rebellion ended only when Napoleon captured their leader, Andreas Hofer, and had him shot.

In Germany, too, the whole population was in a state of great agitation and indignation at the French emperor's wilful brutality. And now that most of the German principalities were under French rule, for the first time in their history they sensed a common destiny: they weren't French, they were Germans. Who cared if the king of Prussia was on good terms with the king of Saxony or not, or if the king of Bavaria had allied himself with Napoleon's brother? The experience shared by all Germans, that of being dominated by foreigners, had given birth to a shared desire: the wish to be free. For the first time in the whole of history, all Germans – students and poets, peasants and noblemen – joined forces against their rulers to liberate themselves. But it wasn't as easy as that. Napoleon was all-powerful. The great German poet Goethe said at the time: 'Shake your chains how you may, the man is too great for you!' And indeed, for a long time no amount of inspiration or heroism could match the might of Napoleon. What finally brought him down was his insatiable ambition. The power he had already never seemed to be enough: to him it was only the beginning. And now it was Russia's turn. The Russians had defied his command not to trade with the British, and for this they had to be punished!

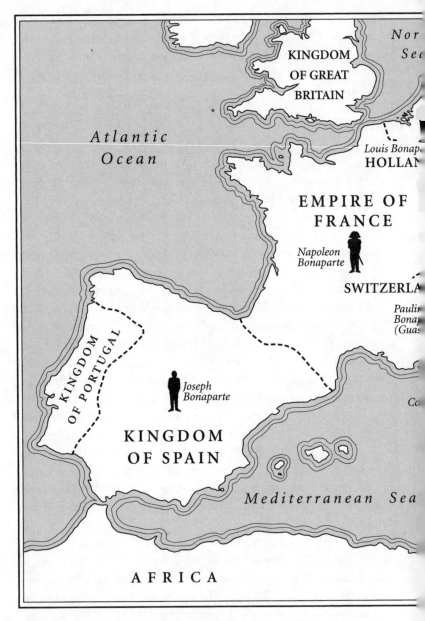

Here you can clearly see the power of the little man from Corsica, who set his relatives up as rulers all over Europe like pieces on a chess board.

Napoleon assembled troops from every region of his vast empire until he had an army of some six hundred thousand men – just think of it, more than half a million human beings! One of the largest armies the world had ever seen. And now, in 1812, this army marched on Russia. As the soldiers penetrated deeper and deeper into the heartland, they met with no resistance. When they advanced, the Russians retreated, just as they had done before the troops of Charles XII of Sweden. At last, outside the gates of Moscow, the mighty Russian army stopped. Napoleon attacked and seemed to be victorious – I almost said 'of course', since for him winning battles was the same as solving puzzles, if you are someone who is good at that sort of thing. He would note the enemy's position and knew immediately where to place his own troops in order to evade or attack them. So he marched into Moscow, only to find the city almost empty and most of its inhabitants fled. It was late autumn. Napoleon installed himself in the Kremlin, the ancient imperial castle, and waited to dictate his terms. Then came news that the suburbs of Moscow were burning. In those days most of Moscow's houses were made of wood, and as the fire spread, large parts of the city were engulfed in flames. The Russians had probably started the fires to put pressure on the French. All efforts to extinguish them were in vain.

Where could six hundred thousand men stay, with Moscow burnt? And how could they be fed? Napoleon had no choice but to retreat. In the meantime, however, winter had arrived and it was bitterly cold. Everything in sight along their route had already been plundered and consumed. The retreat across the endless, frozen wastes of the Russian plains would now become something too terrible to describe. Overcome by cold and starvation, more and more soldiers fell by the wayside. Horses perished in their thousands. The Russian Cossacks rode up and attacked the rear and flanks of the army. The soldiers fought with desperation. Surrounded by Cossacks, and in the midst of a raging snowstorm, they managed to cross the great Berezina River. But little by little their strength ebbed away and they lost hope. Fewer than one in twenty of the soldiers survived this terrible defeat and reached the German frontier in the last stages of sickness and exhaustion. Disguised as a peasant, Napoleon abandoned his troops and hurried back to Paris on a sledge.

His first act was to raise fresh troops, for now that his strength was reduced, there were rebellions everywhere. Yet once again, he succeeded in raising a mighty army, this time made up entirely of young men. These were the last men left in France, whom Napoleon now sent to combat the subject peoples. He marched on Germany. The emperor of Austria sent his chancellor, Metternich, to negotiate a peace treaty. Metternich talked to Napoleon for a whole day: 'And what if this army of boys that you have just raised is mown down?' At these words, Napoleon turned first white, then purple with rage: 'You are no soldier!' he shouted. 'You know nothing of a soldier's heart. I was raised on the battlefield, and a man such as I doesn't give a fig for a million lives!' With this outburst, so Metternich related, Napoleon hurled his hat across the room.

Metternich left the hat where it lay and said calmly: 'Why should I be the only person to hear this, within the privacy of these four walls? Open the doors so that your words may resound from one end of France to the other.' Napoleon rejected the terms of the emperor's peace treaty, telling Metternich he didn't have any choice. If he wished to remain emperor of the French, he would have to fight on and win. In 1813 a battle took place, at Leipzig in Germany, between Napoleon's army and those of his allied enemies. On the first day, Napoleon had the upper hand. But when, on the second, he was suddenly abandoned by the Bavarian troops who were fighting for him, he lost the battle and was forced to retreat. During this retreat he fought with another large army of Bavarians which was pursuing him, after which he returned to Paris.

He had been right: following his defeat the French deposed him. He was given sovereignty over the little island of Elba, to which he retired. However, the princes and the emperor who had brought about his defeat met in Vienna in 1814 to negotiate with one another, and share out Europe among themselves. It was their opinion that the Enlightenment had been a disaster for Europe. The idea of Liberty, in particular, was responsible for all the disturbances and the countless victims, both of the Revolution and of Napoleon's wars. They wanted to undo the whole Revolution. Metternich in particular was determined that everything should be as it had been before, and that no similar upheaval should ever be allowed to happen again. It was therefore vital, or so he thought, that nothing should be written or printed in Austria without the approval of the government and the emperor.

In France the Revolution was totally extinguished. The brother of Louis XVI came to the throne as Louis XVIII (the title of Louis XVII having been given to the son of Louis XVI, who had died during the Revolution). The new Louis ruled with his court in France with the same pomp and the same lack of judgement as his unhappy brother, just as if the twenty-six years of revolution and empire had never taken place. The French became increasingly discontented. When Napoleon heard about this, he secretly left Elba (in 1815) and landed in France accompanied by a small number of soldiers. Louis sent an army to fight him. But as soon as the soldiers saw Napoleon, they deserted and went over to his side, and were joined by soldiers from other garrisons. After a few days' march, the emperor Napoleon entered Paris in triumph, and King Louis XVIII fled.

The princes, still conferring in Vienna, were furious and declared Napoleon to be the enemy of humanity. Under the command of the English duke of Wellington, an army, largely made up of British and Germans soldiers, was assembled in Belgium. Napoleon attacked without delay. A savage battle followed in 1815 at a place named Waterloo. Once again, Napoleon seemed at first to be winning. However, one of his generals misunderstood the order he had been given and led his troops in the wrong direction. Towards evening, the commander of the Prussian troops, General Blücher, gathered together his exhausted men and, with the words 'It looks pretty hopeless, but we mustn't give in', led them back into battle. It was to be Napoleon's last defeat. He fled with his army, was once again deposed and forced to leave France.

He embarked on a British ship, placing himself voluntarily in the hands of his oldest enemies, the only ones he had never beaten. He was counting on their magnanimity, and said that he wished to live as a private citizen under English law. But in all his life Napoleon himself had rarely shown any magnanimity. Instead the British declared him a prisoner of war and sent him to a tiny uninhabited island far out in the Atlantic, known as the Island of St Helena, so that he might never come back again. There he spent the last six years of his life, abandoned and powerless, dictating the memories of all his deeds and victories, and quarrelling with the English governor, who wouldn't even let him take a walk on his own around the island. And that was the end of the little man with the pale complexion, whose strength of will and clarity of mind were greater than those of any ruler before him. Meanwhile the great powers of the past, those ancient and pious princely houses, once again ruled Europe. And the austere and unyielding Metternich, who would not stoop to pick up Napoleon's hat, guided the destinies of Europe from Vienna through his emissaries as if the Revolution had never taken place.

36

❖

MEN AND MACHINES

Metternich and the pious rulers of Russia, Austria, France and
Spain were indeed able to bring about a return to life as it
had been before the French Revolution – at least in its outward
forms. Once again there was all the splendour and ceremony of
courts, where the nobility paraded, their breasts covered in medals
and decorations, and wielded much influence. Citizens were excluded from politics, which suited many of them very well. They
occupied themselves with their families, with books and, above all,
with music. For, in the last hundred years, music, heard mostly as
an accompaniment to dancing, songs and hymns in earlier times,
had become the art which, of all the arts, spoke most to people.
However, this period of tranquillity and leisure, known to Austrians as the Biedermeier era – that of the administrative or profes-
sional middle-class citizen – was only the visible side of things.
There was one Enlightenment idea that Metternich could not suppress – not that he ever thought of doing so. This was the idea
Galileo had had of a rational, mathematical approach to the study
of nature, which had appealed so much to people at the time of the

Enlightenment. And it so happened that this hidden aspect of the Enlightenment led to a far greater revolution and dealt a far more deadly blow to the old forms and institutions than the Parisian Jacobins ever did with their guillotine.

Mastering the mathematics of nature enabled people not only to understand the forces of nature, but to use them. And they were now harnessed and put to work for mankind.

The history of all the inventions that followed is not as simple as you might think. In most cases they began with an idea. This idea led to experiments and trials, after which it was often abandoned, only to be picked up again later, perhaps by somebody else. It was only when a person came along who had the determination and persistence to carry the idea through to its conclusion, and make it generally useful, that that person became known as the 'inventor'. This was the case with all the machines which changed our lives – with steam-driven machinery, the steamship, the steam engine and the telegraph – and they all became important in Metternich's time.

The steam engine came first. A learned Frenchman called Papin had already been carrying out experiments around 1700. But it wasn't until 1769 that a Scottish engineer named James Watt was able to patent a proper steam engine. At first the engine was mainly used to pump water out of mines, but people soon saw the possibility of using it to drive carriages or ships. Experiments with steamships went on in England in 1802, and in 1803 an American engineer called Robert Fulton launched a steamboat on the Seine. Commenting on the event, Napoleon wrote: 'This project is capable of changing the face of the world.' Four years later, in 1807, the first steamship made its way up the Hudson River from New York to Albany, its huge paddle-wheel churning, with much puffing, clanking and belching of smoke.

At about the same time attempts were also being made in England to propel vehicles using steam. But it took until 1803 for a usable engine to be invented, one which ran on cast-iron railway lines. In 1814 George Stephenson built the first effective steam locomotive and named it Blücher after the great Prussian general, and in 1825 the first railway line was opened between the towns of Stockton and Darlington. Within thirty years there were railway lines all over Britain, America, throughout almost all of Europe, and even in India. These lines went over mountains, through tunnels and over great rivers, and carried people at least ten times as quickly as the fastest stagecoach.

It was much the same with the invention of the electric telegraph, the only means of rapid communication before the telephone. First thought of in 1753, there were many attempts from the 1770s onwards, but only in 1837 did an American artist called Samuel Morse succeed in sending a short telegraph to his friends. Once again, hardly more than ten years had passed before use of the telegraph was widespread.

However, other machines changed the world even more profoundly. These were the machines which made use of the forces of nature instead of manpower. Take spinning and weaving, for example – work that had always been done by artisans. When the demand for cloth increased (around the time of Louis XIV), factories already existed, but the work was done by hand. It took a while for people to realise that their new knowledge of nature could be applied to the production of cloth. The dates are much the same as those of the other great inventions. People were experimenting with various sorts of spinning machines from 1740 onwards. The mechanical loom was introduced at about the same time. And again, it was in England that these machines were first made and used. Machines and factories needed coal and iron, so countries which had their own coal and iron were at a great advantage.

All of these developments produced a tremendous upheaval in people's lives. Everything was turned upside-down and hardly anything stayed where it had been. Think for a moment how secure and orderly everything had been in the guilds of the medieval cities! Those guilds had lasted right up until the time of the French Revolution and longer. True, it was no longer as easy for a journeyman to become a master as it had been in the Middle Ages, but it was still possible and the hope was there. Now, all of a sudden, everything changed. Some people owned machines. It didn't take much training to learn how to operate them – just a couple of hours and then they ran themselves. This meant that anyone who owned a mechanical loom could, with the help of one or two assistants – perhaps his wife and children – do more work than a hundred trained weavers. So whatever became of all the weavers in a town into which a mechanical loom was introduced? The answer is that they woke up one day to discover that they weren't needed any more. Everything it had taken them years to learn, first as apprentices and then as journeymen, was useless. Machines were faster, better and very much cheaper. Machines don't sleep and they don't eat. Nor do they need holidays. Thanks to the new machines, the money that had allowed a hundred weavers to live safely and comfortably could now be saved by the factory owner, or spent on himself. Of course, he still needed workers to manage the machines. But only unskilled workers, and not many of them.

But the worst thing was this: the city's hundred weavers were now out of work and would starve, because one machine was doing their work for them. And naturally, rather than see his family starve a person will do anything. Even work for a pittance as long as it means he has a job to keep body and soul together. So the factory owner, with his machines, could summon the hundred starving weavers and say: 'I need five people to run my factory and look after my machines. What will you charge for that?' One of them might say: 'I want so much, if I am to live as comfortably as I did before.' The next would say: 'I just need enough for a loaf of bread and a kilo of potatoes a day.' And the third, seeing his last chance of survival about to disappear, would say: 'I'll see if I can manage on half a loaf.' Four others then said: 'So will we!' 'Right!' said the factory owner. 'I'll take you five. How many hours can you work in a day?' 'Ten hours,' said the first. 'Twelve,' said the second, seeing the job slipping from his grasp. 'I can do sixteen,' cried the third, for his life depended on it. 'Fine,' said the factory owner, 'I'll take you. But who'll look after my machine while you're asleep? My machine doesn't sleep!' 'I'll get my little brother to do it – he's eight years old,' replied the luckless weaver. 'And what shall I give him?' 'A few pennies will do, to buy him a bit of bread and butter.' And even then the factory owner might reply: 'He can have the bread, but we'll see about the butter.' And this was how business was done. The remaining ninety-five weavers were left to starve, or find another factory owner prepared to take them on.

Now you mustn't think that all factory owners were as vile as the one I have just described. But the worst of them, who paid the least and sold at the lowest prices, could be the most successful. Then others, against their conscience and their natural instincts, often found themselves treating their workers in the same way.

People began to despair. Why bother to learn a skill and take pains to make beautiful things by hand? Machines could do the same job a hundred times more quickly, often more neatly and at a hundredth of the price. And so weavers, blacksmiths, spinners and cabinet-makers sank ever more deeply into misery and destitution, running from factory to factory in the hope of earning a few pennies. Many of them raged against the machines that had robbed them of their happiness. They broke into factories and wrecked the looms, but it made no difference. In England in 1812 the death penalty was introduced for anyone found guilty of destroying a machine. And then newer and better machines followed that could do the work, not of a hundred, but of five hundred workers, and the general misery increased.

Some people felt that things could not go on like this. It was simply not right that a person, just because he happened to own or had perhaps inherited, a machine, should be able to treat everyone else more harshly than many noblemen used to treat their peasants. It seemed to them that factories and machines and suchlike, which gave their owners such monstrous power over other people's lives, shouldn't belong to individuals, but to the community as a whole. This idea is called socialism. People had many ideas about how to organise work in a socialist way, so as to put an end to the misery of starving workers, and came to the conclusion that, instead of receiving a wage set by the individual factory owner, workers should have a share of the overall profits.

Among the many socialists in France and Britain in the 1830s there was one who became particularly famous. He was a scholar from Trier in Germany, and his name was Karl Marx. The ideas he had were rather different. In his view it was pointless wondering how things might be if only the machines belonged to the workers. If they wanted the machines, the workers would have to fight for them, for the factory owners would never give up their factories voluntarily. And it was equally pointless for groups of workers to go round destroying mechanical looms now that they had been invented. What they should do was stick together. If each of those hundred weavers had not gone out looking for work for himself, and instead they had all got together and said with one voice, 'We won't work for more than ten hours in the factory, and we each want two loaves of bread and two kilos of potatoes', the factory owner would have had to give in. True, that in itself might not have been enough, since the factory owner no longer needed skilled weavers for his mechanical looms, and could take his pick from men so destitute that they would accept the lowest wages. But this, said Marx, was precisely why unity was so vital. For in the end the factory owner would be unable to find anyone who would do the job for less. So the workers must support each other. And not just those from one district, or even one country. All the workers of the world must unite! Then they would not only have the power to say how much they should be paid, but they would end up by taking over the factories and the machines themselves, and so create a world that was no longer divided into haves and have-nots.

For, as Marx went on to explain, the truth of the matter was that weavers, shoemakers and blacksmiths didn't really exist any more. A worker who did nothing but pull a lever on a machine two thousand times a day hardly needed to know what the machine produced. His only interest was in his weekly pay packet and in earning enough to prevent him from starving like his unhappy fellows who had no work. Nor did the owner need to learn the trade which gave him a living, for the work was all done by machines. Which meant, in fact, said Marx, that there were no longer any real occupations. There were just two sorts – or classes – of people: those who owned and those who didn't. Or as he chose to call them, capitalists and proletarians. These classes were in a constant state of war with one another, for owners always want to produce as much as possible for the smallest amount of money, and therefore pay the workers – the proletarians – as little as they can get away with, whereas workers seek to force the capitalists – the owners of the machines – to part with as much of the profit as they can be made to. This battle between the two classes of people, so Marx thought, could only end in one way. The many dispossessed would one day seize the property of the owning minority, not in order to own it themselves, but to get rid of ownership altogether. Then classes would cease to exist. This was the goal of Karl Marx, one that he thought was near and quite simple to achieve.

However, when Marx published his great appeal to the workers (*The Communist Manifesto*, as he called it) in 1848, the situation was very different from what he had expected. And things have gone on being different, right up until today. In those days few factory owners had any real power. Most of it was still in the hands of those much-decorated noblemen whose authority Metternich had helped to restore. And it was these noblemen who were the real adversaries of rich citizens and factory owners. They wanted a secure, orderly and regulated state in which each had his appointed place, as people had always had in the past. This meant that, in Austria for example, peasants were still tied to inherited estates, and were hardly less bound to the landowners than the serfs of the Middle Ages. Artisans were still governed by many strict and ancient regulations dating back to the time of the guilds – as, to some extent, were the new factories. However, citizens who had become wealthy as a result of the new machines and factories were no longer willing to take orders, either from the nobility or from the state. They wanted to act as they saw fit, and were convinced that this would be best for everyone. All that was needed was for able people to be given a free rein, unimpeded by conventions, rules or regulations, and in time the whole world would be a better place. The world looks after itself as long as it isn't interfered with, or so they thought. Accordingly, in 1830, the citizens of France rose up and threw out Louis XVIII's successors.

In 1848 there was a new revolution in Paris, which spread to many other countries, in which citizens tried to obtain all the power of the state so that nobody could any longer tell them what they might or might not do with their factories and their machines. In Vienna, Metternich found himself dismissed and the emperor Ferdinand was forced to abdicate. The old regime was definitively over. Men wore black trousers like drainpipes that were almost as ugly as the ones we wear today, and stiff white collars with complicated knotted neckties. Factories were allowed to spring up everywhere and railways transported goods in ever increasing quantities from one country to another.

37

❖

ACROSS THE SEAS

Thanks to railways and steamships the world became much smaller. To set off across the seas for India or China was no longer a perilous adventure into the unknown, and America was almost next door. And so from 1800 onwards it is even less possible to see the history of the world as only that of Europe. We must take a look beyond our frontiers at Europe's new neighbours, and in particular at China, Japan and America. Before 1800, China was still in many ways the same country it had been at the time of the rulers of the Han family at around the time of the birth of Christ, and at the time of China's great poets, eight hundred years later. It was a mighty, orderly, proud, densely populated and largely peaceful land, inhabited by hardworking peasants and citizens, great scholars, poets and thinkers. The unrest, the religious wars and the endless disturbances which troubled Europe during those years would have seemed alien, barbaric and inconceivable to the Chinese. True, they were now ruled by foreign emperors who made men wear their hair in a plait, as a sign of their submission. But since their invasion, this family of rulers from inner Asia, the

Manchus, had adopted Chinese ways and had learnt and absorbed the guiding principles of Confucius. So the empire flourished.

On occasion, learned Jesuits came to China to preach Christianity. They were usually received with courtesy, for the emperor of China wanted them to teach him about Western sciences, and about astronomy in particular. European merchants took home porcelain from China. People everywhere tried to match its exquisite fineness and delicacy. But it took centuries of experimenting before they could do so. In how many ways the Chinese empire, with its many, many millions of cultivated citizens, was superior to Europe you can see from a letter sent by the emperor of China to the king of England in 1793. The English had asked for permission to send an ambassador to the Chinese court, and to engage in trade with China. The emperor Ch'ien-Lung, a famous scholar and an able ruler, sent this reply:

> You, O king, live far away across many seas. Yet, driven by the humble desire to share in the blessings of our culture, you have sent a delegation, which respectfully submitted your letter. You assure us that it is your veneration for our celestial ruling family that fills you with the desire to adopt our culture, and yet the difference between our customs and moral laws and your own is so profound that, were your envoy even capable of absorbing the basic principles of our culture, our customs and traditions could never grow in your soil. Were he the most diligent student, his efforts would still be vain.
>
> Ruling over the vast world, I have but one end in view, and it is this: to govern to perfection and to fulfil the duties of the state. Rare and costly objects are of no interest to me. I have no use for your country's goods. Our Celestial Kingdom possesses all things in abundance and wants for nothing within its frontiers. Hence there is no need to bring in the wares of foreign barbarians to exchange for our own products. But since tea, silk and porcelain, products of the Celestial Kingdom, are absolute necessities for the peoples of Europe and for you yourself, the limited trade hitherto permitted in my

province of Canton will continue. Mindful of the distant loneliness of your island, separated from the world by desert wastes of sea, I pardon your understandable ignorance of the customs of the Celestial Kingdom. Tremble at my orders and obey.

So that was what the emperor of China had to say to the king of the little island of Britain. But he had underestimated the barbarity of the inhabitants of that distant island, a barbarity which they demonstrated several decades later when they arrived in their steamships. They were no longer prepared to put up with the limited trade allowed them in the province of Canton, and they had found a ware that the Chinese people liked all too well: a poison – and a deadly one at that. When opium is burnt and the smoke is inhaled, for a short time it gives you sweet dreams. But it makes you dreadfully ill. Anyone who takes up smoking opium can never give it up. It is a little like drinking brandy, but far more dangerous. And it was this that the British wanted to sell to the Chinese in vast quantities. The Chinese authorities saw how dangerous it would be for their people, and in 1839 they took vigorous action to stamp out the trade.

So the British returned in their steamships, this time armed with cannons. They steamed up the Chinese rivers and fired on peaceful towns, reducing beautiful palaces to dust and ashes. Shocked and bewildered, the Chinese were powerless to stop them and had to give in to the demands of the big-nosed foreign devils: they had to pay a huge sum of money and open their ports to foreign trade. Soon afterwards, a rebellion broke out in China, known as the Taiping – or great peace – Rebellion, begun by a man who proclaimed himself Heavenly King of the Heavenly Kingdom of the Great Peace. At first the Europeans supported him, but when the port of Shanghai was threatened, they fought alongside the imperial troops to protect their trade and the rebels were defeated.

The Europeans were determined to expand their trading activities, and set up embassies in China's capital, Peking. But the imperial government would not allow it. And so, in 1860, British

and French troops together forced their way northwards, bom-
barding towns and humiliating their governors. When they
reached Peking, the emperor had fled. In revenge for Chinese
resistance, the British sacked, looted and burned the beautiful and
ancient imperial Summer Palace, together with all its magnificent
works of art dating back to the earliest days of the empire.
Wrecked, and in a state of utter confusion, the vast and peaceful
thousand-year-old empire was forced to bow to the demands of
Europe's merchants. This was China's reward for teaching Europeans the art of making paper, the use of the compass, and –
regrettably – how to make gunpowder.

During these years the island empire of Japan might easily have
suffered the same fate. Japan at this time was much like Europe in
the Middle Ages. Actual power was in the hands of noblemen and
knights, in particular those of the distinguished family which
looked after the emperor – not unlike the way the ancestors of
Charles the Great had looked after the Merovingian kings. Painting
pictures, building houses and writing poetry were all things the
Japanese had learnt hundreds of years before from the Chinese, and
they also knew how to make many beautiful things themselves. But
Japan was not an orderly, vast and largely peaceful country like
China. For years powerful noblemen from the various districts and
islands had fought each other in chivalrous feuds. In 1850 the
poorer ones among them joined together to seize power from the
great rulers of the kingdom. Would you like to know how they did
it? They enlisted the help of the emperor, a powerless puppet who
was forced to spend several hours each day just sitting on the
throne. Those impoverished noblemen rose up against the great
landowners in the emperor's name, claiming that they would give
him back the power Japan's emperors were said to have had, way
back in the mists of antiquity.

All this was happening at about the time when European envoys
first returned to Japan, a land forbidden to foreigners for more
than two hundred years. To these white-skinned ambassadors, life
in Japanese cities – with their millions of inhabitants, the houses
made of paper and bamboo, the ornamental gardens and pretty

ladies with their hair piled high upon their heads, the bright temple-banners, the rigid formality, and the solemn and lordly manner of the sword-bearing knights – was all delightfully comical. In their filthy outdoor boots they trampled over the priceless mats of the palace floor where the Japanese only trod barefoot. They saw no reason to respect any of the ancient customs of a people they thought of as savages, when exchanging greetings with them or drinking tea. So they were soon detested. When a party of American travellers failed to stand aside politely, as was the custom, when an important prince happened to pass by in his sedan chair, together with his entourage, the enraged attendants fell on the Americans and a woman was killed. Of course, straight away British gunships bombarded the town, and the Japanese feared they were about to suffer the same fate as the Chinese. Fortunately, the rebellion had meanwhile been successful. The emperor – known in Europe as the Mikado – now really did have unlimited power. Backed by clever advisers who were never seen in public, he decided to use it to protect the country against arrogant foreigners for all time. The ancient culture must be preserved. All they needed was to learn Europe's latest inventions. And so, all at once, the doors were thrown open to foreigners.

The emperor commissioned German officers to create a modern army, and Englishmen to build a modern fleet. He sent Japanese to Europe to study Western medicine and to find out about all the other branches of Western knowledge which had made Europe so powerful. Following the example of the Germans he established compulsory education, so that his people would be trained to fight. The Europeans were delighted. What sensible little people the Japanese had turned out to be, opening up their country in this way. They made haste to sell them everything they wanted and showed them everything they asked to see. Within a few decades the Japanese had learnt all that Europe could teach them about machines for war and for peace. And once they had done so, they complimented the Europeans politely, as they once more stood at their gates: 'Now we know what you know. Now *our* steamships will go out in search of trade and conquest, and *our* cannons will fire on peaceful cities if anyone in them dares harm a Japanese citizen.' The Europeans couldn't get over it, nor have they, even today. For the Japanese turned out to be the best students in all the history of the world.

While Japan was beginning to liberate itself, very important things were also happening across the seas in America. As you remember, the English trading posts which had grown into coastal cities on America's eastern seaboard had declared their independence from England in 1776 in order to found a confederation of free states. British and Spanish settlers had meanwhile pressed on towards the west, fighting Indian tribes as they went. You must have read books about cowboys and Indians, so you'll know what it was like. How farmers built log cabins and cleared the dense forest and how they fought. How cowboys looked after enormous herds of cattle and how the Wild West was settled by adventurers and gold diggers. New states sprang up everywhere on land taken from the tribes, although, as you can imagine, not much of that land had been cultivated. But the states were all very different from each other. Those in southern, tropical regions lived off great plantations where cotton or sugar cane was cultivated on a gigantic scale. The settlers owned vast tracts of land and the work was done by negro slaves bought in Africa. They were very badly treated.

Further north it was different. It is less hot and the climate is more like our own. So there you found farms and towns, not unlike those the British emigrants had left behind them, only on a much larger scale. They didn't need slaves because it was easier and cheaper to do the work themselves. And so the townsfolk of the northern states, who were mostly pious Christians, thought it shameful that the Confederation, founded in accordance with the principles of human rights, should keep slaves as people had in pagan antiquity. The southern states explained that they needed negro slaves because without them they would be ruined. No white man, they said, could endure working in such heat and, in any case, negroes weren't born to be free . . . and so on and so forth. In 1820 a compromise was reached. The states which lay to the south of an agreed line would keep slaves, those to the north would not.

In the long run, however, the shame of an economy based on slave labour was intolerable. And yet it seemed that little could be done. The southern states, with their huge plantations, were far stronger and richer than the northern farm lands and were determined not to give in at any cost. But they met their match in President Abraham Lincoln. He was a man with no ordinary destiny. He grew up as a simple farm boy in the backwoods, fought in 1832 in a war against an Indian chief called Black Hawk, and became the postmaster of a small town. There in his spare time he studied law, before becoming a lawyer and a member of parliament. As such he fought against slavery and made himself thoroughly hated by the plantation owners of the southern states. Despite this, he was elected president in 1861. The southern states immediately declared themselves independent of the United States, and founded their own Confederation of slave states.

Seventy-five thousand volunteers made themselves available to Lincoln straight away. Despite this, the outlook was very bad for the northerners. Britain, which had abolished and condemned slave labour in its own colonies for several decades, was nevertheless supporting the slave states. There was a frightful and bloody civil war. Yet, in the end, the northerners' bravery and tenacity prevailed, and in 1865 Lincoln was able to enter the capital of the southern states to the cheers of liberated slaves. Eleven days later, while at the theatre, he was murdered by a southerner. But his work was done. The reunited, free, United States of America soon became the richest and most powerful country in the world. And it even seems to manage without slaves.

38

❖

Two New States in Europe

I have known many people who were children at a time before either Germany or Italy existed. It seems incredible, doesn't it? That these great and powerful nations, which play such an important role, aren't old at all. After the revolutions of 1848 – when new railway lines were being built all over Europe and telegraph cables were being laid, when the towns which had turned into factory towns were expanding and many peasants were being drawn into them, and when men had taken to wearing top hats and funny pince-nez spectacles with dangling black cords – the Europe we know was still no more than a patchwork of tiny duchies, kingdoms, principalities and republics, linked to one another by complicated ties of allegiance or enmity.

In this Europe (if we ignore Britain, which was at this time more concerned with its colonies in America, India and Australia than with the neighbouring continent), there were three important powers. In the centre of Europe stood the empire of Austria. There the emperor Franz Josef had been ruling from the Imperial Palace

This is what the map of central Europe looked like before Italy and Germany had become states. At the same time as all these little pieces of land were uniting to create those two powerful states, the Turkish empire was breaking up into an ever-increasing number of independent countries.

in Vienna since 1848. I saw him once myself, when I was a little boy.
He was by then an old man, and was crossing the park at the Palace
of Schönbrunn. I also have a very clear memory of his state funeral.
He really was what an emperor was meant to be. He ruled over all
sorts of different peoples and countries. He was emperor of Austria, but he was also king of Hungary and count-elevated-to-the-
rank-of-prince of the Tirol and had lots of other ancient titles,
such as king of Jerusalem and protector of the Sacred Tomb – a title
that went back to the Crusades. Many provinces of Italy came
under his authority, while others were ruled by members of his
family. Then there were the Croats, the Serbs, the Czechs, the
Slovenes, the Slovaks, the Poles and innumerable other peoples.
For this reason, the words on old Austrian banknotes (for example,
'ten crowns') also appeared in all these other languages. The
emperor of Austria even had some power, at least in name, in the
German principalities. But the situation there was rather complicated. When Napoleon shattered the last remnants of the Holy
Roman Empire of the German Nation in 1806, the German empire
had ceased to exist. The many German-speaking lands – which
included Prussia, Bavaria, Saxony, Hanover, Frankfurt, Brunswick
and so on and so forth – then formed an association, known as the
German Confederation, to which Austria also belonged. All in all
it was a remarkably confusing picture, this German Confederation.
Each speck of land had its own prince, its own money, its own
stamps and its own official uniform. It was bad enough when it
took several days to get from Berlin to Munich by mail-coach. But
now that the same journey took less than a day by train, it had
become almost unendurable.

The patchwork presented by the lands of Germany, Austria and
Italy was quite unlike anything around them on the map.

To the west was France. Shortly after the revolution of 1848, it
had once again become an empire. One of Napoleon's descendants
had been able to reawaken memories of the glory of the past and
although far from great himself, he was first elected president of
the republic and soon afterwards, emperor of France under the
name of Napoleon III. Despite all its wars and revolutions, France

was now an exceptionally rich and powerful country, with great industrial cities.

To the east was Russia. The tsar was not loved in that mighty land. You must bear in mind that by this time many Russians had studied at universities in France and Germany and their outlook was quite modern and up to date. But the Russian empire and its officials was still living in the Middle Ages. Just think: it was only in 1861 that serfdom was formally abolished and then, for the first time, twenty-three million Russian peasants were promised an existence worthy of human dignity. Making promises is one thing, but keeping them is another. In Russia, generally speaking, government was by the lash – or the knout, as it was called. The penalty for speaking freely, for expressing even the mildest opinion, was exile to Siberia at the very least. Consequently, students and members of the middle classes who had received a modern education detested the tsar so much that he lived in constant fear of assassination. This was, in fact, the fate of most tsars, however hard they tried to guard against it.

Beside the immensity of Russia and the battle-hardened might of France it seemed impossible for any other country to make itself heard in Europe. With the loss of its Latin American colonies, beginning in 1810, Spain had become weak and powerless. Turkey, no longer in control of its European possessions, was now referred to in the newspapers as the 'sick man of Europe'. Its various Christian subject peoples had been fighting for their liberty with the enthusiastic support of the rest of Europe. The Greeks were first, followed by the Bulgarians, the Romanians and the Albanians, while Russia, France and Austria fought over the rest of Turkey's European possessions and Constantinople. This was just as well for Turkey, for none of those three countries was willing to surrender such a rich prize to any of the others. So Constantinople stayed Turkish.

Meanwhile France and Austria were still fighting over the Italian dominions, as they had been for hundreds of years. But times had changed. Italians had also been brought closer to one another by their railways and, like the inhabitants of German towns, they too had come to realise that they weren't simply Florentines, Genoese, Venetians or Neapolitans. They were all Italians, and they wished to decide their own fate. At that time there was only one small state in northern Italy that was free and independent. It lay at the foot of the mountains over which Hannibal had once come and was called Piedmont, which means exactly that: foot of the mountains. Now Piedmont and the island of Sardinia together formed a small but strong kingdom under one ruler, King Victor Emmanuel. And he had an exceptionally able and wily minister called Camillo Cavour, who knew exactly what he wanted. He wanted what all Italians had been yearning for, and what so many of them had shed their blood for in bold but often ill-conceived and perilous adventures, both during and after the 1848 revolution: a unified Italian kingdom. Cavour himself was no warrior. He had no faith in the secret con- spiracies and risky surprise attacks favoured by a brave dreamer called Garibaldi and his young fellow fighters in their efforts to win their country's freedom. Cavour was looking for a different and more effective way, and he found one.

He managed to persuade the ambitious emperor of the French, Napoleon III, that he should join in the struggle for Italian free- dom and unity. He encouraged him to think that if he did so he had everything to gain and nothing to lose. For by involving him- self in the struggle for freedom of a country that didn't belong to him, he could only harm Austria, through its possessions in Italy – a prospect which did not altogether displease him. At the same time, being the champion of liberty would make him the hero of a great European nation, and this too was a tempting thought. Thanks, then, to Cavour's cunning diplomacy and to the bold expeditions of the impetuous Garibaldi, and at the cost of a very great number of lives, the Italians achieved their goal. In the two wars they fought against Austria, in 1859 and 1866, the Austrian armies often had the upper hand, but as a result of interventions by Napoleon III and the tsar, the emperor Franz Josef was finally forced to give up his Italian territories. Elsewhere everyone had cast their votes, and the results showed that the whole population wanted to belong to Italy. So the various dukes abdicated. By 1866

Italy was unified. Only one state was lacking, and this was the capital, Rome. But Rome belonged to the pope, and Napoleon III refused to hand the city over to the Italians for fear of falling out with him. He defended the city with French troops and repelled a number of attacks by Garibaldi's volunteers.

In 1866, Austria's stubborn determination might yet have ended in victory if Cavour hadn't cleverly arranged an enemy for Austria with similar intentions. This was Prussia, in the north, whose prime minister at the time was Bismarck.

Bismarck was a noble landowner from north Germany. He was a man of exceptional intelligence with a will of iron. He never lost sight of his goal and wasn't in the least bit shy of telling even King William I of Prussia exactly what he thought. From the outset Bismarck wanted just one thing: to make Prussia mighty and use its strength to make one great German empire out of the jumbled patchwork of the German Confederation. For this, he was convinced it was vital to have a strong and powerful army. Indeed, it was he who famously said that the great questions of history are decided not by speeches but by blood and iron. I don't know whether that's always true, but in his case history proved him right. The Prussian representatives were unwilling to grant him the great sum he needed for this army out of the people's taxes so, in 1862, he persuaded the king to rule against the constitution and the will of parliament. The king feared he would suffer the same fate as King Charles I of England when he failed to keep his word, and Louis XVI of France. He was travelling with Bismarck in a railway carriage and turned to him and said: 'I can see exactly where all this is leading. Down to Opera House Square where they'll chop off your head beneath my windows, and then it will be my turn.' Bismarck merely said: 'And then?' 'Well, then we shall be dead,' replied the king. 'True,' said Bismarck, 'then we'll be dead, but what better death could we have?' And so it came about that, against the will of the people, a great army was equipped with a large number of guns and cannons and was soon proving its worth against Denmark.

With these exceedingly well-armed and well-trained forces Bismarck attacked Austria in 1866, while the Italians were attacking from the south. His aim was to force the emperor out of the German Confederation, leaving Prussia as its most powerful member. Prussia could then lead Germany. At Königgrätz, in Bohemia, he defeated the Austrians decisively in a bloody battle. The emperor Franz Josef had to give in and Austria left the Confederation. Bismarck didn't press his victory too far and made no further demands. This incensed the generals and officers of the Prussian army but Bismarck wouldn't budge. He had no wish to make a lasting enemy of Austria. But, without telling anyone, he made secret pacts with all the other German states, ensuring their support in any war Prussia chose to undertake.

Meanwhile, in France, the growth of Prussian military power was making Napoleon III increasingly uneasy. He had just lost an utterly unnecessary war in Mexico in 1867 and was fearful of this well-armed neighbour across the Rhine. In any case, the French had never felt comfortable with any growth in German military might. King William of Prussia was staying at a hot-spring resort at Ems when Napoleon III's ambassador interrupted his cure with the most extraordinary demand. On behalf of himself and his descendants, the king was to renounce in writing claims that he had never even made. Without the king's agreement Bismarck then seized the opportunity to force Napoleon III to declare war. Against the expectations of the French, all the German states joined in, and it was soon clear that the German troops were better equipped and better led than the French.

At a place called Sedan, the Germans captured a large part of the French army, which happened to include Napoleon III. They hurried on towards Paris where they laid siege to the well-defended city for months. The defeat of France meant that the French troops in charge of the pope's protection had to leave Rome, and this allowed the king of Italy to make his entry. It was all very complicated. Meanwhile, during the siege, Bismarck persuaded the various German kings and princes to propose to the king of Prussia, who was staying at Versailles, that he accept the title of German emperor. You won't believe what happened next. King William insisted on being called emperor of Germany and not German emperor, and the whole thing nearly fell through. Finally, however, in the great gallery of mirrors at Versailles, the creation of the German empire was solemnly proclaimed. But the newly appointed emperor, William I, was incensed at not having the title he had wanted. In full view of everyone, shockingly and intentionally, he strode past Bismarck, refusing to shake the hand of the empire's founder. Despite this Bismarck continued to serve him, and served him well.

In Paris, during the months of the siege, a dreadful and bloody workers' revolt had broken out which was later suppressed with even greater bloodshed. More people died in it than in the whole of the French Revolution. For a while afterwards France was powerless, and the French were forced to make peace. They had to hand over a large part of their country to Germany (Alsace and Lorraine) together with a large sum of money. Because he had ruled so badly, the French dismissed Napoleon III and founded a republic. They had had enough of emperors and kings and they wouldn't ever have any again.

Bismarck was now chancellor, or prime minister, of the unified German empire and he governed with great authority. He was a fierce opponent of the sort of socialist action recommended by Karl Marx, but he knew about the appalling conditions of the workers. He believed the only way to stop the spread of Marx's teachings was to allay the worst hardships of the workers, so that they no longer wanted to turn the whole state upside-down. So he created organisations to give support to workers who were sick or had had accidents, who would otherwise have died from lack of assistance, and did his best to ensure that the worst poverty was reduced. Even so, all workers in those days still had to work a twelve-hour day – including Sundays.

Prince Bismarck, with his bushy eyebrows and his stern and resolute expression, was soon one of the best-known men in Europe. Even his enemies agreed that he was a great statesman. When the peoples of Europe wanted to set about dividing up the world, which was now so much smaller, they met together in Berlin in 1878, and Bismarck led the discussions. But when a new German emperor came along, the two were constantly at odds. After many disagreements with his chancellor, William II could stand it no longer and dismissed him. Bismarck, now an old man, retired to his ancestral estate. There he lived for several more years, sending messages to the new leaders of the German government to warn them of the blunders they were making.

39

❖

DIVIDING UP THE WORLD

And now we are coming to the time when my parents were young. They were able to tell me exactly what things were like. How more and more homes came to have first gas and then electric lighting, and then a telephone, while in the towns electric tramways appeared, soon to be followed by cars. How vast suburbs spread to house the workers, and factories with powerful machines kept thousands busy doing work which used to be done by perhaps hundreds of thousands of artisans.

But whatever happened to all those textiles, shoes, tins of food and pots and pans that were turned out every day in wagonloads by these great factories? A certain amount, of course, could be sold at home. People who had jobs could soon afford many more clothes and shoes than artisans used to own. And everything was infinitely cheaper, even if it didn't last as long, so people had to keep buying replacements. But of course they didn't earn enough to buy all the things the monstrous new machines produced. And if all those wagonloads of cloth and leather just sat around unsold, it was pointless for the factory to keep on producing more. It had to close down. But if it did, the workers lost their jobs and were no longer able to buy anything, and even less was sold. This sort of situation is called an economic crisis. And to make sure it didn't happen, every country needed to sell as much as it possibly could of what its many factories produced. If it was unsuccessful at home it had to try to sell its goods abroad. Not only in Europe, where there were factories just about everywhere, but in countries where there weren't any – countries where there were people who didn't yet have clothes or shoes.

In Africa, for example. And so, all of a sudden, the industrialised countries found themselves falling over each other in a race to get to remote and wild places. The wilder they were, the better. They needed them not only so they could sell their goods, but also because those places often had things that their own countries didn't have, such as cotton for making cloth and oil for petrol. But there again, the more of these so-called 'raw materials' they brought from the colonies to Europe, the more the factories were able to produce, and the more eager was their search for places where there were still people who would buy their vast output. People who were unable to find work in their own countries could now emigrate to these foreign places. In short, it became vitally important for the countries of Europe to own colonies. No one bothered to ask the native inhabitants what they thought about it. And, as you can imagine, they were often very badly treated if any of them tried shooting at the invading troops with their bows and arrows.

Of course, the British did best in this division of the world. After all, they had had possessions in India, Australia and North America for several centuries, and colonies in Africa, where their influence in Egypt was particularly strong. The French had also started early, and by now owned a large part of Indo-China and several parts of Africa, among them the Sahara desert – more impressive, perhaps, on account of its size than for any other reason. The Russians had no colonies overseas, but their own empire was vast and they didn't yet have many factories. They wanted to extend their grasp across Asia as far as the sea, and trade from there. But their way was barred by those good students of the Europeans, the Japanese, who said: 'Stop!' In a dreadful war that broke out between Russia and Japan in 1905, the tsar's mighty empire was defeated, and forced to give up some of its territory by tiny, new Japan. And now the Japanese also began building more and more new factories for themselves, and they too needed foreign lands, not only to sell their goods, but because there wasn't enough room for them all in their tiny island kingdom.

Naturally enough, last in line for the share-out were the new states: Italy and Germany. While they had been fragmented they had been in no position to conquer lands overseas. Now they wanted to make up for centuries of lost opportunities. After much fighting, Italy obtained some narrow strips of land in Africa. Germany was stronger and had more factories, so its needs were greater. And in time, Bismarck succeeded in acquiring several larger stretches of land for Germany, mainly in Africa, together with some islands in the Pacific.

But because of the way the whole thing works you can never have enough land. More colonies means more factories, more factories means more goods and more goods means that even more colonies are needed. The demand isn't driven by ambition or the lust for power, but by a genuine need. But now the world had been shared out. To create new colonies – or merely to prevent the old ones being snatched from them by stronger neighbours – it was necessary to fight, or at least to threaten to do so. So each state raised powerful armies and navies and kept on saying: 'Attack me if you dare!' The countries that had been powerful for centuries felt they had a right to be so. But when the new German empire and its excellent factories entered the game, built a great navy and tried to win more and more influence in Asia and Africa, the others took it very badly. And because everyone knew that sooner or later there was bound to be a fearful conflict, they all went on expanding their armies and building bigger and bigger battleships.

When war finally did break out, however, it wasn't where it had been expected all those years. Nor was it on account of some dispute in Africa or Asia. It was caused by another country, the only great state in Europe to have no colonies at all: Austria. That ancient empire, with its mosaic of peoples, wasn't interested in conquering far-off lands on the other side of the world. But it did need people to buy the goods made in its factories. So, just as it had done since the wars with Turkey, Austria kept on trying to acquire new lands towards the east, lands only recently liberated from Turkish rule where there weren't yet any factories. But these small populations of newly liberated eastern peoples, such as the Serbs, were frightened of the great empire and didn't want it to reach out any further. When, in the spring of 1914, the heir to the Austrian throne was visiting one of these newly conquered regions called Bosnia, he was murdered by a Serb in the capital, Sarajevo.

Austria's generals and politicians thought at the time that a war with Serbia was inevitable. The dreadful murder had to be avenged, and Serbia humbled. Frightened by Austria's advance, Russia was drawn in, whereupon Germany, as Austria's ally, also became involved. And once Germany was in the war, all the ancient enmities were unleashed. The Germans wanted to begin by destroying France, their most dangerous enemy, so they marched straight across neutral Belgium to attack Paris. Britain, fearing that a German victory would make Germany all-powerful, now joined in as well. Soon the whole world was at war with Germany and Austria, and the two countries found themselves surrounded by the armies of the entente (meaning their allied enemies – those who had an understanding with one another). Germany and Austria, in the middle, were known as the 'central powers'.

The gigantic Russian armies pressed forward, but were brought to a standstill after a few months. The world has never seen a war like it. Millions and millions of people marched against each other. Even Africans and Indians had to fight. The German armies were stopped when they reached the River Marne, not far from Paris. From this moment on, real battles, in the old sense, would only very rarely be fought. Instead, giant armies dug themselves in, and made their camps in endlessly long trenches facing one another. Then, for days on end, they fired thousands of guns at each other, bursting out in assaults through barricades of barbed wire and blown-up trenches, across a scorched and devastated wasteland strewn with corpses. In 1915, Italy also declared war on Austria, despite having originally been its ally. Now people fought in the snow and ice of the mountains of the Tirol and the famous exploits of Hannibal's warriors during their crossing of the Alps seemed like child's play compared with the courage and endurance shown by these simple soldiers.

People fought each other in the skies in aeroplanes; they dropped bombs on peaceful towns, sank innocent ships, and fought on the sea and under the sea, just as Leonardo da Vinci had foreseen. People invented horrible weapons that murdered and mutilated thousands each day, the most terrible of which were gases that poisoned the air. Anyone who breathed them died in terrible agony. These gases were either released and carried to the enemy soldiers on the wind, or fired in the form of grenades which released their poison when they exploded. People built armoured cars and tanks which moved slowly and inexorably over ditches and walls, demolishing and crushing everything in their path.

The people of Germany and Austria were destitute. For a long time there was hardly anything to eat, no clothes, no coal and no light. Women had to queue for hours in the cold to buy the smallest piece of bread or a half-rotten potato. But just once there was a glimmer of hope. In Russia a revolution had broken out in 1917. The tsar had abdicated, but the bourgeois government which followed wanted to continue with the war. However, the people were against it. So there was a second great uprising in which the factory workers, under the guidance of their leader, Lenin, seized power. They shared out the farmland among the peasants, confiscated the property of the rich and the nobility, and tried to rule the empire according to the principles of Karl Marx. Then the outside world intervened, and in the fearful battles that followed millions more people died. Lenin's successors continued to rule Russia for many years.

The Germans were able to recall some of their troops from the eastern front, but this didn't help them much because new, fresh soldiers now attacked them from the west. The Americans had decided to step in. Nevertheless, the Germans and Austrians held out for more than a year against overwhelming odds. By putting all their efforts into a last desperate attempt in the west, they very nearly won. In the end, however, they were exhausted. And when, in 1918, America's President Wilson announced that he wanted a just peace in which each nation would determine its own fate, many of their troops gave up. So Germany and Austria were forced to agree to a ceasefire. Those who had survived returned home to their starving families.

The next thing that happened was that revolution broke out in these exhausted countries. The emperors of Germany and Austria abdicated and the various peoples of the Austrian empire – the Czechs and the Slovaks, the Hungarians, the Poles and the Southern Slavs – declared themselves independent and founded individual states. Then, having understood from President Wilson that there was to be a peace treaty, and that negotiations were to be held in the ancient royal palaces of Versailles, St Germain and the Trianon, Austria, Hungary and Germany sent envoys to Paris, only to discover that they were excluded from these negotiations. Germany was held chiefly responsible for the war and was to be punished. Not only did the Germans have to surrender all the colonies and lands which they had taken from France in 1870, and pay vast sums of money to the victors each year, but they even had to sign a formal declaration saying that Germany alone was to blame for the war. The Austrians and the Hungarians fared little better. So this was how President Wilson kept his promises. (What you have just read is what I believed to be true when I wrote this account, but read my explanation in the final chapter of this book.)

Eleven million people died in that war and entire regions were devastated in a way that had never been seen before. The suffering was beyond imagination.

Mankind had come a long way in its mastery of nature. With a telephone you can now sit in your room at home and talk about everything or nothing with someone on the other side of the world in Australia. You can tune in on the radio to a concert in London or a programme on raising geese broadcast from Portugal.

People build gigantic buildings, far higher than the pyramids or St Peter's church in Rome. They make great aeroplanes, each one capable of killing more people than the whole of Philip II of Spain's Invincible Armada. Ways have been found to combat the most fearsome diseases. There have been amazing discoveries. People have found formulas for all sorts of things that happen in nature which are so mysterious and so remarkable that few people understand them. But the formulas are correct: the stars move in exactly the way they predict. Every day we know a little more about nature, and about human nature too. But the horror of poverty remains. There are many millions of people on our earth who cannot find work and every year millions die of starvation. We all hope for a better future – it must be better!

Imagine time as a river, and that we are flying high above it in an aeroplane. Far below you can just make out the mountain caves of the mammoth-hunters, and the steppes where the first cereals grew. Those distant dots are the pyramids and the Tower of Babel. In these lowlands the Jews once tended their flocks. This is the sea the Phoenicians sailed across. What looks like a white star shining over there, with the sea on either side, is in fact the Acropolis, the symbol of Greek art. And there, on the other side of the world, are the great, dark forests where the Indian penitents withdrew to meditate and the Buddha experienced Enlightenment. Now we can see the Great Wall of China and, over there, the smouldering ruins of Carthage. In those gigantic stone funnels the Romans watched Christians being torn to pieces by wild beasts. The dark clouds on the horizon are the storm clouds of the Migrations, and it was in those forests, beside the river, that the first monks converted and educated the Germanic tribes. Leaving the deserts over there behind them, the Arabs set out to conquer the world, and this is where Charlemagne ruled. On this hill the fortress still stands where the struggle between the pope and the emperor, over which of them was to dominate the world, was finally decided. We can see castles from the Age of Chivalry and, nearer still, cities with

beautiful cathedrals – over there is Florence, and there the new
St Peter's, the cause of Luther's quarrel with the Church. The city
of Mexico is on fire, the Invincible Armada is being wrecked off
England's coasts. That dense pall of smoke comes from burning
villages and the bonfires on which people were burnt during the
Thirty Years War. The magnificent chateau set in a great park is
Louis XIV's Palace of Versailles. Here are the Turks encamped
outside Vienna, and nearer still the simple castles of Frederick the
Great and Maria Theresa. In the distance the cries of 'Liberty,
Equality and Fraternity' reach us from the streets of Paris, and we
can already see Moscow burning over there, and the wintry land in
which the soldiers of the Last Conqueror's Grand Armée perished.
Getting nearer, we can see smoke rising from factory chimneys and
hear the whistle of railway trains. The Peking Summer Palace lies
in ruins, and warships are leaving Japanese ports under the flag of
the rising sun. Here, the guns of the World War are still thunder-
ing. Poison gas is drifting across the land. And over there, through
the open dome of an observatory, a giant telescope directs the gaze
of an astronomer towards unimaginably distant galaxies. But
below us and in front of us there is nothing but mist, mist that is
dense and impenetrable. All we know is that the river flows
onwards. On and on it goes, towards an unknown sea.

But now let us quickly drop down in our plane towards the river.
From close up, we can see it is a real river, with rippling waves like
the sea. A strong wind is blowing and there are little crests of foam
on the waves. Look carefully at the millions of shimmering white
bubbles rising and then vanishing with each wave. Over and over
again, new bubbles come to the surface and then vanish in time
with the waves. For a brief instant they are lifted on the wave's crest
and then they sink down and are seen no more. We are like that.
Each one of us no more than a tiny glimmering thing, a sparkling
droplet on the waves of time which flow past beneath us into an
unknown, misty future. We leap up, look around us and, before we
know it, we vanish again. We can hardly be seen in the great river
of time. New drops keep rising to the surface. And what we call our
fate is no more than our struggle in that great multitude of

droplets in the rise and fall of one wave. But we must make use of that moment. It is worth the effort.

40

❖

THE SMALL PART OF THE
HISTORY OF THE WORLD WHICH I
HAVE LIVED THROUGH MYSELF:
LOOKING BACK

It is one thing to learn about history from books, and quite another to experience it oneself. That is what I wanted to remind you of just now when I likened a glimpse into the past of mankind to the view seen from an aeroplane flying at a great height. All we can make out are a few details on the banks of the river of time. But when seen from close up, with the waves coming towards us one by one, the river looks quite different. Some things are much clearer, while others are barely visible. And that's how I found it. In the last chapter I told you about the terrible World War of 1914–18. Although I lived through it, I was only nine years old when it ended. So when I wrote about it I still had to rely on books.

In my final chapter I would like to tell you a little about what I actually did experience. The more I think about it, the stranger it seems. The world is now so utterly different from what it was in

1918, and yet so many of the changes that occurred happened so imperceptibly that we now take them completely for granted.

When I was a boy there were no televisions, no computers, no space flights and no atomic energy. But it's easy to forget the most important change, and that is that there are so many more people in the world than there were then. Towards the end of the 1914–18 war there were more than 2,000,000,000 people on our planet. Since then the figure has more than doubled. Of course, numbers as big as that don't mean much to us because we can't actually picture them to ourselves. But if we bear in mind that a line drawn round the earth at the level of the equator would measure roughly 40,000,000 metres, and that when people form queues in front of a ticket office there are roughly 2 of them to a metre, it means that 80,000,000 people waiting patiently in a queue would reach all the way round the world. The queue when I was a boy would have gone round 22 times, and today, with our 4,500,000,000 fellow inhabitants, the queue would reach more than 50 times round the earth!

Then you must also realise that, throughout the time that the population was multiplying at such a tremendous rate, the globe we all inhabit was imperceptibly growing smaller and smaller. Of course, I don't mean literally shrinking, but technology – and, in particular, that of flying – kept on reducing the distance between the various parts of the globe. This was also something I experienced myself. Whenever I find myself at an airport and hear a succession of announcements for flights to Delhi, New York, Hong Kong or Sydney, and see the swarms of people preparing to depart, I can't help thinking of my youth. In those days people would point at someone and say: 'He's been to America', or 'She's been to India!'

Today there are hardly any places in the world that can't be reached in a matter of hours. Even if we don't go to far-off countries ourselves, they seem closer to us than they were in my youth. Whenever a major event happens anywhere in the world we read about it in the newspapers the next day, we hear about it on the radio and see it on the television news. The inhabitants of ancient

Mexico knew nothing about the destruction of Jerusalem, and it is unlikely that anyone in China ever heard of the effects of the Thirty Years War. But by the First World War things had changed. The very fact that it was known as a 'World War' was because so many nations had been drawn into the fighting.

Naturally, that doesn't mean that all the news which now reaches us from all over the world is true. One of the things I also learned was not to believe everything I read in the newspapers. I'll give you an example. Because I had lived through the First World War myself, I thought I could believe everything I had heard about it at the time. That is why the last chapter, 'Dividing up the world', is not quite as impartial as I had intended. The role played by America's President Wilson (see p. 269) was not at all what I had imagined. I described a situation in which Wilson made promises to the Germans and Austrians which he failed to keep. I firmly believed that what I remembered had to be right – after all, it was part of my own experience – and when I wrote about it later I just wrote down what everyone believed. But I should have checked my facts, as all historians must be especially careful to do. To cut a long story short, President Wilson did indeed make a peace offer early in 1918, but because Germany and Austria and their allies were still hoping to win the war, they ignored it. Only when the war had dragged on for ten more months, and they had been defeated with very heavy losses, were they prepared to accept the President's proposal. But by then it was too late.

Quite how serious and regrettable this error of mine was rapidly became apparent. For, although I did not foresee it, the fact that all those who had been defeated were convinced that their suffering was the result of a gross deception was very easily exploited and transformed by ambitious and fanatical agitators into a raging thirst for vengeance. I am reluctant to name them, but everyone will know that the one I have most in mind is Adolf Hitler. Hitler had been a soldier in the First World War, and he too remained convinced that, had it not been for the supposed deception, the German army would never have been defeated. But he didn't just blame Wilson. In his eyes, the enemy's propaganda had been

crucial in persuading the Germans and Austrians at home to abandon the soldiers at the front to their fate. Hitler was therefore
determined to trump the enemy in the art of propaganda. He was
a brilliant popular orator and drew huge crowds. He knew there
was no better way to incite a mob to action than to give them a
scapegoat, someone they could blame for their suffering, and he
found one in the Jews.

The fate of this ancient people has been touched on several
times in this book. I described their voluntary segregation, and the
loss of their homeland with the destruction of Jerusalem (p. 27),
and their persecution during the Middle Ages (p. 159). But even
though I come from a Jewish family myself, it never entered my
head that such horrors might be repeated in my own lifetime.

Here I must confess to another error that slipped into this history – but one for which I might perhaps be excused. In chapter 33
it says that a 'truly new age' began in which people started to turn
their minds away from the brutality of earlier times, because the
ideas and ideals of the so-called Enlightenment of the eighteenth
century had by then become so widespread that people took them
to be self-evident. At the time that I wrote that it seemed to me
inconceivable that anyone might ever again stoop to persecuting
people of a different religion, use torture to extract confessions, or
question the rights of man. But what seemed unthinkable to me
happened all the same. Such a painful step backwards seems
almost beyond our understanding, and yet it may be no harder for
young people to understand than it is for adults. They need only
open their eyes at school. Schoolchildren are often intolerant. Look
how easily they make fun of their teacher if they see him wearing
something unfashionable that the class finds amusing, and once
respect is lost all hell breaks loose. And if a fellow student is different in some minor way – in the colour of their skin or hair, or the
way they speak or eat – they too can become victims of hateful
teasing and tormenting which they just have to put up with. Of
course, not all young people are equally cruel or heartless. But no
one wants to be a spoil-sport, so in one way or another most of
them join in the fun, until they hardly recognise themselves.

Unfortunately grown-ups don't behave any better. Especially when they have nothing else to do or are having a hard time – or, sometimes, when they just think they are having a hard time. They band together with other real or supposed companions in misfortune and take to the streets, marching in step and parroting mindless slogans, filled with their own importance. I myself saw Hitler's brown-shirt supporters beating up Jewish students at Vienna University, and when I was writing this book, Hitler had already seized power in Germany. It seemed only a matter of time before the Austrian government would also fall, so I was lucky to be invited to England just in time, before Hitler's troops marched into Austria in March 1938. After that, as in Germany, anyone who greeted someone with a simple 'Good morning' and not a 'Heil Hitler!' was taking a very grave risk.

In this type of situation it soon becomes all too clear that in the eyes of the supporters of this sort of movement, there is only one sin, disloyalty to the *Führer*, or leader, and only one virtue, absolute obedience. To bring victory closer every order had to be obeyed, even if it ran counter to the laws of humanity. Of course, similar things have happened at earlier times in history, and I have described many of them in this book – for example, when I wrote about Muhammad's first disciples (p. 119). The Jesuits, too, were said to place obedience above all else. I also touched briefly on the victory of the Communists in Russia under Lenin, and there, too, there were convinced Communists who would not tolerate any opponents. Their ruthlessness in the pursuit of their goals knew no bounds, and millions died as a result.

In the years that followed the First World War, tolerance also vanished in Germany, Italy and Japan. The politicians of those countries told their fellow countrymen that they had been cheated when the world was shared out, and that they too had the right to rule over other peoples. The Italians were reminded of their ancient Roman ancestry, the Japanese of their warriors, and the Germans of the old Germanic tribes, of Charlemagne and Frederick the Great. People, they were told, were not of equal value. Just as some breeds of dog were better at hunting than others, they themselves belonged to the best race, the one designed for ruling.

I know a wise old Buddhist monk who, in a speech to his fellow countrymen, once said he'd love to know why someone who boasts that he is the cleverest, the strongest, the bravest or the most gifted man on earth is thought ridiculous and embarrassing, whereas if, instead of 'I', he says, '*we* are the most intelligent, the strongest, the bravest and the most gifted people on earth', his fellow countrymen applaud enthusiastically and call him a patriot. For there is nothing patriotic about it. One can be attached to one's own country without needing to insist that the rest of the world's inhabitants are worthless. But as more and more people were taken in by this sort of nonsense, the menace to peace grew greater.

Then, when a serious economic crisis in Germany condemned vast numbers of people to unemployment, war seemed the simplest way out. The unemployed would become soldiers or work in the armaments factories, and in this way the hateful treaties of Versailles and St Germain would be wiped off the face of the earth. Not only that, but the Western democratic countries – France, Britain and the United States – had become so softened by years of peace, or so it was thought, that they were hardly likely to defend themselves. Certainly no one there wanted a war, and every effort was made to avoid giving Hitler an excuse to bring calamity down on the world. But, sadly, a pretext can always be found and, if need be, 'incidents' can be arranged. So on the first day of September in 1939, the German army marched into Poland. By that time I was already in England and witnessed for myself the profound sadness – but also the determination – of those who had to march off to war again. This time there were no cheerful battle songs, and no dreams of glory. They were just doing their duty, for the madness had to be stopped.

My task was to listen to German broadcasts and translate them into English so as to know what German listeners were being told, and what they were not being told. This meant that from 1939 to 1945 I was in the curious position of living through all six years of that terrible war on both sides, as it were, if in very different ways. At home in England I saw determination, but also hardship, anxiety for the men at the front, the effects of air raids and fear at the turns the war was taking. From German radio broadcasts all I heard were cries of triumph and outpourings of abuse. Hitler believed in the power of propaganda, a faith which seemed justified when the successes of the first two years of the war exceeded even his wildest expectations. Poland, Denmark and Norway, Holland and Belgium, France, large parts of Russia and the Balkans were overrun, and only Britain, that little island on the edge of Europe, still held out. And even that resistance could surely not last long, for, to the sound of trumpet fanfares, the German radio ceaselessly proclaimed how many ships carrying supplies and armaments intended for the British had been sunk by their U-boats.

But when, without any declaration of war, in December 1941, the Japanese attacked the American fleet at anchor in Pearl Harbor and virtually destroyed it, and Hitler took it upon himself to declare war on the United States, and when, in the autumn of 1942, the German troops were beaten back in North Africa and defeated by the Russians in January 1943 outside Stalingrad, and when the German air force – the Luftwaffe – proved powerless to prevent the Allies' devastating bombardments of German towns, it became clear that it takes more than fine words and fanfares to win a war. When Winston Churchill became prime minister in England, at a time when the outlook was grim, he said: 'I can promise nothing but blood, sweat and tears.' And it was precisely because he had said that that we also believed him when he held out a glimmer of hope. How many German listeners paid any attention to the justifications and promises that I heard, day in, day out on the German radio, is anyone's guess.

What I do know is that neither the German listeners nor we ourselves were aware at the time of the most horrifying of all the crimes committed by the Germans during the war. In connection with this I shall, if you don't mind, take you back to page 280 where it says (speaking of the Spanish conquistadores of Mexico):

'there and in other parts of America they set about exterminating the ancient, cultivated Indian peoples in the most horrendous way. This chapter in the history of mankind is so appalling and so shameful to us Europeans', I wrote 'that I would rather not say anything more about it . . .'

I am even more reluctant to talk about the monstrous crime that was committed in our own century – after all, this book is intended for young readers who should not have to read about such things. But children grow up too, and they too must learn from history how easy it is for human beings to be transformed into inhuman beings through incitement and intolerance. And so it came about that, in the last years of the Second World War, the Jewish inhabitants of every country in Europe under German occupation – millions of men, women and children – were driven from their home countries. Most were put on trains and sent eastwards, where they were murdered.

As I said before, the German radio said nothing about any of this to its listeners, and like many others I couldn't at first bring myself to believe it when the war ended and the unthinkable became known (in 1945). But sadly there is abundant proof of this monstrous crime, and although many years have already passed since it was committed, it is of the utmost importance that it should not be forgotten or hushed up.

With the mingling of peoples on our tiny planet, it becomes more and more necessary for us to respect and tolerate each other, not least because technological advances are bringing us closer and closer together.

The impact of technology was also demonstrated in the Second World War, when the almost inexhaustible reserves of the American arms industry, which benefited both Britain and Russia, made the outcome inevitable. Despite the desperate resistance put up by the German soldiers, the British and Americans were able to land on the French coast of Normandy in the summer of 1944 and drive the Germans back. At the same time the Russians were pursuing a by now unresisting German army and, in April, they finally reached Berlin, where Hitler took his own life. There was no talk of a peace treaty this time. The victors remained in Germany as occupying forces, and for decades a heavily guarded frontier ran right through Germany separating the sphere of influence of Communist Russia from that of the Western democracies.

However, with the defeat of Germany the World War was still not over, for the Japanese, who had meanwhile conquered large parts of Asia, were far from defeated. And because no end was in sight, the Americans brought out an entirely new weapon: the atomic bomb.

It so happened that, shortly before war broke out, I had met a young physicist who told me about an article published by the great Danish scientist, Niels Bohr. Its subject was the theoretical possibility of constructing a 'uranium bomb' whose destructive power would far exceed that of any known explosive. At the time we were both united in hoping that such a weapon might only be dropped on some desert island, to show friend and foe alike that all other ideas of weaponry and warfare had had their day. Although many of the scientists who were working frantically throughout the war to realise this weapon certainly felt as we did, our hope was in vain. In August 1945, the Japanese towns of Hiroshima and Nagasaki became the first victims of an unimaginable catastrophe, and Japan was finally defeated.

It was clear to all of us that with this invention an entirely new chapter in the history of the world had begun, for the discovery of atomic energy might be likened to the discovery of fire. Fire, too, can warm, and it can destroy, but its destructive power is nothing next to that of today's even greater atomic weapons. One can only hope that this development has made it impossible for such weapons to be used ever again against human beings. It must be clear to everyone that if they were to be used, neither side would be likely to survive and vast areas of the globe would be turned into uninhabitable deserts. Of course, the world has changed enormously since the last war. The inhabitants of whole continents that belonged to the British empire have since then become largely independent – although, unfortunately not yet any more peaceable for it. Yet despite the brutal conflicts and worrying crises that have broken out since 1945 in various parts of the globe, we have been spared a third world war because we all know only too well that it could mean the end of the history of the world. It isn't a great comfort, but it's better than none at all.

Not surprisingly, this entirely new situation in human history led many to condemn out of hand all the achievements of a science that had brought us to the edge of the abyss. And yet those people should not forget that, without science and technology, it would not have been possible for the countries concerned to make good, at least in part, the damage and destruction caused by the World War, so that life could return to normal much earlier than anyone had dared to hope.

Finally, I should like to make one more small correction to my book, to make good an omission that lies close to my heart. My chapter 'Men and machines' is not exactly incorrect, but it is a little one-sided. While it is indeed true that the switch from artisans and craftsmen to factories and machines entailed a great deal of suffering, I should nevertheless have mentioned that without the new techniques of mass production it would have been quite impossible to feed, clothe and house the steadily increasing population. The very fact that more and more children were being born, and fewer and fewer of them were dying soon after, was largely due to the scientific advance of medicine which insisted on such things as piped running water and proper sewerage. True, the growing industrialisation of Europe, America and of Japan has meant the loss of much that is beautiful, but we must not forget how many blessings – and I mean blessings – it has brought us.

I well remember what people meant in my youth when they talked about 'the poor'. It was not only the destitute, the beggars and the homeless who looked different from the middle-class inhabitants of large towns, but factory workers too – both men and women – could be recognised at a distance by their dress. The women usually wore shawls on their heads against the cold, and no factory worker would ever have dreamed of wearing a white shirt, for it would have instantly shown the dirt. And when I think about it, I remember people used to talk about 'the smell of the poor', because the majority of a town's inhabitants lived in poorly ventilated tenements with, at most, a single tap at the foot of the stairs. A middle-class household (and not just the wealthy ones) usually included a cook, a parlour-maid and often a nursery-maid to take care of the children as well. Such women often had a better life than they would have had if they had stayed at home, but it can't have been very pleasant, for example, to have had only one day a week when you were allowed out, and to be generally looked upon as a servant. It was during my childhood that people were just beginning to think about such things, and after the First World War, servants became officially known as 'home helps'. Even so, when I visited Berlin as a student, houses often had a sign at the entrance which read 'Entrance for Gentlemen and Ladies only'. Even in those days this made me feel uncomfortable. Servants and tradesmen had to use the back stairs and weren't allowed to use the lift, even if they had a heavy load to carry.

Thankfully, all that is over now, like a bad dream. To be sure, life is still hard for many people, and there are wretched and joyless neighbourhoods in the towns of Europe and America. But most people who work in factories and even most of the unemployed live better today than many medieval knights must have done in their castles. They eat better, and above all they are healthier and as a rule live longer, which was not the case only a short while ago. Since time began people have dreamed of a 'Golden Age', and now that something close to one is true for so many, no one is willing to admit it.

But the same could not be said of those countries in Eastern Europe which were forced by Russia's armies to adopt the

Communist system. It was especially hard for the inhabitants of East Germany, who, as the years went by, saw how much better the lives of their Western neighbours were, until the day came when they were no longer prepared to make the heavy sacrifices that the Communist system of economics demanded. And so, in 1989, quite unexpectedly, the unthinkable happened. The East Germans succeeded in forcing open their border and both parts of Germany were once more united. The mood took hold of Soviet Russia, where the political system collapsed, as it did in all the remaining countries of Eastern Europe.

I ended my account of the First World War with the words: 'We all hope for a better future, it must be better.' Has such a future come? For many of the people who live on our earth, it is still remote. Among the constantly growing populations of Asia, Africa and South America the same misery reigns that, until not so long ago, was accepted as normal in our countries as well. We have no easy remedies, not least because there too, as ever, intolerance and misery go hand in hand. And yet improvements in sending information have made the consciences of richer nations a little more attentive. Whenever an earthquake, a flood or a drought in a far-off place leaves many victims, thousands of people in wealthier countries put their money and their efforts into providing relief. And that, too, used not to happen. Which proves that we still have the right to go on hoping for a better future.